Are You Still Coaching?

Are You Still Coaching?

41 YEARS COACHING YESHIVA UNIVERSITY BASKETBALL

Johnny Halpert

authorHOUSE®

AuthorHouse™ LLC
1663 Liberty Drive
Bloomington, IN 47403
www.authorhouse.com
Phone: 1-800-839-8640

Published by AuthorHouse 11/26/2013

ISBN: 978-1-4918-2859-5 (sc)
ISBN: 978-1-4918-2858-8 (hc)
ISBN: 978-1-4918-2857-1 (e)

Library of Congress Control Number: 2013918966

She opens her mouth with wisdom;
And the teaching of kindness is on her tongue.
Proverbs 31:26

Dedicated To:

Aviva

5 children
19 grandchildren
938 games
3,360 practices
1 million phone calls

In Gratitude

To My Parents
Max and Ida, z"l[1]

To My Brother
Danny

Rabbi Joseph and Martelle Urivetsky

To My Teachers
Rabbi Moshe Kahana, Teacher, Yeshiva Rabbi Moses Soloveitchik
Hy Wettstein, z"l, Coach, Yeshiva University High School (MTA)
Rabbi Louis Bernstein, z"l, Teacher, MTA
"Red" Sarachek, z"l, Coach, Yeshiva University
Rabbi David Weinbach, z"l, Owner and Director, Camp Raleigh and
Principal, MTA
Rabbi Chaim Faskowitz, z"l, Rabbi, Congregation Ohr Yitzchak
Rabbi Simcha Krauss, Rabbi, Young Israel Hillcrest

To My Children
Tzippora and David
Ariella and Jonah
Tzofit and Jason
Yehuda and Shoshana
Rafi and Michelle

To My Grandchildren
Daniella, Eytan, Talia, Yael
Nachshon, Avital, Yair, Yedida
Aliza, Naomi, Elie, Dani
Aryeh, Avigayil, Ezra, Leora
Ari, Alyssa, Ben

---

[1]   Of blessed memory

Acknowledgments

All successful endeavors require the efforts of a team and the completion of this book is no exception. I am indebted to the following people without whose help this book would never have been attempted, let alone completed.

To my daughters, Tzippora and Ariella, who repeatedly said, "You're always telling us stories; why don't you write a book?" To my daughter Tzofit, the Research Guru, whose technical knowledge guided me through the minefields of the publishing process.

To my son Yehuda, the rabbi, who translated Hebrew terms to English, and to my son Yehuda, the lawyer who counseled me on the consequences of seeking vengeance. To my son Rafi who upon reading each chapter felt compelled to practice tough love.

To Rabbi Simcha Krauss, whose scholarship and perspective served as an invaluable resource.

To David Kufeld, whose guidance I always sought.

To my sister-in-law Tamar for sharing her photographic skills.

To Norman Goldberg and Peter Robertson of Yeshiva University's Department of Communications for capturing through pictures the events of the past forty-one years, and to Derrick Henry, who for twenty-five years preserved through his videography the wins and last-minute shots that are recounted in the book.

To Shulamith Berger, Yeshiva University's curator of special collections for providing access to the Yeshiva University archives. To Moshe Kranzler for providing easy, unlimited access to his personal Yeshiva College yearbook collection, and to Mayer Fertig and Matt Yaniv for their continual support and professional guidance.

I am indebted to Yaffa Karp for arranging the book's photographs, to Moshe Isaacson and Edwin Maleve for developing the design of the website www.backdoorhoops.com and to Rabbi Yechiel Simon and Suzanne Muench for reading the book cover to cover.

To my children and grandchildren especially Daniella, Eytan and Aryeh and to Tamar and Joey for taking the time to read and comment on my initial drafts, and finally to my wife, Aviva, for providing a very insecure writer with professional but gentle editing by always prefacing her suggestions with "I am just going to tweak a few things."

I must also acknowledge the owners of Bagels N' Cream of Queens, New York, for providing sustenance while I wrote—and for allowing me to use their store as a virtual office.

Unsung Heroes

Although my forty-one years of stories could not have been written without the support of family, former players, and YU staff, there would not have been any stories to write if not for the support of Yeshiva University's past athletic directors. I wish to acknowledge and express my gratitude to Rabbi Abraham Avrech, Hy Wettstein, z"l, Red Sarachek, z"l, Arthur Tauber, Gil Shevlin, Steve Young, and especially Richard Zernick for their help and support.

These stories are also the stories of Yeshiva University's deans, administrators, and office personnel who helped the players achieve their dreams. On behalf of myself and the players, I thank the past directors of admissions Abner Groff, Paul Glasser, Judy Paikin, and the current director, Moish Kranzler, and his staff, Gerry Mansdorf, Murray Srago, Heidi Fuchs, and Martha Decaille; I thank the deans, Daniel Kurtzer, Norman Rosenfeld, z"l, Norman Adler, Ira Jaskol, and Fred Sugarman; I thank the directors of student financial aid, Jack Nussbaum, z"l, and Bob Friedman; the administrators of student services, Rabbi Josh Cheifitz, Rabbi Mitchel Serels, Jonathan Mantel, and Elaine Thompson; Meyer Edelstein, associate registrar, and the secretaries of the athletic office, Florence Miller and Debra Soto.

Finally, I would be remiss if I did not acknowledge and thank Mr. Stan Watson for his 28 years of devotion to the athletes and students of Yeshiva University

Hakoras Hatov[2]

I wish to express my profound appreciation to Rabbi Dr. Norman Lamm, chancellor of Yeshiva University, for not only providing me the opportunity to represent Yeshiva University but also for his constant support throughout his tenure as president (1976-2003).

Despite the many pressing financial challenges that he inherited upon taking office, the needs of the students always remained a priority as evidenced by his focus on fulfilling the fifty-year-old dream of bringing an athletic center to the campus of Yeshiva University. It was only through his tireless efforts that this dream was realized in 1985 with the opening of the Max Stern Athletic Center.

Through his integrity and inspired leadership, Dr. Lamm created an environment where thousands of YU students could simultaneously engage in Torah study while pursuing their dreams of becoming rabbis, doctors, dentists, lawyers, accountants, businessman, and even basketball coaches.

---

[2]   Gratefulness

Contents

---

[3]   Ecclesiastes 7:5

---

[4] Although the original intent was to include within the book the results of all games played from 1930 to 2013 accompanied by individual team pictures, an Excel spreadsheet does not lend itself to a book format. Therefore, game results accompanied by team pictures can be accessed by going to www.backdoorhoops.com.

Preface

Mens sane in corpore sano (a healthy mind in a healthy body) is a classical concept in modern times. Health consciousness via sports activities has even "made it" into Jewish thought.

HaRav Avraham Yitzhak Kook zt"l (of saintly blessed memory) who publicly supported and encouraged various sports activities in the nascent settlement of mandatory Palestine was the great defender of sports activities as legitimate expressions of Judaism. Against vehement attacks by the traditional leadership that these sports activities destroy the essence of Judaism, Rav Kook argued that the healthy Jewish soul and Jewish spirit can only survive in a healthy Jewish body. Rav Kook's position has been accepted by most American Jews—even Orthodox Jews—and most Yeshiva High Schools now support various sports teams that compete against other yeshiva and non-yeshiva high schools.

Yeshiva College is, of course, unique. It began its basketball program in 1930 and is currently completing its eighty-third year of athletic competition. Perhaps to celebrate the longevity of the YU basketball team Dr. Jonathan Halpert is releasing a brief but important memoir of his forty-one years as coach.

In it, the interested reader will find important facts and data about what is, after all, the history of the first "Torah-sponsored basketball team of an Orthodox school of higher learning." And here Dr. Halpert's stories, reminiscences, and vignettes become important. When Dr. Halpert scours the globe for good player-athletes who will lead the team to victory, he looks for athletic promise. But in searching for the best, he is cognizant that, in the final analysis, his team will be the YU team. Hence his search is value laden. He knows that the players must be the best but also informed by values—Jewish values, universal values, and values touched by the breath of Torah.

The best example of Dr. Halpert's fidelity to this mission is his promise given to Rabbi Israel Miller in the story "The Israelis Are Coming." In other words, during his forty-one-year tenure as coach of the YU basketball team, Dr. Halpert was also a great Mechanech, Jewish educator, and Marbitz Torah.[5] That is no small feat.

All that remains for me to do is to wish Dr. Halpert well. May he continue in this path for many happy, healthy, and winning years.

Simcha Krauss
Rabbi Emeritus
Young Israel of Hillcrest

---

[5]   Disseminator of Torah

Chapter 1

IN THE BEGINNING

The Hebrew Typewriter

My relationship with Yeshiva started in September 1930 when my father arrived from Jerusalem at the age of seventeen with only the clothes on his back and his Hebrew typewriter. It was his good fortune that his arrival coincided with Dr. Bernard Revel's[6] search for what was then the rarest of commodities in New York, a Hebrew typist. When he presented with the skill to type Hebrew—and his own typewriter—he was hired immediately to type Dr. Revel's Hebrew correspondence.

He had learned his skill during his years at the Diskin Orphanage in Jerusalem, which had taken him in after the expulsion by the Ottoman Empire of his father, a Russian national, and the premature death of his mother soon after. With no money, he bartered his typing skills to pay his tuition at YU and after graduating in 1938, he again bartered his typing—this time to convert the YU cafeteria into a wedding hall where he married my mother, Ida, in 1939.

Although distinct because of the number of years it spans, my family's story is not unique. For more than a hundred years, Yeshiva University has distinguished itself as an outstanding institution of higher learning and as a caring and supportive environment where less fortunate students and families have been able to realize their dreams. My father's story is only one example of a student who was not only educated by Yeshiva, but also clothed and fed.

Competitive sports are all about the pride that accrues from winning. Although I live in the world of wins and losses—and therefore value victories—my proudest achievement is being able to declare that because of a Hebrew typewriter there has been a Halpert at Yeshiva University for eighty-three consecutive years.

---

[6] The first president of Yeshiva University

On behalf of my family and all the families that have been nurtured by Yeshiva University, I say thank you.

One Year at a Time, Forty-One Years Later

"Are you still coaching?" is the comment I hear most often when I meet former players and fans. My usual response is to profess how much I enjoy the players or to confess my fear of life without coaching. As one year has turned into forty-one, however, I have come to realize that it is neither fun nor fear that motivates me—it is my need to chase dreams.

It began when I was ten years old and living in a one-bedroom apartment across the street from Yeshiva University. I had the apartment to myself because my parents traveled to Brooklyn every night to visit my brother in the hospital. There I was, alone in the living room, faking right and cutting behind a pick set by our living room chair. Moving gracefully toward the piano, I would loft my imaginary basketball, a pair of rolled-up socks held together by rubber bands. The ball would bounce softly off our ceiling and drop into the taped tissue box hanging on the living room wall. In 1955, no one dunked.

What a shot, what a play! The fans were going wild. Not even the banging of a broomstick from our downstairs neighbor or his screams of "What the hell are you doing up there?" could drown out the cheering of my imaginary fans. Yeshiva Rabbi Moses Soloveitchik[7] had defeated Yeshiva Salanter on a last-second basket from their star, Johnny Halpert. Ironically, my son Rafi is the varsity basketball coach of SAR[8] (Salanter, Akiva, Riverdale) High School, the 2000 version of Yeshiva Salanter.

After my imaginary game, I would lie in bed with my radio hidden under my pillow, listening to Marty Glickman's signature call, "It's good—just like Needicks."

Although much has changed since my jump shot from the piano, I continue to dream about winning shots. The difference is that now

---

[7] Yeshiva Rabbi Moses Soloveitchik and Yeshiva Salanter were Yeshiva day (elementary) schools that combined secular and religious studies.

[8] Yeshiva high schools combine secular and religious studies. Examples noted are Valley Torah, Hebrew Institute of Long Island (HILI), Rabbi Jacob Joseph (RJJ), SAR, Ramaz, and Yeshiva of Flatbush.

it is Yeshiva University that is losing by one, and I am not shooting but drawing plays. This year's star executes a perfect backdoor cut, and Yeshiva wins. My season starts every year with dreams of a championship and is sustained throughout the year by the same visions. I know the season is coming to an end when my dreams of perfect backdoor cuts are supplanted by the reality of missed layups. Once again, I begin to think that this is my last year; after all, how many missed shots can I endure? Five months later, the dreams begin again, and one more year turns into another.

Dreaming is one of the things we all do but somehow just take for granted. It is a key prerequisite for sustaining a healthy psychological outlook because the natural consequence of not dreaming is giving up. If you no longer believe what you do matters, there is nothing to dream about.

One of the great values of competitive sports is that it teaches kids that dreams can come true. Anyone who has ever played competitive sports, whether during a schoolyard recess or in an NCAA basketball game, has dreamed about making the winning shot. It does not matter if the shot is realized in front of one fan or ten thousand fans because when the dream is achieved, it is always fulfilled in front of the most important person, the dreamer. It is why wives say, "You remember a shot that you made thirty years ago, but you cannot remember what you ate for breakfast." Players and coaches always remember their shots because the shot was their dream coming true.

Over time, I have come to understand that coaching not only allows me to pursue my own personal dreams, but more importantly, it enables me to give young men the same opportunity. At some moment and at some place, a player's dream is realized. The time and place are irrelevant. All that matters is that I have enabled another young man to believe that everything is possible. Everyone needs and deserves one of those moments.

On Saturday night December 13, 2008, with nine seconds remaining and Yeshiva trailing Maritime College by three, I substituted Aryeh Magilnick. Aryeh had started his college career as a team manager and it was only after a year of hard work on the practice squad that he was elevated to the varsity. Although he was an excellent shooter, he was not among the nine-man rotation that received playing time. The last-second play blew up immediately, and it was by fate—not design—that the ball landed in his hands with one second left. In front of fans and friends, he rose up and hit nothing but net. The shot enabled Yeshiva to gain a 74-71 overtime victory, but more importantly, it provided Aryeh with his moment.[9]

Sometimes special moments take time to evolve. In March 2008, I watched Dovie Hoffman rebound and score for Valley Torah High School. Impressed by his potential, I encouraged Dovie to try out for the Yeshiva varsity team. In October 2009, following a year of study in Israel, I sat with Dovie to discuss his status. I said, "You have potential, but right now you are the eighteenth man on a fifteen-man varsity. If you want to learn, I'm willing to teach."

Dovie accepted the offer to spend eight hours a week practicing without the goody bag of playing time. For ten weeks, he practiced in silence. One night at the end of a blue-white scrimmage, his rebound and game-winning put-back basket caught my attention. Two nights later, on December 12, 2009, against Baruch College, in my desperate search for a rebound, the eighteenth man got his name called. He played five minutes, got two rebounds, and made two foul shots.

Two months later, against St. Joseph College, his stat sheet showed thirteen points, four rebounds, and a very unusual three. By accident, not design, Dovie found himself unguarded in front of the St. Joe's bench. Suddenly, and very out of character, the St. Joe's bench yelled loud enough for everyone to hear, "Shoot." Dovie, who had earned playing time for rebounding, not for three-point shooting, dutifully obeyed and hit nothing but net. As he ran back on defense, I also yelled loud enough for everyone to hear, "I'm your coach. You are supposed to listen to me—not to them."

On March 1, 2012, two years after our sit down, Dovie was named to the Skyline Conference 2012 all-star team. In 2013, he became the twenty-fifth player in the history of Yeshiva University to score a thousand points.

Aryeh and Dovie will always remember their moments—and so will I. It is why one year has turned into forty-one.

---

[9]   To view Aryeh Magilnick's shot and full game video, go to www. backdoorhoops.com.

Photo Courtesy of Yeshiva University
Aryeh Magilnick Shoots a Three to Send the Maritime versus Yeshiva Game
into Overtime. December 13, 2008.

Summertime in the Fifties—The Early Years

The only basketball I shot before my bar mitzvah was my pair of
rolled-up socks held together by rubber bands. It was not because playing
basketball violated a biblical commandment; the ball was simply too big.
My childhood was spent playing baseball. There were no Little League
teams, just choose-up games. We didn't have uniforms, and our parents
never watched us strike out. I played punchball in courtyards and curb
ball against apartment house stoops. When I got older, I played stickball
in the streets, and dodged oncoming buses while hiding stickball bats
from the police. To this day, I can hear my mother asking, "Where are
all my broomsticks?" I was chosen into every game because my brother
was a three-sewer stickball player. We bought Spaldings by redeeming
bottles; when we couldn't find bottles, we retrieved our lost Spaldings by
fishing in the sewers with wire baskets.

In seventh grade, although I didn't play basketball, I listened to
Knicks games on the radio; only on rare occasions did I actually get to
watch Richie Guerin and Carl Braun lose to Dolph Schayes. Back then,
I didn't even know that Dolph Schayes was Jewish. When it got too dark

to play stickball, we didn't go to a gym to shoot jump shots—we played ring-a-levio.

In the summer of 1957 I celebrated my bar mitzvah in the Rockaways. When I returned home, I discovered that my stickball buddies had disappeared. John and Brian were in Greenwood Lake, Eddie went to Florida, and Robert and Dean moved out of state. To make matters worse, my brother was back in the hospital. The block was suddenly deserted.

There were players in the PS 187 schoolyard, but my parents wouldn't let me go there. "Too many gangs," they warned. "Stay out of the schoolyard." Each day, instead of playing baseball, I sat alone on my stoop and listened to Russ Hodges broadcasting New York Giants games.

You never know from where help will come, and I certainly never expected my savior to come from apartment 2B.

"Hey, Halpert!"

He knew my name because I always broke his windows. It wasn't my fault. He was the one who chose to rent a second-floor apartment with a window next to our left-field foul pole. What was I supposed to do—hit the ball like a girl?

"Our team is short a player. Want to catch?"

Within minutes, I was on the Fort George field playing with guys who were twice my age and certainly not on my parents' play-date list. I had two doubles that day, and at the age of thirteen, I became an official member of the O'Donnell's Bar team. The players bought beer from the bar, and I ate Bungalow Bar from the ice cream truck. My neighbor from 2B paid. The field was adjacent to a park with a basketball court that doubled as a wading pool with a sprinkler. I had no use for the basketball court, but I used the sprinkler to cool off after games.

After one of my post-game showers, the park attendant approached me. "Want to sign up for a foul-shooting contest? You can win a silver dollar." A silver dollar in 1957 was like mega millions today. I signed up and a week later I took five foul shots and made only two. I shot the ball underhand because it was the only way I could reach the basket. I forgot about the contest until the next bar league game.

"Hey, Johnny," called the park attendant. "You made the finals."

I tried again, and this time, I made only one shot. Disappointed, I sat down and waited to see who would claim the silver dollar. I had listened to enough Knick games to know that one out of five doesn't win you any championships. That's still true today. The park attendant finally emerged holding the silver dollar.

"Congratulations. You are the foul-shooting champion of Fort George Park."

"I won?" I said with astonishment. "What did the other guys shoot?"

"What other guys? You're the only one who signed up."

I took the dollar home, and I still have it fifty years later.

My foul-shooting triumph did not come a minute too soon. The next day, my bar league career ended when my father found me standing outside the bar. I tried to calm him down by claiming that I was just obeying his order to stay out of the schoolyard. My pleadings did not impress, and a few days later, under orders from my father, Mr. 2B cut me.

I am not sure if it was boredom or the silver dollar, but without baseball, I went to the park everyday to play basketball. I didn't own a ball, but I got one from the park house by leaving my house keys as collateral. My routine was always the same. I started by first bringing a cold soda to my elderly neighbors who sat on the bench outside the park. On my way back, they gave me the empty bottle, which I redeemed for two cents. I used the money to treat myself to a pretzel stick, which I would dunk into my egg cream.

With the end of summer, my basketball routine was replaced by visits to the Yeshiva University High School Manhattan (MTA)[10] gym. I would go there at night to watch the high school team practice and on Thursday nights, I played three-on-three with YU college students. Although I did not know it, one of my Thursday night teammates was the future Rabbi Blau whose advice I still seek today.

Mr. Wettstein, my future high school coach, was a spectator during those half-court games. After watching me shoot underhand, he warned, "You will never make the team shooting that way."

After eighth grade graduation, I resumed my park routine of buying soda and shooting hoops. I listened to Mr. Wettstein's advice and made the MTA junior varsity team by shooting foul shots overhand. At the end

---

[10] A yeshiva high school operated by Yeshiva University and located on its Manhattan campus. It was earlier known as Manhattan Talmudical Academy—hence MTA—and today, as the Marsha Stern Talmudical Academy

of my freshman year, I was called to the high school office. A complete stranger handed me ten dollars. "I just want to say thank you for always stopping to bring my parents soda."

My first year junior varsity experience intensified my obsession with basketball. That summer, I shot jump shots instead of hitting baseballs and practiced in Rockaway instead of Washington Heights. Every morning, I would dribble from our bungalow on Beach 73rd Street to the empty schoolyard on Beach 54th Street.

There were no gangs in the Rockaway schoolyard. In fact, there wasn't anyone in the schoolyard. All alone I would move from court to court, endlessly driving and shooting jump shots. My goal to make the varsity in my sophomore year, however, fell short and although I practiced with the varsity one night a week, I played a second year on the JV.

The following summer, I returned to Rockaway, determined not only to make the starting team, but the league's all-star team. I doubled my workout routine and achieved both goals. The team, captained by Neil Katz, went undefeated in regular league play, but an upset by the Hebrew Institute of Long Island (HILI) in the playoffs knocked us out of the championship game in Madison Square Garden. In need of new challenges, I prepared for my senior year by returning to the Beach 54th Street schoolyard, determined to break the MTA scoring record and get to the championship game in Madison Square Garden.

My first-quarter report card almost put an end to both goals when my Hebrew teacher, Rabbi Bernstein, or "Rocky Louie" as he was fondly called, gave me a ten in Hebrew language. When I asked Rabbi Bernstein why he couldn't fail me with an inconspicuous sixty, he said, "You got a twelve on the test, and you lost two points for talking during class."

Mr. Perlmutter, my Bible and Jewish History teacher had less flair for the dramatic and failed me with a traditional fifty-five and fifty. Mr. Abrams, the principal, summoned me to his office to pronounce my sentence. Fortunately, Mr. Wettstein accompanied me to court.

"You have received a ten in Hebrew," said Mr. Abrams, "and a fifty-five in Bible. The teachers are demanding that I drop you from the basketball team."

Mr. Wettstein didn't hesitate and pounced on the word *demand*. "Who is running the high school—you or the teachers? Give Johnny two weeks, and he will improve his grades."

Mr. Wettstein had hit the right nerve. Mr. Abrams did not like to be told what to do by anybody. He stayed my execution and gave me two weeks to improve. Fear is a great motivator, and I received passing grades on my next Hebrew and Bible exams.

Mr. Abrams was so impressed by my turnaround that I became his personal farmer cheese courier. Every Thursday at the start of lunch hour I walked ten blocks to Daitch Supermarket on Broadway where I bought him two pounds of farmer cheese. I turned the fifteen-minute walk into a ninety-minute expedition, arriving back at school just in time to miss my first period history class with "Doc" Schapiro. When asked by Mr. Abrams what took so long, I blamed it on the long farmer cheese lines.

We finished the year in fourth place and found ourselves once again playing the now first-place HILI in the playoffs. In the last minute, I made a jump shot that broke the school scoring record and propelled us into the championship game in the Garden. Once again, however, my season ended with a loss as we were defeated by the Yeshiva of Flatbush.

At the end of my high school career, my attention turned to the summer. Despite my grade of ten in Hebrew, I had developed a close relationship with Rabbi Bernstein and one day after class, he asked me what I was doing for the summer.

"Playing basketball."

"How would you like to work and play at Camp Massad?"

"Camp Massad? That's a camp where they only speak Hebrew. You want to take someone who can barely speak Hebrew to a Hebrew-speaking camp?"

"It won't be a problem," he assured me. "You will work in the kitchen as the bread and milk boy and be free all day to play ball. As for the Hebrew, all the kitchen workers are parolees from South Philly. They don't speak much Hebrew either."

There would be an extra perk to the position that neither Rabbi Bernstein nor I could have ever predicted. Shortly after arriving in camp, I met a sixteen-year-old camper-waitress, Aviva Margolis, who within twenty-four hours became my first girlfriend and four years later, my wife.

Part of my job was to wake up each morning at 5:30 and cut the freshly baked bread. Through the intervention of G-D, Aviva's favorite food was the rye bread ends. Every morning, I would select the best ends and present them as a gift. Who needed to buy jewelry? I had unlimited access to rye bread.

The job was everything that Rabbi Bernstein had promised. No one knew or cared that I could barely speak Hebrew. I had time to practice by myself in the morning and had a shooting companion to keep me company in my afternoon workouts. We were not only rye bread-compatible but Aviva was a starter on the Ramaz girls' varsity basketball team. The summer went on without incident until one day I received a frantic message from Rabbi Bernstein.

"Shlomo Schulsinger, the camp director, is visiting the camp. Don't take any chances. Hide out in the laundry room until he leaves."

Schulsinger's vision for Camp Massad was to promote and teach Zionism. Speaking Hebrew, therefore, was paramount—and failure to do so could lead to a one-way ticket back to New York. I had too much to lose so I hid in the laundry shack, which was a quarter-mile behind the kitchen.

There I sat, me and the dirty tablecloths, eyes glued to the dining room's back door, anxiously waiting for a messenger to signal the all clear. Suddenly the back door opened and not one but two messengers started walking toward me. One was Rabbi Bernstein, my "messenger of freedom" but to my horror, the second was Shlomo Schulsinger, my "messenger of doom." Schulsinger, who was a tyrant, obviously had planted a spy in the camp to search for NHS's (non-Hebrew speakers). Some rival for Aviva must have ratted me out in order to get my rye bread concession. How else did Schulsinger know to look for me among the dirty tablecloths? None of that mattered now. In another minute, he would be at the laundry shack, asking me questions in Hebrew that I could barely understand, let alone answer.

Oh G-d, I thought. *Why hadn't I studied more Hebrew?*

Miraculously, with Bernstein and Schulsinger only a few feet away, I had an epiphany. Although I could not speak Hebrew fluently, my twelve years of Yeshiva education had taught me how to count in Hebrew. I jumped to my feet and started counting the tablecloths in Hebrew.

"*Echad* (one), *shtaim* (two), *shalosh* (three)."

I kept my back turned to Schulsinger to avoid making eye contact and just kept counting.

"There are hundreds of tablecloths here," I muttered to myself. "I'll just keep counting real slowly. Maybe he will get tired of waiting and go away."

"*Chamesh* (five), *shesh* (six)."

My plan was working to perfection. I was counting, and he was standing. More importantly, he wasn't asking—and I wasn't answering.

I had it made. "*Sheva* (seven), *shmona* (eight)." When I got to *tesha* (nine), I was seized with fear. I could only count to ten!

"*Esser* (ten)," I said with a quivering voice.

I paused and waited for Schulsinger's inevitable questions that would send me back to New York. To this day, I have no idea what fired the neurons in my brain, but before Schulsinger could utter a word, I started counting again. "*Echad, shtaim, shalosh, arba, chamesh, shesh, sheva, shmona tesha, esser.*" As soon as I got to ten, I started counting again. "*Echad, shtaim, shalosh, arba, chamesh, shesh, sheva, shmona tesha, esser.*"

I have no idea how many sets of ten I counted that day, but I finally outlasted him. The messenger of doom never got to ask a question and finally retreated. I was still standing and could return to my rye bread ends. The experience was so frightening, however, that even after they left I continued counting in Hebrew. I didn't stop until they disappeared through the back door of the dining room and only then did I sit down, this time surrounded by table cloths neatly piled in groups of ten. I stayed there until it was time for dinner preparation. After dinner, I passed Rabbi Bernstein on the path. He looked at me, shook his head, and started laughing. We never discussed the incident.

When the summer of 1962 ended, I returned home. The fifties were over and everything had changed for me. My brother was out of the hospital, but my mother was in the hospital. High school was replaced by college, hoops were practiced at sleep away camp not Rockaway, Red Sarachek replaced Mr. Wettstein, and Aviva Margolis was my best friend.

Photo courtesy of Yeshiva University
Johnny Halpert, 1962, Yeshiva University High School.

Coachette

The sixteen-year-old high school junior stood on Camp Massad's foul line, poised to launch her potential game-winning hook shot and I stood under the basket waiting to rebound and score the certain miss. Regardless of the game's outcome, it was a very unusual first date. It was a cost-free opportunity to meet a pretty girl and simultaneously play basketball. What could be better than that?

Not even those idyllic conditions, however, would interfere with my competitive drive to win. A date is one thing, a loss to a girl, even a pretty one, is something else. The hook shot left her hand with a perfect arc and with a follow-through right out of Clair Bee's manual on shooting. The ball sailed through the air and hit nothing but net. I caught the ball before it hit the ground and then stood for a long second stunned that I had actually lost. I turned slowly toward the future Mrs.

Halpert who was standing without celebration on the foul line. Her only outward show of emotion was her smile. I took another second and then overwhelmed with male machismo, declared, "I let you win." The pretty girl, without missing a beat, smiled and asked, "Do you want to play again?" Throughout the years when people ask how we met I retell the story but always end with the declaration that "I let her win." Aviva never offers a word of dissent. She just smiles and reminds everyone that at sixteen she was the MVP in the 1964 Metropolitan Jewish High School League, Girls' (MJHSLG)[11] All-star game.

What began with a simple game of twenty-one has become a fifty year coaching partnership. My wife attends all games because she wants to share in the thrill of winning but also wants to be there to ease the disappointment of losing. At home or on the road she can be found sitting anxiously with arms folded, three rows directly behind the bench. She understands the etiquette of being the "coach's wife." No yelling at referees who are tormenting her husband with missed calls, no responding to irate fans who are criticizing the coach, no reactions to players' turnovers and certainly no post-game discussions with parents about their sons' playing time. Even after the game is over there is no gloating at victories and no despair at losses. The only show of emotion permitted is a small kiss after a victory and a quiet handhold after a loss.

The greatest challenge to her self-imposed standards of coaching etiquette has been the questionable calls by refs, especially in close games. Despite often experiencing "Referee rage" she always maintained her self-imposed silence. However, that did not stop our younger son from using his mother to gain an advantage from the refs. In a could-have-gone-either-way call the ref chose the other way and whistled Rafi for a foul. Rafi angled up to the ref and whispered, "That was a bad call; remember my mother's watching." The ref, who had officiated many Yeshiva games, took notice and gave Rafi the next call sending him to the line for two shots. As he handed Rafi the ball, he whispered, "Tell your mother that was for her."

Aviva's presence impacted not only the coach and referees but also the players. Although college players do not want their mothers hovering over them, a mother's presence can still provide players a sense of

---

[11]   The Metropolitan Yeshiva High School Athletic League for girls is made up of teams from the New York metropolitan area.

security, as long as she remains in the shadows. This was especially true for players who were thousands of miles from home. When requested she provided Tylenol for pregame headaches, orthopedic referrals for game injuries, entrée to part time jobs for rent money and a Shabbos retreat when school became overwhelming. On those rare occasions when she missed a game they always noticed by asking me if she needed "a night off."

Perhaps it was at our Sabbath retreats that Aviva's presence was most keenly felt. The centrality of the Jewish mother is never more evident than on the Sabbath and therefore Sabbath meals at our home always stood in stark contrast to the training tables of Duke. The Sabbath was not ushered in with a pep talk by the coach but by the lighting of Sabbath candles by the coach's wife. The candles served as a quiet reminder to the players of their own homes.

Aviva's presence was so muted that I never imagined that she would be the subject of a player's request for a meeting. I began the player-coach meeting expecting a typical conversation about basketball. Instead of a demand for more playing time, however, I heard a plea for more food.

"Coach, can you get me your wife's carrot kugel recipe? I want to give it to my mom, but I am too embarrassed to ask."

I wish I could testify that eating Aviva's carrot kugel turned guards into centers, but unfortunately, kugel eaters usually grow wider, not taller.

Over the years, we have been very fortunate that our relationships with many former players have extended past jump shots and graduations. Among our great thrills is to be introduced by former players to their wives and children. The conversation always begins with the question, "Are you still coaching?" and concludes with "Don't retire, in ten years, I'll have a shooting guard for you." Unfortunately, they never offer a big man.

Very often, the relationship with former players evolves and becomes more parallel than vertical; it is Aviva who captains this evolution, and although her relationship is no longer from the third row, it still retains elements of distance. This subtlety is captured by the title "Coachette," which was bestowed by Daniel Aaron, a former player who had a part-time job working for Aviva. The work environment was purposefully informal with everyone on a first-name basis, but Daniel couldn't bring himself to address the coach's wife by her first name and Aviva felt uncomfortable being formally addressed as Mrs. Halpert. In a stroke of creativity, Daniel created the title of "Coachette."

Today, when former players introduce us to their children, they often say, "This is my former coach, and this is Coachette."

The Code of the Court

I played my first basketball games in the schoolyards and parks of Washington Heights. We played three-on-three half-court, winners out, and ten baskets wins. The games were intense because a loss meant a forty-five minute wait for "next." Despite the high stakes, players resolved all disputes. Traveling and out-of-bounds calls were decided by "Odds, one takes it" or the great compromise "No basket, your ball." Fouls were adjudicated via the honor code; a player's verbal whistle of "I've got it!" stood even if you didn't think he had anything. The court gave great respect to anyone who accepted the call and shunned anyone who abused the code by making phantom calls.

My step from a park "participant" to a park "player" occurred in 1960. I spent my one-hour lunch breaks playing against my yeshiva classmates and spent after school and days off playing against the Washington Heights locals.

On the Sunday before the Passover vacation, the park was packed with players, including a recent *New York Post* all-city all-star. With the game tied at nine and the losing team looking at a forty-five minute wait, the all-star faked right and drove left to the basket. I blocked his shot, but before I could score the winning basket, he yelled, "I've got it!"

The court murmured against the call. I abided by the code, gave him the ball, and yelled, "Play it back." He scored on the ensuing possession, and I spent the next forty-five minutes waiting for "next." Although enraged by his sham call, the high-fives from the other players for honoring the code consoled me. The all-star may have won the game, but I had won the court. The experience taught me that respect from the court is better than any win.

In December 1974, with Brooklyn Poly leading by two with two minutes to play, Paul Merlis, YU's six-foot-six center, was whistled for a foul. Everyone in the gym knew it was his fifth—except Poly's official scorer. Although Yeshiva's book had Paul for five fouls, the official Poly book had him for four. After a few moments of waiting patiently for the referees to sort out the discrepancy, Joe Martini, the Poly coach, took matters into his own hands. "That's his fifth," he declared. "The Poly book is wrong, and everyone knows it."

While the refs debated whether they could overturn the official book, Joe made one last plea to the court. "Come on, Johnny. You know he's got five!"

I hesitated for a long second and said, "Poly's book is wrong. He's got five."

The refs thanked me, Paul fouled out, and Poly went on to win 83-77, making us 0-5 for the season. I went home frustrated with the loss but feeling good that I had done the right thing.

In the summer of 2012, I attended the wake of Nick Gaetani, a highly respected collegiate referee who had officiated many Yeshiva games over the years. As I paid my respects to his family and got up to leave, a complete stranger approached me. "Thank you very much for coming. Nicky always talked about the Yeshiva coach. He said you always respected the game." I thanked him for his kind words and left.

Nick Gaetani had refereed the 1974 Brooklyn Poly game.

Knock, Knock—Is Anyone There?

I ended my high school career lying at mid-court of Madison Square Garden with a badly twisted ankle. I had scored seven points in the first quarter of the Metropolitan Jewish High School League championship game, but I would score only two more, a half-court fling to beat the halftime buzzer. As I lay there, I saw my mother, who was attending her first basketball game, heading for the court. The embarrassment of my mother hovering over me on the Garden floor got me up. Halftime pleading got me back into the game, but there would be no miracle finishes. I ended my high school career with nine points and a loss.

I took a month off to heal and then returned to the MTA gym to pursue my dream of playing college basketball. Every night, I bribed the custodian fifteen cents to open the gym. It was 1962, a time when Orthodox kids played hoops not Nintendo, wore hats in public not yarmulkes, and never marched in protest. Advocacy was a word on the

SAT exams, and Russia was a question on the world history regents exam. My passion was playing basketball. I would wake up early to practice, and despite living across the street, always came late to school.

"You got stuck in traffic again?" Rabbi Weinbach would ask as he wrote my daily late pass.

That was my world a week before Passover when Bernie Kabak, a former teammate, walked into the gym and introduced me to the world of Russian Jewry.

"Want to play one-on-one?" I asked.

"No," he responded. "Want to attend a protest march for Russian Jews?"

"What are we protesting against?"

"The Russians are not letting Jews bake Matzoh."

I have no idea why I decided to attend the march. Maybe it was because a former teammate was asking, but more likely it was because it was an excuse to cut school. It was certainly not out of conviction. I knew nothing about Russian Jewry, and there was no revolutionary DNA in my genes. The only message that resonated was that Jews would not have Matzoh.

Bernie and two Yeshiva students, David Froelich and Benjy Silverberg, spent the week banging on Yeshiva dormitory doors in search of more "Matzoh protesters." The door-knocking succeeded, and on Thursday April 12, 1962, a few hundred MTA high school and Yeshiva college students participated in the first organized protest on behalf of Russian Jewry.

The following Monday, two days before the start of the Passover vacation, all high school marchers were summoned to the auditorium and addressed by our legendary principal, Mr. Norman B. Abrams. There was no political correctness in the sixties, and neither students nor faculty felt any guilt when referring to Mr. Abrams as the "Jap." The title was bestowed because Mr. Abrams not only possessed Japanese features but he acted like the stereotypical Japanese soldiers in American war movies. Throughout the school day, he would stalk the halls, spying through the small windows of our classroom doors. Due to his short stature, only his eyes reached above the door windows, which made it impossible for even the best lookout to sound the alarm, "Chickie the Jap". Without warning he would burst through the door and capture the transgressing students. The prisoners would be herded to his office where they would hear him declare in his unique cadence, "You are suspended until your mother, your father, or one of your parents comes to school."

We sat in the auditorium waiting for the arrival of the prison commandant. We foolishly believed that he would spare us from punishment since our absences had been for a just cause. In 1962, however, neither Mr. Abrams nor anyone in the Jewish establishment believed that Jews should engage in public protest. They firmly believed that change could be best achieved through quiet, behind-the-scenes negotiations.

Mr. Abrams stood at the podium, barely reaching the microphone, and declared that we were all suspended since Thursday's absences were not excused. The auditorium was filled with seniors who had spent four years dreading the suspension sentence but now two months away from graduation, suspension held no fear. More importantly, a suspension before Passover meant an extended vacation.

Mr. Abram's announcement was followed by a five-second pause as we processed the implications of the punishment. Suddenly and spontaneously, a scream of joy erupted from the protesters, and all the seniors jumped to their feet and ran screaming through the auditorium doors. Within five minutes of the announcement every "Matzoh protester" was on his way home. Mr. Abrams was left standing at the podium, stunned. No one looked back.

As for me, the kid who lived across the street, within minutes I was back in the gym playing ball. The march of protest had not freed our Russian brothers, but it had freed the protesters. Talk about positive reinforcement. No wonder we participated in future marches.

Unfortunately our freedom was short-lived and that night all our parents were called and directed to send their children back to school. The following day, the parents of all high school protesters received official unexcused absence letters, which I proudly present as certification that I was a member of the original "Matzoh protesters."

Two years later, in the spring of 1964, Mr. Jacob Birnbaum[12] knocked on a Yeshiva University dormitory door. Inside were former high school

---

[12] Jacob Birnbaum and Glenn Richter founded the Student Struggle for Soviet Jewry movement in 1964.

"Matzoh protesters." We listened as he pleaded with us to attend another protest on behalf of Russian Jewry.

Four days later, on May Day, we, along with approximately a thousand students from the New York metropolitan area, showed up at the Soviet Union United Nations Mission and participated in the first Student Struggle for Soviet Jewry (SSSJ) protest rally. With each succeeding year, the SSSJ-sponsored rallies increased in size and intensity. The protests grew to fifteen thousand people in 1966 and culminated in the 1987 March on Washington when a quarter of a million people participated. Yeshiva high schools no longer suspended students for attending but actually chartered buses so that students could participate.

Years later Jacob Birnbaum reflected, "In one decade, I went from knocking on dormitory doors at Yeshiva University to knocking on doors in Congress."[13]

Learning theory teaches that future behavior is a function of past experiences. My frayed fifty-year-old Matzoh letter, which I proudly show to my children and grandchildren, taught me that one dedicated person can make a difference provided that he has the passion to knock on dormitory doors.

---

[13]   Yossi Klein Halevi, "Jacob Birnbaum and the Struggle for Soviet Jewry," *NCSJ,* Spring 2004.

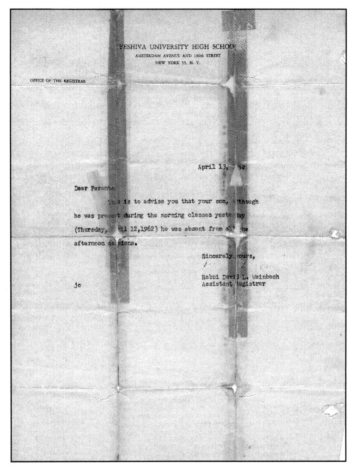

YESHIVA UNIVERSITY HIGH SCHOOL
AMSTERDAM AVENUE AND 186th STREET
NEW YORK 33, N. Y.

OFFICE OF THE REGISTRAR

April 13, 62

Dear Parents

This is to advise you that your son, although
he was present during the morning classes yesterday
(Thursday, April 12,1962) he was absent from all the
afternoon sessions.

Sincerely yours,

Rabbi David L. Weinbach
Assistant Registrar

jc

Yeshiva University's Unexcused Absence Notification Letter. April 1962

If There Are No Baskets, Is It Still A Gym?

Just as our ancestors wandered in the desert for forty years en route to a homeland, Yeshiva University basketball players wandered for fifty years through the greater New York metropolitan area in search of a home gym. Although practice was routine at other colleges, it was always a mystery bus ride at Yeshiva. From the uncertainty of where the next practice was being held to the suspense of whether the chosen gym would have high ceilings, the site of Yeshiva's practices was always an adventure.

The first stop in the journey took place in 1930 when workouts were held in the MTA gym, a converted *mikvah* (ritual bath) located in the bowels of the earth. If that was not distinctive enough, it also featured a fourteen-foot ceiling that made shooting outside shots not only difficult, but also fraught with danger. Legend has it that Yeshiva's long history of moving without the ball comes from the fear of being decapitated by flying basketballs ricocheting off the low ceiling. Even today, when I want to reinforce the principle of pass first, shoot second, I return to my roots and hold practice in the height-challenged gym.

The only experience that could surpass the adventure of practicing in a gym with low ceilings was to practice in a gym with no baskets. In my senior year of college, after years of traveling the trains through the five boroughs of New York, we were greeted by the news that practice that year would be held in the brand-new Eleanor Roosevelt Junior High School, two short blocks from the campus. For the first time there would be no one-hour train rides at ten at night. The opening of Eleanor Roosevelt was equivalent to the coming of the Messiah. Unfortunately, just like other disappointments in Jewish history, Junior High School 143 would prove to be a false Messiah.

There was enormous anticipation as the date of our first practice drew near. In previous years, I would leave class early, catch the Amsterdam Avenue bus to 168th Street, change to the "A" train, get off at 59th Street, and walk five blocks to Power Memorial High School. I would arrive at 8:00 for the 7:30 practice and be greeted by Coach Sarachek who would "gently inquire" why I was late. On Monday night, October 25, 1965, I walked out of class at 7:25—and Red was already yelling at me by 7:30.

Although the gym was virtually on campus, some things remained the same. When we arrived that first night the outside doors were locked so we continued the long Yeshiva tradition of banging on locked gym doors, hoping that someone would hear us. After five minutes of banging the custodian appeared. We raced onto the court, vying to score the first baskets. Basketballs came flying out of the ball bag as ten players wrestled for six balls. The excitement abated when everyone suddenly recognized what was so obvious. There were no baskets. We had practiced in gyms with low ceilings, and we had practiced in gyms without lights, but now we were experiencing the ultimate philosophical dilemma that only Talmudic scholars could answer. If there are no baskets, is it still a gym? We pondered the question but only briefly and in testimony to our ability to engage in denial, we started shooting at the imaginary baskets.

In retrospect, we were the first college basketball team to play virtual basketball. In a matter of moments we had completely adjusted and the legend of the low ceiling morphed into the legend of no baskets. As for Red, the lack of baskets did not bother him at all. "What difference does it make," he barked, "you could never shoot anyway."

We practiced for almost two months without baskets and learned to take the concept of making the extra pass to its infinite extreme. We still ran our full-court shooting drills, but we emphasized technique rather than made shots. For me personally, it was a blessing in disguise. For two months, I never missed a layup. Perhaps the most amazing outcome was that during the first half of the season when we had no baskets, we led the metropolitan area in foul shooting. When the baskets arrived in January, our foul shooting percentages returned to mediocre.

So You Want to Be a Coach? It's All about the Little Things

I called time-out and the Camp Raleigh[14] waiters' team gathered around to hear my last-shot instructions. I used one of Red Sarachek's plays, and Stu Poloner made a last-second shot on an inbound pass from Larry Schiffman, Camp Raleigh's version of Bill Russell.

I was only a twenty-year-old college junior, but then and there I knew I wanted to coach. Each waiters' team victory reinforced that desire, but final reinforcement only came in my senior year of college when Mr. Wettstein, injured in a car accident, asked me to coach the MTA varsity during his convalescence.

On Monday and Wednesdays, from 6:15 to 7:45, I would teach Red's "C" play to the high school varsity and at 8:00, I'd execute the same play at my college practice. On Thanksgiving Eve, 1965, the undefeated MTA varsity overcame a 37-22 halftime deficit to defeat archrival Albertus Magnus 54-49 before a standing-room-only crowd. The game featured great individual performances by Stu Poloner and Larry Schiffman—as

---

[14]   A private, coed Orthodox summer camp that was located in Livingston Manor, New York.

well as Steve Singer's acrobatic dive into the stands to save an errant pass.[15]

Although Steve's takeoff was amazing, it was his landing on the laps of the Albertus Magnus nuns dressed in full white habits that will always be remembered. The startled nuns, unfazed by their flying visitor, helped Steve back onto the court and proceeded, along with the YU fans, to applaud his hustle. The thrill of the come-from-behind victory left me believing that coaching was all about wins. It did not take long, however, before my JV players taught me that coaching was also about the little things you do. Forty-six years later, my JV players are still reinforcing that lesson.

Upon graduation from College in 1966, Rabbi Weinbach, MTA's principal, asked me to coach the JV team. Too excited to understand how difficult it was going to be to build a high school team, I immediately accepted the offer. I continue to marvel how a conductor can induce a hundred individual musicians to perform together in perfect harmony with a flick of a hand, yet I struggle to get five individuals to play as one unit. When my awe turns to envy, I rationalize that the conductor, unlike the coach, does not have to worry that an opposing musician is going to steal his players' instruments while they perform Beethoven.

All seasons begin with tryouts, which in 1966, I viewed as nothing more than choosing the best players. I quickly realized, however, that tryouts were more about the kids who didn't get *chosen-in* than about those who did. My final cuts triggered immediate pleas of "I know I can play better than I did tonight. Can I have another chance?"

In my first year, I stood firm, but pleas from players, parents, and even Rabbi Weinbach about second chances taught me how important it is for fourteen and fifteen-year-olds to be *chosen-in*. As a result, my subsequent JV teams opened the season with fifteen to eighteen players. In my pre-gym college coaching years, I had no problem with tryouts because there were not enough players interested in trying out. Desperate to find players to fill the last spots anyone who appeared was issued a uniform. With the opening of our new gym, however, my earlier tryout dilemma returned as multiple players showed up to vie for the fifteenth

---

[15]   Others members of the 1966 MTA varsity include Harry Bajnon, T. Bernstein, Marty Genauer, Harvey Gertel, Larry Jacobs, David Kramer, Jake Krieger, David Maizel, Sam Wilzig, and Efrem Zuroff.

spot. This time, I not only heard the earlier claim of a "bad night," but a new appeal, "If I can't be on the team, can I still practice with the team?"

My initial reaction was to observe the tradition of fifteen-man rosters, but the collegiate need to be *chosen-in* was equal to that of my JV teenagers of twenty years prior and made me question the sacredness of the number fifteen. I solved the problem by inviting the last five candidates to start practicing with the team, thus allowing them to decide on their own whether being *chosen-in* was worth the time and effort. Invariably, after a few weeks, some chose not to sacrifice the time and opted out. For those who were willing to practice four times a week without the possibility of playing, I always found room for one more. I had learned that regardless of age, the exhilaration of feeling *in* was just as important as a game-winning steal or foul shot.

In my first month of coaching, I taught a new play at every practice. By the time my JV players got to their first game, they had received so many plays that every offensive possession resulted in chaos. Although Red had given me great offensive schemes, I had failed to grasp that fundamentals—not schemes—enable players to neutralize their opponent's skills. As I began to understand the importance of fundamentals, drilling replaced scrimmaging. Although my current college players still echo the complaint of too much drilling and not enough scrimmaging, I still believe in "Drill, baby, drill."

My belief in teaching fundamentals was immediately challenged by a disappointing first year record of five wins and five losses. Fortunately, Mr. Wettstein supported my approach, and I was able to maintain my stubborn commitment to teaching and drilling. My stubbornness was rewarded with a 14-3 record in my second year, which taught me that if you want to be a coach, you better remain true to what you believe.

Beyond the lesson of keeping the faith, I also learned to never assume anything. With twenty-two seconds left in the half against Ramaz, I stood up and yelled, "One shot" and just for emphasis added, "Hold for one."

I assumed that everyone, even a JV freshman playing in his first game, understood the coaching command of one shot. As soon as my words reached his ears, my high school freshman stopped his dribble and hoisted up a half-court jump shot. The shot crashed off the front rim and fell into the hands of a stunned defensive player.

The player, along with the spectators, was so shocked that he remained frozen in surprise for a few seconds. Then, realizing the great opportunity that had just fallen into his hands, he dribbled the length of the court, making a layup as time expired. In the halftime locker room it took me a few minutes to compose myself before I asked the obvious question.

"Didn't you hear me yelling one shot? What were you thinking?"

The freshman looked up and with pure innocence, he said, "You said take one shot, and that's exactly what I did. I took one shot."

The November 1970 Albertus Magnus JV game taught me that anything can happen in a basketball game—and it usually does. Trailing by twelve points, I called time-out to set up an inbounds play against their full-court pressure. Having learned my lesson *to never assume* anything, I carefully reminded each player of his individual responsibility. Unfortunately, I neglected one small detail. The press-break play worked to perfection, and Harold Landa received the inbound pass completely unguarded under his defensive basket. He did not hesitate upon receiving the pass and did what any fifteen-year-old would do when left unguarded under a basket. He shot the ball. It was a perfect shot with a perfect follow-through; unfortunately, it was at the wrong basket. His teammates stood frozen, I stood speechless, and the fans stood and yelled. As for Harold, he realized immediately that his field goal "was not like the others" and ran down the court, hoping to get as far away from his mistake as possible.

In February 1998, Joel Jacobson scored thirty-eight points—thirty-six for Yeshiva and two for Pratt. An errant half-court inbounds pass landed in Joel's hands, and with no defender within ten feet, he dribbled to the wrong basket and made the easiest two points of his 1,330 career total. Fortunately, the basket only bruised Joel's ego and had no bearing on the game's outcome. We went on to win 80-43.

In the locker room after the game, everyone ignored Joel's thirty-six points and focused on his two-point layup. I stood in the locker room, unfazed. When my players asked why I was so calm, I said, "That's not the first time I've seen that. Twenty-eight years ago, Harold Linda prepared me to expect the unexpected."

During a spring 1970 gym class, I watched freshman Terry Rifkin steal the ball five consecutive times and lead his team to a 10-0 intramural game win. Impressed by his quickness, I encouraged him to improve his skills at Camp Raleigh where I was head counselor. Terry came to Raleigh and approached me on the third day.

"I am in bunk three, but I want to play with the better players in bunk one."

It is impossible to remember what I was thinking forty-two years ago, but I am confident that I said yes simply because I recognized that it was important for Terry and it was an easy request to accommodate. It would take many years before I learned just how important.

That fall, Terry used his quickness to make the JV. In March 1971, with two minutes remaining in the championship game and trailing 37-33, I substituted Terry and told him, "We need the ball; play for the steal!"

Thirty seconds later, still, trailing 37-35, Terry used his speed to steal the inbounds pass and dribble the length of the court to tie the game. Although it was Donnie Berman's three points and Mark Hoenig's put-back basket in the last minute that gave us the 42-40 championship victory, Terry's steal was the play of the game. Since the game was a championship win, I always remembered Terry's steal but completely forgot about his odyssey from gym class to Bunk One. In May 2012, Terry called me in response to an invitation to my floor-naming tribute.

"I have never thanked you for what you did, but you changed my life. My freshman year at MTA was very difficult. I was from public school, didn't know anyone, and wasn't in with the good players. I would have transferred if you hadn't brought me to Camp Raleigh and let me play with boy's Bunk One. Who knows where I would be today if I had transferred."

In March 1972, one year after my first championship, fourteen-year-old Jonathan Heller stepped to the foul line in the junior varsity championship game between MTA and Ramaz. With the score tied at fifty-nine in overtime, Jonathan made the two foul shots that gave MTA its first lead and ultimate 63-59 championship win. Although I lost all contact with Jonathan after his family relocated to Florida, I never forgot his two foul shots.

Twenty-five years later, in response to my request for a referral to a Florida attorney, Rabbi Davis of the Young Israel of Hollywood recommended the law firm of Deborah Chames. An hour later, my phone rang. "Hi, Coach Halpert, I'm sure you don't remember me. I am Jonathan Heller, Ms. Chames' partner."

Before he could say another word, I said, "Remember you? I've never forgotten you. You're the freshman who made two foul shots in the last seconds of overtime to give me my second championship."

In May 2012, Jonathan flew to New York to attend my floor-naming tribute and followed the visit with an e-mail. "Coach, I know we only spent one short JV season together . . . but I have felt your influence in my life virtually on a daily basis."

I was stunned by Terry and Jonathan's remarks because I had no recollection of doing anything other than giving them opportunities to make steals and foul shots, let alone something that changed their lives. Their expressions of gratitude confirmed once again that coaching is not just about moments of triumph, but about the little things you do simply because they are the right things to do.[16]

---

[16] See Appendix A for a listing of all junior varsity players from 1966 through 1972.

Chapter 2

G-D AND BASKETBALL

Why?

I blew the whistle and directed the offensive team to run the "C" play. "Remember—Pass right and pick left."

At most colleges, players respond by passing and cutting. At Yeshiva, players ask, "Why." "Why pick and spin? Maybe I should pick and slide?" Insubordination or the tradition of Talmudic[17] study?

The team completed its pre-game warm-ups and returned to the locker room to listen to my Knute Rockne inspirational speech. The players listened while off on the side Simon Brookhim, my six-foot-five starting forward devoured a plate of fried chicken and French fried potatoes. Player disrespect or pangs of hunger?

Following our last minute, three-point loss, I delivered my postmortem speech. I completed my harangue by challenging the team to return to our next practice with more focus.

Benjy Lockspeiser, our captain, immediately stood up and addressed the team. "Okay, guys, before we leave, let's settle this. Who is bringing the challah and wine Friday night?" Was it player disinterest or echoes of Ecclesiastes ("There is a time and place for everything.")?

The above vignettes succinctly capture the struggles and perspective of the Yeshiva basketball player as well as the challenges inherent in coaching those players.

Asking "why" is a trait that has been nurtured by two thousand years of Talmudic study. From the ancient study halls of Babylonia to the modern study halls of YU, the Jewish people have been imbued with the tradition of asking questions. Questioning is how we learn, and it is the

---

[17] The Talmud, also referred to as Gemara, is a sixty-volume exposition of Jewish law where Talmudic scholars reach legal conclusions via a process of back-and-forth questions and responses.

reason why we answer a question with a question. It is the phenomenon of "why" more than weight training or limited practice times that makes the YU athlete distinct from his opponents. It is not surprising, therefore, that YU players do not leave their "whys" in the study halls when they come to the gym. The "why" is so embedded that when a player follows my directives without hesitation, I immediately stop practice and ask, "What? No whys? Are you sure you're Jewish?"

As for Simon, it would be easy to interpret his eating as an act of disrespect, and most coaches would react by throwing out the food followed by the player. At Yeshiva, the player's actions do not represent acts of defiance but the reality of not having eaten all day. The typical player's day is 7:30 wake-up, Jewish studies classes from 9:00 to 1:00, secular classes from 2:00 to 8:00, and basketball from 8:00 to10:00. The unusual act of eating a pre-game meal at a pre-game meeting is really an example of dedication. After all, an unmotivated player would quit after missing his first meal.

As for the captain who was seeking accountability for wine and challah, he was merely practicing King Solomon's dictum that "there is a time and place for everything." For the Yeshiva player, "everything" means religious observance, Jewish studies, secular studies, pursuit of career, pursuit of a wife and, oh yes, three-point jump shots. Prioritizing these objectives is the only way a YU player can accommodate all his goals. This orientation starts in preschool when he simultaneously learns two languages and two cultures.

Each advance in age and grade is accompanied by additional goals. This process of compartmentalization is further nurtured by the reality that, regardless of the Yeshiva player's level of religious observance, he will always be accommodating himself to his secular and Jewish worlds. Inevitably as the player approaches college, his dreams of victories are supplanted by the importance of study and career. It is not by chance that although Jews comprise only 2 percent of the population, they comprise 37 percent of all American Nobel Prize winners.[18]

The challenge of coaching the Yeshiva player is to balance the demand for basketball focus against the player's multiple objectives and "why" personality. I have attempted to achieve this balance by requiring

---

[18]   Arthur's Anything Index, http://en.wikipedia.org/wiki/
American_Jews#Socioeconomics

basketball dedication only when players are engaged in basketball. The perspective that basketball is not "all-important-all-the-time" is not often written on locker-room walls, but I have learned never to demand from players what I cannot expect them to produce.

On Wednesday, March 5, 1997 the Yeshiva basketball team traveled to Staten Island to play the College of Staten Island in the postseason ECAC[19] championship tournament. Despite the usual hysteria over post-season play, the Yeshiva players attended their five o'clock classes, arriving only forty minutes before tip-off. As we entered the gym, we were greeted by the following posting. "Due to the class commitment of the Yeshiva student-athletes, our game will tip off at 8:00."

We lost to Staten Island and finished the season at 15-6. As we left the gym, I took home the student-athlete announcement and hung it with my other memorabilia. I have always cherished that sign because it was a public affirmation that we could go to class until 6:00 and still play in the ECAC at 8:00. The announcement remains far more meaningful than any ECAC trophy.

On the trip back to school, the team decided to stop in Manhattan for an end-of-season dinner. It took the team only ten seconds to decide to stop—and only five seconds to decide that the coach should pay. However, in the true tradition of Talmudic study, it took thirty minutes of questioning to decide where to stop. The dinner had a nostalgic air as it symbolized the end for the graduating seniors and the beginning for the returning players.

As we rose to leave, the new captain asked, "Coach, where is our team trip next year?"

"We are going to Boston," I answered.

Before the word Boston left my lips, a voice from the back yelled, "Boston? Why not Florida?"

On or Off? That Is the Question

The accommodation of wearing yarmulkes[20] while playing basketball has a long history both in the religious world of Yeshiva University and the

---

[19]   Eastern College Athletic Conference

[20]   A head covering also referred to as a skullcap.

secular world of the NCAA.[21] Yeshiva, out of devotion to observance, wanted the yarmulke on and the NCAA, out of devotion to safety, wanted the yarmulke off. Due to multiple judicial decisions supporting the principle of individual rights and the lack of evidence supporting yarmulke-related injury, the debate has faded into memory. In 1979, however, the tension between on and off was still very much alive.

The referee's reminder that players wearing yarmulkes could warm up with their head coverings on, but had to remove them once the game started quickly changed my pre-game focus from Drew University to Yeshiva.

"My players wear their yarmulkes for religious reasons," I responded. "If some can't play, then we're all going home."

The ref's response was quick and decisive. "NCAA rules prohibit all appendages, and head coverings are considered appendages."

I would like to claim that my threat to go home was predicated on principle only, but in truth I was equally motivated by the tempting prize of avoiding another loss.

Before I could secure either points or prize, the Drew coach rose up to advocate on our behalf. If I was determined to escape a loss, he was equally determined to secure a win.

"It's not a problem. Yeshiva always plays with yarmulkes," he pleaded to the refs.

Of course it's okay, I thought. *He's looking at a certain win. He would play if we were wearing sombreros.*

"No," I insisted in righteous indignation. "We are a team; if some players can't play, then no one will play."

My threat to leave only energized the Drew coach and he filed the following amicus brief with the court. "Referees always allow Yeshiva to play with yarmulkes." The refs, who in their defense were only invoking the NCAA bible, conferred momentarily, unsure what to do.

In that moment of hesitation, my newfound advocate declared with Solomonic wisdom, "Call the supervisor of officials; he will give you the okay."

His appeal to the supervisor signaled that *on this night* Yeshiva would be awarded neither points nor prizes. The supervisor had just refereed a YU game and allowed yarmulkes to fly all over the court.

---

[21]   National Collegiate Athletic Association

In a flash, the Drew coach was dialing the supervisor's number. My only hope was that the supervisor wasn't home. Unfortunately, he picked up on the third ring. It took the refs a minute to explain the problem—but only five seconds for the supervisor to okay the yarmulkes.

The refs dutifully obeyed the supervisor's verdict. We returned to the gym with yarmulkes firmly in place and lost 79-49, proving that if you don't have the players, not even G-D can save you from a thirty-point loss.

Pre-Game Warm-Ups and Prayers

The best way to earn an invitation to a tournament is to demonstrate the correct balance between being skillful enough to compete but not skillful enough to win. We were on everyone's tournament invite list and usually proved to be very gracious guests. We played well, but ultimately succumbed to the host team. On those occasions when we upset the host, we were treated as ungrateful guests and were not invited back. To quote a host coach moments after we upset his team, "Congratulations, you played great. I'll never invite you again."

Despite our past drubbings by Trinity College, the opportunity for a championship trophy and all-star selections was enough incentive to accept an invitation to their 1980 holiday tournament. Little did I know that their tournament would also provide a unique opportunity for religious observance.

The pre-game routine proceeded according to custom. Players dressed, got taped, and warmed up. Midway through the warm-ups, the worlds of religious practice and game preparation collided, providing an excellent example of how the religious and secular worlds can be accommodated. According to Jewish law, the Mincha (afternoon) prayer must be recited before sundown.

Fifteen minutes before tip-off, one of my players approached, "Coach, it is thirty minutes before sundown; we have to recite Mincha now."

I had no idea how to react since I had never thought about integrating prayer and layup drills. While I was thinking, the captain was acting. "Let's go guys."

In a flash, the team ran into the twenty-degree parking lot and offered afternoon prayers in their basketball shorts. The sight of ten young men standing in Yeshiva University uniforms offering silent prayer was startling to the arriving fans. It was equally startling to the spectators inside the gym as they watched the Yeshiva players abruptly run to the parking lot, apparently to board the bus to return home.

When I explained to the referees that my players had merely left to recite their afternoon prayers but were coming back, they were very sympathetic.

"I don't blame you for praying. They're a tough team, and you're going to need all the help you can get." Their words were prophetic. On this night, G-D was rooting for Trinity College—and we were soundly defeated.

After the game, we climbed onto the bus, grabbed the eight-hour-old tuna fish sandwiches, and started back to school. On the way back the bus stopped and we said our evening prayers.

Purim at the ECAC

The drive to make the 1993 ECAC postseason tournament was so intense that it wasn't until we received the invitation that we realized the game time would conflict with the reading of the Purim Megillah.[22] Coaching at Yeshiva teaches you many life lessons, but none more important than that "for every problem, there is a solution."

My phone call to Jersey City State was short and simple. "We are looking forward to the game, but we need some assistance."

Coach Brown, expecting the traditional coaching requests responded without hesitation. "No problem. I'll get you our game tapes, and we'll provide the trainer."

"Thank you, Coach, but we don't need tapes or taping; just a large classroom where we can read the Purim Megillah after the game."

---

[22] The holiday of Purim commemorates the deliverance of the Jewish people in ancient Persia in the wake of a plot by Haman, the king's vizor, to annihilate the Jews. The story of Purim is recorded in the Book of Esther and is read on Purim from a scroll referred to as a Megillah.

"That's a new one," he said, "but it's not a problem. We have a large room near the gym."

Two hundred cheering fans who chose to combine Megillah with basketball watched Yeshiva take the top seed into the second half before succumbing 76-62. The atmosphere associated with a loss, especially a tournament loss, is traditionally characterized by a lingering silence rather than voices of celebration. At Yeshiva, however, a victory that has been celebrated for over twenty-four hundred years easily trumped a single loss, even if it was the ECAC.

Within ten minutes of the final horn, Yeshiva's players, fans, and even Steve Podias (my Greek Orthodox assistant coach) piled into a classroom and intently followed the reading of the Purim Megillah, booing loudly at the mention of the evil Haman's name while simultaneously quietly celebrating the miraculous victory of the Jewish people. We capped our post-game loss with homemade Hamantashen.[23],[24]

If It's Good Enough for G-D

Even the casual reader of the Bible will recall that when G-D completed each day's creations, he looked at his work and simply declared, "It is good." In the highlight world of ESPN, however, "good" is never enough. In fact, in order to make ESPN's nightly highlights, the play has to be preceded by the adjective "best" or "top ten."

Even Yeshiva University players and fans who are steeped in the study of the Bible and should know better succumb to ESPN hype and ask me to name my best players. I never respond because naming a top ten would make ten players happy at the expense of the other three hundred who believe they were the best, not a very good risk-benefit ratio.

In reality, I have never chosen the best because I cannot find objective criteria on which to base my choices. Is scoring more important than passing? You cannot score a basket if no one makes a pass, but you cannot receive an assist if no one scores a basket. After all, where

---

[23]   Small pastries made in the shape of Haman's three-cornered hat.

[24]   To hear the audio broadcast of the YU-Jersey City State game go to www. Backdoorhoops.com.

would the six-seven centers be without the five-ten point guards? If you compare points scored, the best scorer may only be a function of the quality of his teammates rather than his skill. The debate can be endless but without some objective standard, it is not possible to reach a conclusion.

The absence of objective criteria is always an obstacle when making choices, but the real impediment to choosing the best may be the assumption that the status of best is superior to the status of good. When you step back from the initial thrill of being anointed the best, you realize that best may not be the ultimate accolade. The status of being "better than" is a relative term with finite value because it only declares that you are better than everyone else at a particular moment in time. Therefore, you only maintain that status until someone else surpasses your performance. Since records are meant to be broken, it is only a matter of time before that someone appears.

In contrast, the status of good is absolute. If you are declared good, it means that you have reached a certain standard of excellence totally independent of the performance of any other player. Good can be equaled, but it can never be taken away from you and therefore, the accolade of good attaches forever. Why prefer the fleeting fame that comes from being deemed the best when you could have the permanent acclaim that accrues from being *good*?

It is interesting that G-D does not distinguish between any of his creations by declaring one creation best. G-D raises the level of praise to very good[25] only after he witnessed that all his individual creations were working together in perfect harmony. Who would believe that right there in the first chapter of Genesis, G-D would be teaching basketball coaches the importance of team play? The lesson for coaches and players is obvious. You cannot select one best player, just as you cannot declare that the waters are more important than the grass. The value of each player, just like each creation, is interdependent.

So next time when you ask me who my best players were, you will forgive me when I respond that I do not have best players, only good players. If good was good enough for G-D, then good is certainly good enough for me.

---

[25]   Genesis 1:31, "And God saw everything that he had made and behold it was very good."

G-D Roots for Both Teams

I'm always taken aback when I hear an athlete in his post-game TV interview thank G-D for his last-second heroics. Although I acknowledge G-D's presence in my life, when it comes to shooting foul shots, I place my faith in the fundamentals of shooting rather than divine intervention.

After a weekend spent watching multiple last-second baskets followed by hallelujahs to G-D, I offered the following cynical tongue-in-cheek comments at the weekly Metropolitan Basketball Writer's Luncheon.

"With the proliferation of cell phones," I began, "it is now possible to create a dial-a-prayer hotline where coaches, for a small fee, can have a rabbi or priest offer prayers for foul shots and three-point field goals. The fee structure could be based on the importance of the game and a prayer request in an NCAA Division I championship game could command thousands of dollars. Money could even be made on both ends with the defending team willing to pay an equally large amount for a prayer requesting a missed foul shot. The only complication, for everyone except the Yeshiva coach, is what happens when the coach is Jewish but the shooter is Christian. Does the coach call a rabbi or a priest? Perhaps he should spare no expense and place a call to a rabbi and a priest. Once again, the high-revenue teams gain the advantage."

My proposal received some laughs. Following the luncheon, George Blaney, who was suffering through a losing season at Seton Hall, took me aside, and with tongue firmly planted in cheek, asked if he could be my dial-a-prayer partner. The following year Coach Blaney involuntarily left Seton Hall and became UConn's assistant coach. Not surprisingly, his Connecticut players renewed his faith in fundamentals.

Touch Fouls

Among the leading coaching nightmares is the touch foul that results in the star player's fifth foul. At Yeshiva, the fear of a touch foul created a whole different nightmare.

In the Orthodox tradition, a man may not touch a woman other than his wife. This practice, observed by some, but not all Yeshiva basketball players, never impacted our games until the passage of Title IX, which allowed women to compete on men's teams. In 1987, Stevens Tech, decimated by injuries, promoted their female manager to the varsity. Coaches in the conference felt no need to react.

I immediately called Wally Whitaker, Stevens Tech's coach. "Is she getting any playing time?"

"Only in blowouts."

I breathed a sigh of relief because our games with Stevens were always competitive.

"So she probably won't play against us?" I asked more as a prayer than a question.

"Boy, you really do a thorough scouting report. You even scout the reserves."

"Only when they are women," I responded. "Because if she plays, half my team will opt out—and we will all have to opt out."

"Tell them not to worry; they'll be able to guard her."

"No, they won't. They can't risk committing a touch foul."

After a brief explanation of Jewish religious law, Wally agreed to speak with the young lady, but reminded me that the "opt-out" decision ultimately rested with her. I assured him that we would respect her decision and underscored that our decision not to play was based on religious obligations and not intended as a bargaining chip.

A few days later, the Stevens coach related that the young woman had decided that it was in everyone's best interests, especially her teammates, to opt out.

Prior to tip-off, my captain expressed the players' appreciation to the young lady and further explained the rationale for our "no-touch" obligation. My leading scorer, who needed the game to break the all-time YU scoring record and did not abide by the no-touch rule, attempted to express his appreciation by planting a socially acceptable, but certainly not religiously permissible, touch kiss on her cheek. Fortunately, our captain tackled him at the last second, thus avoiding an in-depth philosophical discussion about the diversity of religious practice among Orthodox Jewish basketball players.

Chapter 3

BASKETBALL AND FAMILY

A Strong Bench Needs A Minyan

The requirement of ten men for prayer, a Minyan, is based on the belief that communal prayers have more impact than the supplications of individuals. The seven players on the '75-'76 basketball team learned that lesson firsthand as their yearlong prayers for wins were answered only twice. As my seven dedicated congregants were about to end their season in the Manhattanville tournament, help was finally arriving. When you are down to seven[26] players, any help is welcome—even if it's your three daughters (ages eight, six, and four).

The sudden appearance of the new recruits was the result of my wife's post-operative vigil at our ten-month-old son's bedside. Unable to find a babysitter, I found myself writing plays on the blackboard with my right hand as I cradled four-year-old Tzofit in my left arm. Fortunately, Tzippora and Ariella were content to scrawl with magic markers on the other side of the blackboard. As for the players, they were just pleased to have three more fans. I am not sure if it was the valet water service during time-outs or the wild cheering from the bench, but we held a five-point lead at halftime. My halftime coach talk was routine except for a brief interruption to accompany the children to the bathroom.

The second half was punctuated by coaching instructions from the sideline interspersed with the girls asking repeatedly if the game was over yet. We entered the final two minutes of the game carrying a two-point lead—and the memory of past leads lost due to late-game fatigue. But this night would be "different from all other nights" because we had new congregants schooled in the fundamentals of sharing nicely

---

[26]   The season started with nine players but by the Manhattanville tournament only seven remained.

with others. Their willingness to share snacks with teammates provided the extra energy to earn a 63-59 victory, proving that a winning team must have a bench that is willing to share its snacks as well as the ball.

By championship Sunday, my sister-in-law, Tamar, had arrived and was prepared to babysit the children. My young recruits, however, refused their demotion from bench to bleachers and initiated howls of protest equal to any player's demand for playing time. I calmed the insurrection by offering up their snacks, a decision that would come back to haunt me.

The bench repeated its stellar contribution in the championship game, but my coaching decision to use snacks early rather than late cost us the victory. Without enough snacks to share, we fatigued in the last two minutes and lost the championship game 59-53.

Every game teaches new lessons. The Manhattanville tournament reinforced the wisdom that although a Minyan is a must for synagogues, victories require kosher Twinkies.

Tzippora and Ariella, April 1972 Tzofit, July 1974

The Eleventh Commandment: Have Faith in Your Children

Down by one point with three seconds remaining, my older son stepped to the foul line to shoot one-and-one. I closed my eyes, too scared to watch. After what seemed like an hour, my assistant, Evan Goldstein, nudged me, "It's okay to look; we're up by one."

This story captures the conflicting emotions that accompanied me throughout my personal father-son coaching odyssey. I desperately wanted to witness my son's triumphs, but fearing failure, I was initially too afraid to watch. It is not only the father who lives with fear, but also the son who risks failing in the presence of his father. In the good old days when parents neither had the time to attend games nor the inclination to watch, children could fail in anonymity.

Further complicating the coach-son dyad is the assumption by fans and players that the father/coach will favor his son. Although there are examples of favoritism, there is also ample evidence of the son being unfairly held to higher standards.

Coaching my older son, Yehuda, was inevitable. He wanted to attend Yeshiva University, and I wasn't prepared to stop coaching. Our experience began in 1993 when I substituted him into his first college game. The moment confirmed my worst fears. At first, I ignored the crowd noise accompanying his substitution, but after a few seconds, I realized that the muffled sounds were boos. My son had not committed a turnover or missed a shot, but for some fans, his mere appearance engendered feelings of favoritism. The barely audible booing ended quickly and never occurred again. Years later, I discovered that my captains had intervened to suppress future boo birds. The booing had no consequences for my son, but it served as a constant reminder for me that my son was always playing under a policy of zero tolerance.

Those suppressed allegations of favoritism surfaced again during a typical player-coach discussion regarding lack of playing time. When the disgruntled fifteenth man conceded his arguments, he did not end the discussion by saying, "Thanks for listening." but signed off with, "Your son should not be the starting point guard!"

"Can you play point guard?" I asked.

"No, but he still should not be playing instead of me!"

My older son and I never had any sit-downs regarding how we would handle our relationship. There was nothing to discuss. We both understood that all decisions would be based on the principle of "not any better, not any worse." Years later, he confided that he was never bothered by what fans thought because he always believed that he deserved to be the starter. His performance his junior and senior years justified that self-confidence.[27] In 1996-97, he captained the team to a 15-6 record, earning Yeshiva an invitation to its fourth post-season ECAC tournament. In the last two minutes of games, he shot 96 percent from the foul line. I kept my eyes open for every shot, although I was very careful never to publicly display my joy. Today, I can admit publicly that those foul shots and that season were among the highlights of my coaching career.

Five years later, my younger son Rafi began his father—son odyssey accompanied by his most partisan fan, his mother. There has never been a more supportive wife in the annals of coaching. Neither work, nor sickness, nor sitting on bleacher seats during five pregnancies could prevent her from attending our games. However, with the addition of our younger son to the equation, her support was occasionally challenged.

All rides home after losses had a certain routine. I would spend the drive quietly obsessing over the team's mistakes while my wife occasionally interjected her own insightful comments. After one particular loss, however, she was unusually silent.

I did not realize how upset she was until we reached the Whitestone Bridge. "Are you okay?" I asked innocently.

She said, "I'm fine," however, her tone indicated that anger had supplanted her usual support.

I immediately scrolled through the usual list of husband transgressions and concluded that today had been a transgression-free day. What could she possibly be mad at me about? Rather than being prudent and dropping the subject, I foolishly stirred the pot with the flippant comment, "What are you mad at me about? I didn't miss any shots."

Like a bolt of lightning from the passenger seat, she fired back, "You didn't miss any shots but whatever happened to 'not any better, not any worse?' Why didn't you play Rafi tonight?"

Right then and there, I should have realized I was a dead man. I not only stood accused of the ultimate coaching crime, providing insufficient playing time, but the aggrieved party was our younger son. Worst of all, the prosecutor was his mother. Having never been confronted with

---

[27]   To view Yehuda, Joel Jacobson, and Alan Levy's performance in Madison Square Garden on January 31, 1996, go to www.backdoorhoops.com.

this dilemma before, I committed the ultimate coaching mistake of not freezing before shooting off my mouth.

"He played exactly the same minutes as he did in all his other games," I said.

She responded by employing the playbook used by all wives in moments of heated husband-wife debates. She stopped talking to me. The time-out continued until I parked the car in the driveway and reached for the game video. Suddenly I remembered Warner Wolf's signature line, "Let's go to the videotape."

We proceeded to the VCR where we sat with stopwatch in hand, meticulously calculating the exact number of playing minutes I had bestowed upon Rafi. At 2:15, after two hours of watching game film, we laughed and agreed that I had indeed played him less than I thought but more than Aviva thought. As any husband and wife who have been successfully married for forty-six years can attest, marriage is all about compromise.

On February 16, 2002, I experienced the ultimate victory—all thanks to the all night video session with my wife. A victory against Mount St. Vincent would guarantee a fifteenth consecutive winning season, entrance into the conference playoffs, and my three hundredth career victory. Despite, or because of, the game's importance, the team played poorly. As Mount St. Vincent stepped to the foul line ahead by three with nine seconds remaining, Rafi found himself praying for a miracle from the bench. Hoping for a miss and a three to send the game into overtime, I substituted Rafi.

Mount St. Vincent answered our first prayer by missing, and G-D answered the second by directing the pass into Rafi's hands. With one second remaining, Rafi rose up and hit nothing but net sending the players into a frenzy and the game into overtime.[28] As poorly as we had played for thirty-nine minutes and fifty-nine seconds, that's how well we played in the five-minute overtime and secured the 81-75 victory.

On our victory walk back to the locker room, Rafi captured the father-son emotions in one sentence, "That shot makes it all worthwhile."

---

[28]   To hear the rebroadcast of the last-second three-point shot, go to www. backdoorhoops.com.

Three weeks later, Ira Berkow of the *New York Times* memorialized the game.[29]

Upon reflection, I regret that I obsessed so much over the pain I would feel if my kids failed rather than just enjoying their triumphs. However, to their great credit, they were never worried about failing. and, therefore triumphed mightily.

A Mother's Perspective

As a five-year-old, I loved to watch construction workers pour cement and drive bulldozers. As I watched, I would tell my mother, "When I grow up, I am going to build tall buildings."

"Wonderful," she would respond. "Someday you are going to be a great architect."

I grew up in the typical American modern Orthodox home where a career as a doctor, accountant, or rabbi was expected. Parental reminders about the importance of study were continuous, Torah study was paramount, and G-D help you if your parents were called to school.

It is within this world that potential Yeshiva basketball players practice their jump shots—and parents come to cheer their victories.

Although all parents root for their children, the intensity of the Orthodox parents' cheers is fueled by communal bragging rights rather than expectations of athletic scholarship or professional contracts. Despite their intense rooting, however, these parents would never allow their children to sacrifice studies for a better foul shot. Consequently Yeshiva High School athletes spend forty-five hours a week in the classroom and only four to six hours a week on the basketball court. It is this emphasis that also explains why the Yeshiva basketball team has graduated professionals from every walk of life but has not produced one professional basketball player.

The first time I met David Kufeld, he was a high school student sitting with his father behind our bench watching Kings Point outrebound Yeshiva. As I stood up from our time-out, I saw a young man who possessed two very important characteristics. He was very tall and was

---

[29] "Longtime Yeshiva Coach Gains a Memory," *New York Times*, February 26, 2002.

wearing a yarmulke. Desperate for a rebounder, I asked, "Are you ready to play?" He smiled and said, "Next year."

Next year came, and David quickly established himself as the team's leading rebounder and scorer. In his senior year, he broke Shelly Rokach's all-time rebounding record and led the nation with 17.6 rebounds per game. I always joked with David that it was the team's poor shooting that gave him the extra rebounding opportunities.

In between practice and games, David served as the school's sports information director, enabling him to send out press releases. While David was rebounding and mailing on the East Coast, (there were no faxes in 1980), Larry Weinberg, the owner of the Portland Trail Blazers, was on the West Coast, searching for the best Jewish basketball player in America.

Friday afternoon phone calls from players usually announced acceptance to a medical, dental, or law school—not a selection in the NBA draft. David's call, therefore, announcing his invitation to the Trail Blazers rookie camp was quite a surprise. The news spread quickly through the Orthodox world, and my phone did not stop ringing. The calls all began with "Did you hear" and ended with "Isn't it great?" Well, almost all the calls. There was one notable exception, the one from Mrs. Kufeld.

"Johnny, did you hear the news?"

"Yes," I responded. "It's wonderful. Congratulations."

"No, no" Mrs. Kufeld said. "The news is not good; it's terrible."

I was surprised by her reaction since she and her husband were David's greatest supporters, attending every game—home or away.

"Why are you upset, Mrs. Kufeld? The selection is recognition of David's achievements."

"That's what worries me," she answered.

"When he makes the team, he may feel a conflict with playing on Shabbos!"

For David, the draft selection was not a conflict but a moment to savor. He had realistic expectations and faith that transcended basketball. However, for an Orthodox parent convinced of her son's ability to succeed, the draft selection created a potential conflict. I knew I could not allay Mrs. Kufeld's fears by challenging her expectations that David would play for Portland, so I reminded her of the values that she had instilled in him.

"Mrs. Kufeld," I responded. "There are very few things in this world that I can guarantee, but the one thing I am certain of is that David will never play on Shabbos for the Portland Trail Blazers."

David attended rookie camp, but did not play on Shabbos. After a week of memories, he returned home and although rookie camp ended in 1980, his draft story lives on within the Orthodox world. [30]

Thirty years after the draft, Mr. Larry Weinberg was introduced at a Yeshiva University dinner as "the man who selected David Kufeld in the NBA draft."

Surrogate Parents

Coaches often find themselves playing the role of surrogate parent. It was never a position that I sought or a role in which I felt comfortable, especially since I had my hands full with my own five children. Giving guidance when asked presents one challenge, providing good advice. Giving guidance when not requested, however, presents many challenges.

I arrived at our Saturday night game focused on basketball, but I went home worried about intermarriage. As the team came out of the locker room for warm-ups, I headed for the bench. I rarely pay attention to fans in the stands, but one fan could not be ignored that night. There, sitting two rows directly behind my chair, was a very attractive African American young lady wearing a very large gold cross. My immediate reaction was that she had mistakenly sat down behind the wrong bench.

"Excuse me?" I said. "I think your bench is on the other side."

"No," she responded politely. "I'm number twenty-four's girlfriend."

Taken aback, I clumsily apologized and tried to regain my focus. We played, we won, and I went home hoping that the problem would disappear before our next game. As we all know, ignoring problems only makes them bigger—not better. At our next game, she was there again, cheering even louder for her number twenty-four.

The next day, I called my captain. "What's the story with the girl?"

"No story. They have been dating for a while."

---

[30] "Yeshiva Athlete Tries the Pros," *New York Times*, June 7, 1981.

Number twenty-four was a sensitive young man who arrived at Yeshiva with limited knowledge of Jewish traditions and a lack of Jewish identity. His YU experience at first was difficult, but over time through his exposure and studies, he began to develop a greater sense of Jewish identity, which now was at serious risk.

I hung up the phone and did what we all do when we are forced to confront. I searched for rationalizations to avoid the confrontation.

"I am a basketball coach—not a social worker. It is my responsibility to win games—not change minds."

"He is a nineteen-year-old kid with a limited sense of Jewish identity. What do you expect?"

"This is between him and his parents; it's not my role to interject my personal beliefs."

No matter how many times I tried to convince myself that it was not my place, I couldn't drown out the little inner voice that kept whispering, *"You have to speak to him."*

With the little voice growing louder every day, I finally called. "Hi, this is Coach. I'd like to talk to you after practice."

"Sure. Is everything okay?"

"We need to talk."

I would like to say that my call was motivated purely by a sense of responsibility, but it was also anger that made my fingers do the walking.

"Does he think he was recruited to YU to reject his Jewish identity?"

"How could he be so indifferent and bring her to a YU game."

"If he wants to abandon who he is, he can, but I'll be damned if I stand by and say nothing.

By the time I got to our meeting, Chaim Ginot's[31] philosophy of "criticize the behavior not the person" had calmed my visceral emotions.

"You're a good kid," I began, "but you're making a mistake dating a non-Jewish girl."

Based on his reaction, he had obviously never read Ginot.

"You're just a racist. The only reason you are upset is because she is black."

I tried Ginot one more time.

"This is not about the girl. I am concerned about you doing something that you will regret in the future."

---

[31]   Ginot, Chaim, *Between Parent and Child*, 1965, New York: McMillan.

"Everyone is telling me the same thing. You just don't like anyone who is not like you."

"There are a lot of people who care about you. I just thought you needed to hear what I had to say, and I needed to say it. If you want to date her, you can, but just do me a favor and don't bring her to any more home games."

"What are you going to do? Throw me off the team?" he shouted.

"I'm not going to do anything. I'm just asking you for a favor. You can say no."

There was no point continuing. I was not going to change his mind, and now I could quiet my inner voice by telling myself that I had tried. The subject never came up again. He hedged on my request by bringing the young lady to only one more game. Our relationship for the rest of the year was confined to basketball. We said our good-byes after the season, and I assumed that he had fallen into the loss column.

Five years later, on a warm summer night, my wife and I were walking in our old stomping grounds of Forest Hills. We had stopped at a corner, waiting for the light to change when a red convertible screeched to a stop in the middle of the intersection. A tall young man jumped out of the car.

"Coach, it's me!"

I looked up at the familiar voice and it was number twenty-four. Before I could utter a word, he was on top of us.

"I just wanted to let you know that I'm engaged to a Jewish girl."

Without waiting for a reply, and with car horns blaring, he jumped back into his sports car and sped off. My wife and I spent the rest of the walk trying to recreate the events of five years ago. At the end of our discussion, we moved his name back into the win column.

Four years later, while waiting on a checkout line in Costco, we heard the same voice coming from the back of the line.

"Hi, Mrs. Halpert?" he called out. "I have two kids, and we're going to send them to a Yeshiva kindergarten."

"Mazal Tov," we called back as the cashier rang up our kosher chicken.

"We're looking to buy a house in Fresh Meadows. We're going to be your neighbors."

My wife and I left the store after a few more shout-outs, guessing when and where Mr. Twenty-Four would reappear. My wife declared my guess the winner.

"One night we will be sitting in Madison Square Garden watching a Knicks game when a voice will come over the loudspeaker. 'Hey, Coach, it's me. My daughter is marrying a Breslov Chasid.[32] Will you and your wife come to the wedding?'"

My guess, although amusing, proved wrong. In September 2012, a few days before Rosh Hashanah, Mr. Twenty-Four walked into the bagel store where I was having a cup of coffee. "Hi, Coach. This is my son. We just took haircuts for Rosh Hashanah. We're going to go to *shul* together."

---

[32] Breslov is a branch of Hasidic Judaism founded by Rebbe Nachman of Breslov (1772-1810), a great-grandson of the Baal Shem Tov, the founder of Hasidism. Hasidism, literally meaning piety and is a branch of Orthodox Judaism that promotes spirituality and joy through its teaching of Jewish mysticism.

Chapter 4

WINNING AND LOSING

The Ghosts of City College

For players and fans, the January 8, 1992, City College game was just another game. For me, all City College games were special.

In 1950, City College, led by their coach Nat Holman, reached the zenith of the college basketball world by winning both the NCAA (National Collegiate Athletic Association) and NIT (National Invitation Tournament) championships. Many coaches chafed under the shadow of Nat Holman's City College, but none more than Yeshiva's Red Sarachek. Red and his many admirers always believed that if not for the strange vicissitudes of life, he would have lived in the spotlight rather than in the shadow of Nat Holman.

Red chose to live primarily in the small-time world of Yeshiva basketball while living vicariously in the big time through his mentoring of such well-known coaches as Lou Carnesecca, Red Holzman, Eddie Kassler, Danny Lynch, and Pat Rafferty. Although Red remained at Yeshiva because he was an incredibly proud Jew, his thirst for the fame of the big time never diminished.

City College—and especially Nat Holman—represented that fame and therefore, the December 1959 Yeshiva-City game was Red's opportunity to leave the sidelines of Amsterdam Avenue and enter the spotlight of big-time basketball. When Red and Yeshiva defeated City College 58-51 they basked for a brief moment in the glory of the *New York Times* headline, "Yeshiva, Paced by Goldstein's 15 Straight Points, Downs City College Five."[33] Red had finally, in some small measure, claimed the spotlight that his supporters always believed he justly deserved.

---

[33] *New York Times*, Tuesday, December 8, 1959, Page 64

I attended the game with Mr. Wettstein and watched as Irv Bader and Willie Goldstein led YU to victory. To this day, I can still feel the atmosphere of the standing-room-only crowd. As I grew closer to Red, I learned just how much the 1959 win still meant to him. Starting in 1989 with the renewal of our City College rivalry, Red would always call from Florida the day of the City game to talk strategy, and I would call the next day to discuss the results.

Now fifty years later and completely removed from the glory of 1959, I still feel the same emotion that I felt as a high school sophomore. Perhaps it was my attachment to Red or the recollections of my high school years when things appeared more important than they really were. Or perhaps it is for me just as it was for Red—my one chance to fantasize that I was exiting the shadows of Division III basketball and living in the spotlight of the big time. There is nothing wrong with living in fantasy as long as you eventually wake up.

The January 1992 game was close throughout and with fifteen seconds remaining, Yeshiva in-bounded the ball, leading by two points. The pass was deflected and the ref ruled, "Side out, Yeshiva." Out of time-outs, I shouted an inbounds play, which resulted in another deflection. With each deflection, the City College defenders became more aggressive and closer to an outright steal, score, and victory.

From my position on the bench, I recognized the play that we needed to execute, but the dilemma was how to call the play without alerting the City defenders. The solution came from my childhood memories of my parents speaking Yiddish when they didn't want us to know what they were talking about. Although neither I nor any of my players knew Yiddish, we all understood Hebrew. I immediately started yelling in Hebrew "*Rutz aroch, rutz aroch*" (go long, go long). No sooner had the words left my lips than Elisha Rothman faked one way and cut the opposite way to the basket. He caught a perfectly thrown pass and scored, sealing the 62-57 victory. We had won just like in 1959 but this time I had made the call.

It is not often that a coach not only makes the correct call, but also disguises it so cleverly. I could not wait to get to the locker room and receive high-fives for my deception. Although there was much shouting and celebration for the cut and pass, there was not even a whisper of praise for me. I waited patiently, believing it was just a matter of time before my contribution would be recognized.

After a few more minutes of waiting, it became apparent that no one was going to say anything. "How could this be?" I mumbled to myself. "Yes, it was a nice move and an excellent pass, but it was my call that made the play."

I quieted the team and without any shame, I asked, "What did you guys think of *my* call?"

The team gave me a blank look, and my captain responded, "What call?"

"What call?" I declared forcefully "*Aroch, aroch,* that call, you know the one that won the game."

The captain took a deep breath, and trying hard to restrain himself from laughing, said, "Oh, that's what you were screaming about. We heard you screaming something, but we had no idea what the hell you were yelling."

The ensuing laughter quickly awoke me from my City College fantasy. Kids will do that to you all the time. As each player left the locker room, I received a handshake and a sympathetic, "Good call coach."

As for me, I went home comforted that at least they had done what I taught them in practice.

Mr. Clutch

On December 18, 1991, with five seconds remaining and Yeshiva trailing Mount St. Vincent College by two points, a thousand fans rose to their feet to watch Yeshiva attempt the final shot. The shot was missed but rebounded and put in, seemingly tying the game.

Unfortunately, the screams of jubilation were muffled by the simultaneous sounds of a whistle indicating a foul and a buzzer ending the game. The order of these two sounds would determine the game's outcome. The two referees conferred while the fans and players watched.

The Mount St. Vincent coach ran up and down the sideline, lobbying that the buzzer came first. I just stood still and prayed.

Jerry Loeber, the former NBA referee, stood at the scorer's table and in a clear voice stated, "The shot was before the buzzer."

"Thank you G-D," I whispered.

"But the whistle came before the shot," he continued, "foul on Mount St. Vincent." Yeshiva's number forty-two shoots one-and-one."

The reaction of the crowd was instantaneous. Yeshiva fans screamed in protest. The Mount Saint Vincent coach jumped up and down in disgust. I continued to pray.

Yeshiva's Daniel Aaron ignored everyone and demonstrating both skill and confidence made both shots, sending the fans into a frenzy and the game into overtime. The game had a storybook ending as Yeshiva won 73-68. Daniel punctuated his clutch performance with a game-ending dunk. One thousand fans carried him off the court, anointing him as Mr. Clutch.[34]

Very often, the clutch moment results in a scenario where the star misses the foul shots and loses the game. In those cases, fans leave the arena, branding the foul shooter a "choker." Although labels are convenient ways to characterize performances, they do not provide insight into why some athletes succeed under pressure and others fail. In reality, performance in clutch moments is tested not only in athletics, but in all of life's endeavors. It is evident in how students perform on examinations, how soldiers perform in battle, and how a pilot lands an airplane in the Hudson River. The compelling question is what qualities create a clutch player—and how are these qualities acquired?

The transformation from player to clutch performer begins with the blessing of athletic ability. Physical skill alone, however, will not elevate the talented player to the status of clutch. The player who makes the game-winning foul shots must not only bring skill to the foul line but a belief that he is going to succeed. This self-belief is a function of how the player has reacted to past criticism. The player who has learned to accept criticism views each correction as a challenge to improve and is motivated to overcome his initial failure. The foul shooter who cannot accept criticism views each correction as an attack and reacts by rejecting the criticism.

Before this athlete even hears what the coach is going to say, he will already have two excuses for why it was not his fault. Constructive criticism—and not unconditional praise—nurtures the development of the clutch performer. The player who can accept criticism is like the child who falls off his bike, but refusing to give up, gets back on. This child

---

[34] To view the foul shots and full game video, go to www.backdoorhoops.com

not only eventually learns to ride, but more significantly, gains the sense of conquest that comes from succeeding after failing.

Criticism transforms talented players into clutch performers because the next clutch moment becomes just another challenge that needs to be confronted. He has overcome previous challenges and believes he will also prevail in his newest challenge. The foul shooter who misses under pressure does so because his past rejections of constructive criticism have effectively denied him any opportunity to confront new challenges. He stands alone on the foul line, possessing only his excuses for past failures rather than the confidence that accrues from overcoming past challenges.

Each time the player successfully overcomes a challenge, he reinforces a belief in his own abilities. As this belief in himself increases, his need for the affirmation of others decreases. Although all athletes enjoy the cheers of the crowd and do not want to fail, the self-confident athlete does not need the approval of fans in order to succeed and he is not afraid to fail.

Athletes who merely possess athletic skill but lack self-confidence will continually require the affirmation of others because if you do not believe in yourself, your feelings of self-worth are dependent upon whether others value you. As the moment of performance goes from routine to decisive, the consequences of failure also increase. It is a counterintuitive phenomenon, but the more importance the athlete places on the outcome, the greater the likelihood is that he will fail. If you believe that your entire status is based upon what others think, you are doomed to fail. Who is able to carry that burden on his shooting hand?

The inability to accept criticism is not the result of one event but is the culmination of repeated past experiences. It begins when a young athlete demonstrates superior skills and is anointed as the best player. His parents, blinded by the acclaim, praise him unconditionally. Friends and fans, enthralled by his skills, ignore his shortcomings. Coaches focused on winning are more preoccupied with praising his current status than challenging him to reach his future potential. The young talented player, through no fault of his own, believes there is no need to improve because he has never been challenged to do so. Family, fans, and coaches have told him so often that he is great that he *believes* he is great. Therefore, when the moment of criticism arrives, he rejects it because he *believes* that the coach is not attempting to improve his skills but rather is threatening his status as a great player.

Clutch performance is predicated on skill and self-confidence, which are not achieved randomly due to the laws of probability. Even a blind squirrel can occasionally find an acorn. Unfortunately for the blind squirrel, random success still leaves him blind and without the skills and confidence to find new acorns.

Photo courtesy of Yeshiva University

Daniel Aaron making the second of two foul shots with no time left in regulation to send the Mount St. Vincent versus Yeshiva game into overtime on December 18, 1991.

Don't Be Afraid to Lose

Coaches and players fear losing because they believe that the consequences will be dire. Although each loss may produce criticism and bad memories, the consequences are never fatal and life goes on. Once you have internalized that lesson, you are free to risk failure by following your instincts instead of being bound by the principles of conventional wisdom. I am not knocking the importance of wisdom that accrues from knowledge, but instincts that accrue from experience also produce wins. If you are paralyzed by the fear of losing, you will always opt for the safety of the conventional and never listen to the inner voices that urge you to do the opposite. Just a word of caution—be careful that you do not allow your instincts to become your conventional wisdom.

With nine seconds remaining and the game tied at fifty-seven, the Manhattanville point guard drove to the basket and created the referee nightmare of "he said, he said." The referee, serving as judge and jury, called a block not a charge. The Manhattanville point guard stepped to the foul line and calmly sank both foul shots. I followed conventional wisdom and called time-out. Down by two with nine seconds remaining, only one decision remained. Do we play for the tie or play for the win? As the dejected players returned to the bench, I began my internal dialogue.

The two is a higher percentage shot. Go inside.
My big man hasn't made a shot all night.
More chances for a rebound from a two.
Are you kidding? We only have one offensive rebound the entire game.
Better chance for a foul when you go inside.
Not with these refs.
Everyone goes for the two.
Who cares what they do!
We're exhausted. Even if we tie, we'll never win in overtime.
They believe in conventional wisdom and will expect the two.
Follow your instincts. Go for the three.
You're out of time! Stop debating! Just decide!
You've lost 450 games, so you'll lose another one. Life will go on.

The time-out clock ticked down as the players waited for my decision. Free of fear, I listened to my inner voices. I bent down as the first horn sounded. "Run side, side, but fade to the corner and take the three."

I came out of the time-out confident with my decision, but anxious that I had abandoned reason. We ran side, side to perfection, and with three seconds remaining, Yitz Ribald rose up and hit nothing but net. The horn sounded, and the scoreboard read Yeshiva 60 and Manhattanville 59. I pumped my fist and exhaled. I had rolled the dice and won. "Who needs conventional wisdom?"

The win re-energized the 2003-2004 season, and we went on to win six of our last ten games. In four of those wins, the game was decided in the final minutes. I went for the two each time and won all four. Thank G-D for conventional wisdom.

Two months later, I met Dean Meminger, Manhattanville's coach, at an awards dinner. "What the hell were you thinking?" he said. "You've been coaching thirty-five years and you go for three?"

I didn't respond. What was I going to tell him—that losing four hundred and fifty games had set me free?

Thank G-D We Lost

With eleven seconds remaining and Yeshiva winning by eight points, I sat down and exhaled. The victory was secure; we were going to the playoffs. The 2007-2008 season had started with great expectations. Skilled players with great attitudes will do that. In reality, my expectations were being fueled by the realization that my thirty-six-year coaching career was drawing closer to its inevitable end.

Although I had no retirement date, the thought of retiring had suddenly made my personal achievements very important. I had always managed to avoid the hype of "championship" where victories were only valued within that context. At Yeshiva, each victory was valued as a championship. To paraphrase Pirkei Avoth (*Ethics of the Fathers*), "Who is the content coach? The one who just won tonight's game."[35]

I began my career in 1966 coaching the MTA junior varsity and won back-to-back championships in 1971 and 1972. I took over at Yeshiva, assuming that I would win many more. Now thirty-six years later, I was still searching for another ring. My dreams of the 2007-2008 season had been put at risk by injuries. We lost our six-eight center, Shuki Merlis, in the fifth game and played without three of our five starters through the first half of the season. But now we were healthy and with the win tonight, we were in the playoffs. Unfortunately, the playoffs were no longer enough for me. The number thirty-six had seduced me. The seduction was only going to get worse.

I started planning for our playoff opponent as soon as I pulled my car out of Yeshiva's garage and headed for home. Despite having lost to

---

[35] *Pirkei Avoth* is a compilation of the ethical teachings and maxims of the Rabbis of the Mishnaic period. They appear in the Mishnaic tractate of *Avot*, in the order of Nezikin in the Talmud.

Old Westbury 71-63 during the season, I thought, we could beat them this time with some adjustments. By the time I reached the Whitestone Bridge, I was convinced. By three o'clock in the morning, I had become completely delusional. I went to sleep not worrying about the quarterfinal outcome, but dreaming about the semifinals.

Practice preparation was great and I approached the Old Westbury game with great confidence. At halftime, we were down by seventeen—and the game wasn't that close. Every new defensive and offensive scheme we had practiced for three days was forgotten in three seconds. I returned to the locker room very dejected. Halftime was very quiet. No fire-and-brimstone speeches and certainly no new schemes.

After five months of drills and rants, we were on the verge of a first-round elimination. As we left for the second half, I gave the team the following *profound* insights. "Play hard and win the first five minutes."

With nine minutes left in the game, we had cut the deficit to eleven points. With five minutes left we were only down by seven and with thirty seconds remaining we tied the game. We held our collective breaths as Old Westbury missed three put-back layups in the last five seconds to send the game into overtime.

We fell behind by two points in overtime but then went on a seven-point run and won 88-82.[36] We had come from seventeen points back and now had a chance to win a championship. We walked off the court to the announcement that Yeshiva would be playing St. Joseph's College in the semifinals on Thursday night.

On the drive home from Old Westbury, all I could think about was the championship game. We were only one win away. The Old Westbury victory was twenty minutes old and I had already forgotten it. My seduction by a championship dream was complete.

Everyone was energized and confident as we traveled to Long Island to play St. Joseph's College. The game plan was simple—move without the ball and take good shots. The strategy worked perfectly for seventeen minutes. Unfortunately, a half is twenty minutes and in the three remaining minutes we went from a three-point lead to a twelve-point deficit. We never recovered. St. Joseph's advanced to the championship

---

[36]   To view the highlights of the Old Westbury quarterfinal game, go to www. backdoorhoops.com.

game, and we went home. There were no more "next" games to think about. The seduction should have ended.

The day after a loss is usually melancholy. The ego needs time to recover. In the good old days, when I was not consumed with dreams of championships, I was able to get past a loss in a few hours. Unfortunately, I was still preoccupied with the desire for a championship and spent most of Friday daydreaming about coaching the Saturday night game. After all, I had only needed one more good half. Once seduction sets in, it's not easy to break free. It would take until Saturday night to regain my perspective.

On Saturday, I followed my usual Sabbath routine, but I was still dreaming about Saturday night's game. Between my praying, eating, and dreaming, I did not pay much attention to the aches and pains that I was experiencing. At 4:30, I started the four-block-walk to the synagogue with my friend Alan Fruchter. After a few minutes of conversation Alan said, "If we don't walk a little faster, we are going to be late." I told him that I was tired and he should walk ahead. I continued to walk, but realized that although it was twenty-five degrees outside I was sweating. I stopped at the corner to rest and started to experience shooting pains down my arm.

At first, I denied what was happening but after a few more shots of pain I realized I was having a heart attack. There I was standing all-alone, next to a sewer cover, having a heart attack. I guess it was the image of that sewer that got me to the synagogue.

Fortunately, every synagogue has at least one doctor and the Young Israel of Hillcrest is no exception. Upon my arrival, I greeted Dr. Larry Rosman with a, "Good Shabbos, I'm having a heart attack."

I was calmly led into the synagogue kitchen, my wife was summoned, and we waited for the ambulance to arrive. There we sat amid the aroma of chopped liver and potato kugel, the very items that had clogged my arteries.

By 5:15, I was on my way to the hospital and by 5:30, I was in the operating room being told not to worry, which of course made me worry even more. I remember lying there wide-awake, shivering in disbelief that this could really be happening to me. Sometime in the next hour, the surgeon, who talked throughout the procedure about the value of Omega-3 fish oils, told me that I was about to feel much better. I don't know if he was right about the fish oils, but he was certainly right about my feeling better. Suddenly, the three-hundred-pound piano that had been sitting on my chest was gone. It is amazing what three little stents can do. By 6:30, they had wheeled me into the recovery room, where my wife and children were waiting. We all looked at each other with tears of relief as the surgeon continued to talk about the importance of fish oils.

The entire ordeal from first pain to recovery room took about three hours, about the same time that it takes to play a championship game. By 7:00, I was upstairs in the ICU, all hooked up to wires.

A resident came in around 8:00 and said, "Hi, Coach. How are you feeling?"

"Okay," I responded. "How do you know I am a coach?"

"I was undergrad at Yeshiva; everyone knows you." He looked at my chart, took my pulse, and said, "You're going to be fine. Thank G-D you were not out coaching when this happened; you would never have made it." It was 8:30, and the championship game was over. So was my seduction.

Thank G-D we lost.

Chapter 5

OFF THE COURT

Season Ticket Holders

We offered no marching bands, no VIP seating, and certainly no cheerleaders. When home games were played at George Washington High School, we barely offered lights and a place to sit.

Despite the hardships, the Yeshiva basketball team still had a significant number of season ticket holders. In the early years the most loyal were a group of parents who attended every game in order to share their children's triumphs. In 1966, Joseph Faber watched his son, Albie, play in my first game as a JV coach and in 1972 watched as Albie competed in my first game as a college coach. (Albie's mother, better known as Morah Rachel never watched me coach, choosing instead to coach my two sons as their kindergarten teacher.) The Merlises were blessed to watch their son Paul from 1972-1976 and their grandson, Shuki, from 2005-2008. Lou and Sidonia Wenig earned platinum cards as they watched Bruce captain my high school junior varsity team in 1969 and lead the Yeshiva College team from the point position from 1972-1976. Samuel and Harriett Rosenbloom also earned platinum cards as they watched their son, Robert, win a junior varsity championship in 1972 and compete for YU from 1974-1978. The Rosenblooms could not get enough of Yeshiva basketball and re-upped in order to watch their youngest son Michael compete from 1980 through 1983. Not to be outdone, Harold Hoenig watched his son Mark earn a JV championship in 1971 and then team with Robert Rosenbloom to lead YU from 1974-1978. The Kufelds' four years of perfect attendance at home and on the road were rewarded with box seats for the 1980 NBA draft. The parents not only provided support for their children but were a great source of strength to a very young coach. Despite the losses of the seventies, their support and encouragement never wavered; for that, I am eternally grateful.

The most dedicated and enthusiastic fan was my brother Danny who did not believe in the notion that silence is golden. At home or on the road, his presence was felt by both players and fans but he saved his best insights for the refs. I would often be forced to feign ignorance when refs would ask, "Who is that guy?"

The longest-tenured fan was Robert Shotten, known to all as "The Rabbi," not because he had earned the title in the *Beis Medrash* (rabbinic study hall), but because he dressed and looked like a rabbi. In actuality, he was a librarian at the Jewish Theological Seminary. What made him legendary was not just his uninterrupted attendance dating back to the glory days of the fifties, but his game arrival-times. It was not uncommon for "The Rabbi" to travel two hours by train and arrive just in time to catch the last two minutes of the game.

Aaron Kinderlehrer may have lacked the flair of *The Rabbi's* grand entrances, but his home-and-away attendance record remains second to none. Aaron was a devout fan during his Yeshiva undergrad days and he renewed his season tickets in 1980 after a brief respite at Yale Law School. Beginning in the nineties, Aaron was joined on a regular basis by his son Baruch, who parlayed his attendance into a position as team manager in 2010.

Derrick Henry earned his season's ticket from behind his video camera, and hundreds of former players relive past glories and "Candid Camera" moments thanks to Derrick's watchful eye.

Starting in the mid-80s, parental attendance dropped to three years as many yeshiva high school graduates spent their freshman year learning in Israel. Rabbi Mickey Orlian, who played from 1951-1955, came not only as a parent to cheer his son but as a professor of Bible to root for his students.

When I first met Sol and Soshy Teichman, friends from Queens, they told me that their five-year-old son would someday become a great Yeshiva player. Their words were prophetic. Yudi scored 1,109 career points, and in 1989, shot 95 percent to lead the nation in foul shooting.

Other loyal parents who religiously attended games were Elliott Aaron, Zev Furst, Howard Rhine, Barry Rosner, Ilene Himber, and her two-year-old daughter Alana, the Kupfermans, the Aronoffs, who kept a stash of water bottles for Barry, and Moshe and Vivian Neiss who even tagged along on our Boston road trip. More recent fans included Helen Lockspeiser and her husband Alan, who held the distinction of being only one of two father-son captain duos and the Schaulewicz family who continued to travel to games from New Jersey even after their son, Dovid, graduated.

Starting in 2005 Jeff Rothstein, former MTA varsity coach, renewed his 1980 season tickets and along with his son and daughter became loyal team followers.

We now boast long-distance season ticket holders as well. The Hoffmans flew twice a season from Los Angeles to see their son, Dovie, the Weissbergs come from Chicago to cheer their son, Shlomo and the Eckmans fight the New Jersey Turnpike traffic from Philadelphia to watch Yoni play. Toby Shapiro earned the grandparents' platinum season ticket by driving to Newburg, New York, in a rainstorm to watch his grandson Shlomo perform.

Perhaps our greatest fans were the numerous six-to-nine-year-old boys who would use our Saturday night or Sunday afternoon home games as a setting for their destination birthday parties. The festivities included a pre-game shoot around, halftime cake, and post-party pursuit of player autographs. In the lean years of home games at John Bowne High School, birthday guests could double our attendance.

The seventies witnessed two significant media events—the launching of ESPN and the introduction of WYUR, YU's radio station. Among WYUR's first DJs were Nachum Segal and Robert Katz. Nachum, upon graduation, replaced David Kufeld as the host of WFMU's fledging morning radio show "The Hebrew and Jewish Program." Under his leadership, the show was re-named "JM in the AM" and quickly became a drive-time fixture among Jewish audiences living in Manhattan, Brooklyn, and New Jersey.

Although I had to wait until 1997 to get an ESPN interview, in 1988, I was invited to WFMU's studio at Upsala College to discuss Yeshiva's first-ever appearance in the ECAC post-season tournament against Jersey City State. The interview, along with Nachum's continual promotion, brought hundreds of fans to the Saturday night game, including Sheldon Silver, the current speaker of the New York State Assembly and a former Maccabee player and manager. Nachum's attendance at YU games and continued support earned him and his family VIP half-court seats to all Yeshiva home games.

Since Speaker Silver's Albany commitments didn't afford him the time to attend our home games, we brought the 2009-2010 men's and women's basketball teams to his home court, the New York State Assembly. The speaker doubled down by attending our game against Sage College and inviting both YU teams to a session of the New York State Assembly where we were introduced on the floor.

Simultaneous with Nachum's building of WFMU, Robert Katz and Larry Hartstein began their live broadcasts of Yeshiva's games, quickly becoming WYUR's version of Marv Albert and John Andreise. They also served as the first hosts of my pre—and post-game show, which was sponsored by a fifty-dollar ad from San Juan Car Service.

In 2002, Adam Cohen and Avi Bloom began streaming the games and my show on the Internet. Suddenly, I was a big-time coach. What I didn't realize was that the shows had only seven listeners, which dropped to six in 2007 when Max Ribald stopped tuning in from Dallas. When Yitz Ribald graduated that year, I not only lost a thousand-point career scorer but my radio show as well. Despite the cancellation, the game broadcasts continued. Bill Gris, a 1955 alumnus, continues to listen to every broadcast, and follows up with post-game calls of congratulation or consolation.

Yeshiva also had dedicated basketball alumni in Jewish communities throughout the United States who were thrilled to host the team for the Sabbath during our weekend road trips. One of the most exciting road trips occurred during our 1987 visit to Barry University. We entered the gym, expecting two hundred fans from Rabbi Eddie Davis's Hollywood, Florida, community and were greeted by more than five hundred loyalists, including YU students spending their intercession in Florida. When we returned in 1989, attendance at the game swelled to 700 leading Billy Mims, the Barry coach, to officially proclaim, "Tonight's game is a Yeshiva home game." A similar experience took place during our 2007 Dallas trip when Rabbi Ari Perl's Shaarei Tefilla congregation, the rest of the Orthodox Dallas community and fans from as far away as Houston watched Yeshiva defeat University of Texas, Dallas, 54-46. Sabbath road trips to Albany, Baltimore, Brookline, Harrisburg, Los Angeles, Memphis, North Miami Beach, Philadelphia, and Washington—where we were greeted by senator Joe Lieberman and his wife Hadassah—featured lunch with the community, packed houses for our Saturday night games, and requests from young fans for player autographs. In the eyes of Jewish youth, we were the pros.

With the arrival of the Internet and the blogger phenomenon, our fan base has even spread to the Yeshivish[37] world of vozizneias.com.[38] Stories posted from the *New York Times* or *Wall Street Journal* immediately generated the following profound blogger debates:

"*Kol Hakavod*!!!"[39] YU Rocks"

"Such *bitul zman* [waste of time]. I don't understand why they are really allowed to have the word Yeshiva in their name. It's a misrepresentation."

"*Bitul zman*? As opposed to sitting on the Internet and kvetching? Do you even realize how retarded you sound?"

"I totally agree with you. How dare they call themselves Yeshiva for providing an organized outlet for their *talmidim* (students)! It sounds more like Amalek University."

Over the years, there has also been a long tradition of faculty and administrators attending games. The tradition started with Dr. Hyman Grinstein, director of the Teachers Institute for Men, Dr. Eli Sar, director of medical services, Rabbi Abraham Avrech, director of alumni affairs and Sam Hartstein, public relations director, all devoted supporters of the basketball program in the 1950s. Rabbi Israel Miller continued the tradition attending in his capacity as executive vice president and, as a proud grandfather, shepherding his grandchildren to Sunday afternoon games.

Perhaps the most unique visit from a faculty member came in 2010 when Ms. Norma Silbermintz, the director of Yeshiva's English as a Second Language program honored her Israeli students' request to come see them play. It was her first encounter with basketball, and by her own admission, she knew absolutely nothing about the game or its rules.

"I didn't understand anything about the game," she commented after the game, "but now I understand why they are always tired in my class. They are exhausted from running up and down the floor."

---

[37] The Yeshivish world is a self-defined subset of the Orthodox community that places an increased emphasis on the study of Talmud over all other areas of Jewish observance and attempts to minimize interaction with the secular community via the rejection of secular academic studies, sports, and other recreational activities.

[38] Vozizneias.com (What is news?) is a blog that focuses on the current events of the day that are relevant to the Yeshivish community.

[39] Loosely—Way to go!

Fantasy Camp

Starting in 1972, some home games and practices were moved from anywhere we could find a gym to George Washington High School, a short ten-minute walk from the university. It was our hope that the elimination of lengthy travel time would enable more players to play— and more fans to attend home games. Despite all the efforts, however, rosters remained below ten, and attendance rarely climbed above fifty, including players' parents and my family. The absence of players at practice and fans at games created a surreal quiet more reminiscent of a library. Visitors at practice were rare and were limited to school custodians sweeping the gym floor or non-English-speaking, ESL night students looking for their classrooms. If a sweeping custodian or wandering night student did enter the gym, he was immediately drafted to replace the chairs that were being used as the tenth man. There wasn't a chair or sweeping custodian that we couldn't score against; it was just the opposing players that gave us a problem.

After we opened our new gym in 1985, I would receive frequent calls from the pre-gym alumni who wanted to attend practice. They all wanted to play and experience firsthand what they had missed. The most unusual visitor request however, came not from an alumnus who wanted to fantasize but from my periodontist. I will always remember the stunned look on my players' faces when I opened practice by introducing my periodontist. He was the stereotypical New York City Jewish pickup basketball player. He had a 4.0 undergrad grade index, a Harvard dental school degree, and loved to stand outside shooting threes. He was one of numerous successful Jewish professionals who secretly believed that only their pursuit of academics prevented them from playing varsity ball.

It was at my routine dental visit, where he simultaneously poked and talked while I sat and nodded, that he confided, "I have this need to know if I could have played in college. Could I come to a practice and find out?"

Considering that he was holding a drill and my mouth was full of cotton, I had no choice but to nod yes. He really could shoot, but unfortunately played defense like a dentist. He loved his experience and left convinced that he could have been a player. Since I had to see him every three months I said nothing to dispel his belief. My players also loved the experience, especially Steven Kupferman, my pre-dental center, who secured a letter of recommendation that helped him gain admission to Harvard School of Dental Medicine.

Although we cannot boast that basketball scouts visit our practices, we can claim to be the only basketball program that provides letters of recommendation from three-point-shooting periodontists.

Johnny Goes Big Time

All Division III coaches fantasize about entering the world of Division I basketball—even if going back door is the only way to get in. I got my foot in the door because of my association with Lou Carnesecca and because I knew the Israeli scene.

My first experience came in 1989 when I guided Nadav Henefeld through the Israeli neighborhoods of New York. The goal of the tour was simple—demonstrate to Nadav that he could feel just as comfortable playing in New York as he could in Tel Aviv. Our common experiences gave us much to talk about, but from the first red light, our conversation was more like a fencing match than a dialogue. I would thrust and Nadav would parry.

"Here is Naomi's Pizza Store," I declared with great fanfare. "You can eat falafel, play backgammon, and read all the Israeli papers."

Nadav parried by asking "Is it safe to walk here at night?" I proclaimed that it was only twenty minutes by subway to the heart of New York City nightlife. He chose to focus on the transportation rather than the destination. "Are the subways safe?"

I made one final attempt to impress by stating that thousands of Israelis living New York would embrace him. He countered by quoting his own demographics. "Aren't there a lot of squeegee people in New York?"

We continued our sightseeing tour and remained focused on our own separate agendas. I talked about falafel and Nadav talked about crime. The tour ended with the usual thanks and wishes of good luck.

As Nadav exited the car his parting remark foreshadowed the future. "Do you know if the University of Connecticut has a gate around its campus?"

An hour later, I received my debriefing call from Lou. "What do you think, Johnny, are we going to get him?"

"Not unless you are going to build a moat around your school."

Connecticut had a fence and Henefeld chose Connecticut, proving that his fear of crime was stronger than his need to eat falafel.

Given my frequent trips to Israel, I was not surprised by Nadav's focus on safety. In the late 1980s, the average New Yorker was afraid to travel to Israel because of terrorist acts, and Israelis were equally frightened by crime in New York. In my conversations with parents of Israeli recruits, their top concern was whether their six-foot-four son who had served three years fighting in the Israeli army would be safe in New York City subways.

I entered the world of D-I a second time when I attended an open workout for two Israeli recruits shopping their basketball skills. The bleachers were packed with D-I coaches and I tried to sit unobtrusively in the corner.

"What the hell are you doing here?" was the refrain from my Division I colleagues. "Is Yeshiva offering scholarships now?"

After a few minutes of watching the scrimmage, I took notice of a man with a big video camera attached to his shoulder. What I found unusual about Captain Video was that he wasn't just filming the action on the court—but the big time coaches in the bleachers. I waited patiently until the scrimmage ended and then moved in to give the recruits my best sales pitch, all in my grammatically challenged Hebrew. Everyone listened respectfully, but without interest. Captain Video, the boys' father, did not bother to video my pitch. We said our good-byes, and I went home to await my follow-up call.

"So what do you think, Johnny? Can they play? Are they coming?"

"They can play, but they're not coming to the States."

"What are you talking about? They are auditioning up and down the East Coast."

"They're not auditioning; they're making a video entitled 'D-I American Coaches Love My Kids.'"

Although the video was never distributed in the States, it was apparently a big hit with Israeli coaches, especially the scene "Faces in the Bleachers." Two weeks after the workout, both brothers signed professional contracts to play in Israel.

Although both my predictions had proved accurate, I had struck out on both my assignments. I did not get a chance to strike out again.

I had entered the world of D-I basketball through the back door and exited quietly through the same door.

Where Are They Now?

In the world of college basketball, securing an assistant coaching job is the surest path to the position of head coach. Assistant coaches at Yeshiva, however, often get sidetracked.

Dr. Jeffrey Gurock, my first assistant coach, did not pursue a head coaching chair, but he opted for the Lilly Klaperman Chair of American Jewish History. Jeff and I were a perfect pair. I learned my basketball directly from Red Sarachek, and Jeff learned at the feet of Marvin Hershkowitz, one of Red's favorite players. More important than learning at the Sarachek Institute of Advanced Basketball Studies was our shared obsession with the backcourt combo of Oscar Madison, sportswriter, and Felix Unger, "Portraits a specialty."[40] We always followed Felix's sage guidance and "Never ass-u-med" when making player evaluations. Jeff, however, brought more than knowledge and loyalty to the sidelines. He was also the assistant to the president, which provided great comfort during those five-game losing streaks. For twenty years, we coached and laughed together. It has been a wonderful ride.

In 1988, Greek Orthodox Steve Podias arrived from basketball powerhouse Rice High School, focused on a head coaching position. Before he became Brooklyn College's big whistle, he spent ten hours a day living the life of a married-with-children Orthodox Jewish breadwinner. He taught public school from nine to three, worked after-school programs from four to six, and coached the Yeshiva Maccabees from eight to ten. He attended Purim Megillah readings, bar mitzvahs, player weddings, and even took his children to an Orthodox pediatrician. I knew that Steve had completed his Orthodox internship program when he told Nachum Siegel's radio listening audience, "On Friday nights, the one night a week without basketball, my wife and I eat a quiet dinner together, collapse from fatigue on the couch, and say to each other, 'Thank G-D for Shabbos.'"

Steve Post, Evan Goldstein, and Jody King followed Podias to my assistant coach's chair. Steve had already filled the head coach's seat at Stevenson High School, but Evan and Jody arrived with their eyes

---

[40] Tony Randall as Felix Unger and Jack Klugman as Oscar Madison, starred in *The Odd Couple,* a television situation comedy based on the play by Neil Simon and broadcast in the 1970's.

glued on the director's chair. It took only one year, however, before they transferred their energy from March Madness to June graduations. Evan graduated from YU's Cardozo School of Law, and Jody followed him a few years later, graduating with a PhD from YU's Ferkauf Graduate School of Psychology. Evan currently fulfills his coaching dreams through his work as a sports attorney, and Jody is a psychologist by day and the successful coach of Hostos Community College by night.

Starting in 2000, my assistant coaches were recruited from the ranks of former players. Tzvi Himber, Yossy Gev, Yishai Pliner, and Harel Vatavu all spent time seeing what life was like from the sidelines. After a few years, they all opted for the less stressful careers of insurance, banking, and marketing with Yossy and Harel returning to Israel.

Ronnie Rosenblatt, my assistant coach from 2008-2012, was also a former player, however he played for Brooklyn Poly Tech against Yeshiva; for three years, he repeatedly tortured me with his last-second three point shooting. I finally stopped him by co-opting him as my assistant coach. To paraphrase the sage advice from "The Odd Couple," "The best way to deal with a troublemaker is to give him a hat and a whistle."

Continuing the trend of filling the assistant coach's chair from the ranks of former players, my son Rafi signed on in 2012. Although there are obvious benefits to coaching your child, those perks come with the whispered accusations of favoritism. Coaching with your son, however, is a 100 percent win-win. For the father, it is an opportunity to watch your son build on what you have taught him. For the child, it is a socially acceptable opportunity to critique the father, something that every son relishes.

Chapter 6

RECRUITING AT YESHIVA

Searching for Just Right

Too Little

My recruiting odyssey began in 1972 at the home of Avi Haar, an all-star point guard at the Hebrew Institute of Long Island (HILI). Even as a rookie coach, I knew that a floor leader was a must and therefore, Avi was a high priority. He grew-up in an Orthodox home, attended yeshiva day schools for twelve years, and dedicated his freshman year to learning Gemara at Rabbi Chait's Yeshiva B'nai Torah,[41] all factors that should have made his recruitment a slam dunk. I arrived at his home at the height of a driving rainstorm that foreshadowed an Alfred Hitchcock ending. I ignored Alfred, and even worse, drew the wrong conclusion regarding Avi's learning at B'nai Torah.

I gave my recruiting mantra, "At Yeshiva, you can have it all. You can play, learn, and represent the Jewish people."

He listened respectfully, asked a few questions, and promised to call. Two weeks later, he said, "If I play basketball, there will be *too little* time to learn Gemara. Thank you, but I'm going to stay at Brooklyn College and learn at B'nai Torah."

In the 70s, very few yeshiva high school players gave up basketball to devote more time to learning. Today, Yeshiva recruits routinely defer basketball in order to spend a year learning in Israel. The only variable in their decision is the length of their deferment. Most sign up for only one year, but many feel that one year is *too little* and spend an additional six or twelve months. Still others opt out permanently, choosing to spend additional hours learning in the *beis*

---

[41] Many graduates of a yeshiva high school may continue to learn Gemara exclusively at a yeshiva such as B'nai Torah.

medrash[42] instead of running on a basketball court. More recently, players resolve their playing-versus-learning conflict by returning to the *beis medrash* after practice for two hours of night Seder.[43]

Too Much

My recruiting efforts were not restricted to the yeshiva high school world; they included the New York City public high schools as well. In the spring of 1973, I pitched the virtues of Yeshiva to two all-city players from Forest Hills High School. The recruits were comparable to Red's public school recruits of the fifties and sixties. Their grandparents were Orthodox, their parents knowledgeable, but non-practicing, and they were the products of afterschool Talmud Torah programs.[44] Both they and their parents listened attentively and called two weeks later. "The Jewish studies are going to be *too much.* We're going to Queens College." Two years later, they helped Queens defeat us 75-58.

The *too much* responses continued unabated until 1977 when, in an attempt to expand my pool of recruits, I launched the first ever National High School Jewish All-Star Basketball Game. Sam Stern (Yeshiva's former coach and then coach at New York Institute of Technology) and Ed Krinsky (then coach of Old Westbury High School) helped me gather nominations from schools and Jewish community centers throughout the United States.

The games attracted more than seventy-two Jewish players, including future NBA star Danny Schayes, who despite all my recruiting efforts, chose to play in Syracuse University's Manley Field House rather than on Yeshiva's rented home courts.

The game also became a recruiting stop for big-time metro area coaches; by 1979, everyone except me, was reaping the benefits of my work. The players heard scholarship offers, the coaches heard yes, and I heard, "Sorry, the Jewish studies are going to be *too much.*" The game

---

[42] A *beis medrash* is a study hall where students learn Gemara in a small group or with a chavrusah, a study partner.

[43] A Seder is a structured time, place, and chavrusah to study. Night Seder takes place after class or work.

[44] Hebrew school classes are traditionally scheduled 3-5 days a week after public school and sometimes on Sunday.

was designed to be my personal toy, and I had no intentions of playing "Share, Share, that's Fair." If I couldn't have the toy all to myself, then no one would have it. In 1979, tired of hearing *too much*, I ended the game.[45]

Despite the time devoted to recruiting in the public high schools, after twelve years of searching, I had identified only fifteen public school players with the potential to succeed in Yeshiva's double academic program. From the fifteen, only three said yes, and of the three, only Ronnie Schwartz managed to succeed both on and off the court. Ronnie not only scored 1,176 career points but also graduated with honors.

Jeff Weisman, a six-foot-seven center from Buffalo, New York, was one of the twelve who answered "too much." Jeff Gurock and I flew to Buffalo in the midst of a snowstorm to deliver our recruitment speech. His response was positive enough to enlist the assistance of Rabbi Avi Weiss of the Hebrew Institute of Riverdale. One week prior to Passover, Rabbi Weiss, a noted advocate of Jewish outreach, traveled to Buffalo to seal the deal. For his efforts he got stuck in a classic Buffalo blizzard, barely making it back to the Bronx in time for the first Seder. His powers of persuasion were good enough to convince Jeff that New York would be the best venue in which to enhance his Jewish identity. Unfortunately, his powers of persuasion overshot the 185th Street campus of Yeshiva University and landed my potential recruit at Columbia University on 116th Street.

My most exotic "Jewish Hope" was a self-proclaimed member of the national team of Kazakhstan. Before he could even utter "too much," he broke his nose trying to catch a pass during tryouts. Apparently in the eighties, kids from Kazakhstan were not being taught the fundamentals of how to pass and catch. He was never heard from again.

Not long after my national player disappointment, my hopes were dashed again when a letter arrived from a seventeen-points-a-game, former all-city player. Due to some personal problems, he had to defer college but was now ready to resume his studies and basketball career. His contact information, however, was a real turnoff. "You can reach

---

[45]   See Appendix B for a listing of players that were selected to the 1977, 1978, and 1979 Yeshiva University High School Jewish All-Stars Basketball Game.

me at the Manhattan Correctional Center for the Criminally Insane." Needless to say, I chose not to make a home visit.

Enough

Undeterred by the response of *too little* and *too much*, I narrowed my recruiting search to yeshiva high school players who wanted to learn more—just not too much more. My initial search took me to Elizabeth, New Jersey and Brooklyn, New York in the hope that Gary Aboff, Saul Goldberg, or Pete Kessel would be those someones. They each had a yeshiva education, possessed Hebrew language skills, and were devoted to the learning of Talmud—but not to the exclusion of other pursuits.

I repeated my "You can have it all" presentation, but despite thinking I had heard it all, Gary said, "Twelve years of intense Jewish studies is *enough*. I am going to enroll at, and play for, Brandeis."

Saul doubled down on the theme of *enough* by deciding that twelve years of Jewish studies was *enough,* and four years of competitive high school basketball was also *enough*. He left his sneakers at home and went to Boston University.

Peter added another variable to the theme of *enough*. "I want to come and play, but my parents do not have *enough* money without an athletic scholarship." Rather than play on Shabbos, Peter rejected D-II scholarship offers and chose to play-professionally in Israel for Elitzur,[46] Netanya.

Just Right

Although finding *just right* has often been elusive, for every player who said *"too little, too much,* or *enough"* there has been an equal number who yelled *"just right."* The New York metropolitan area, the largest natural pool from which to draw, produced 122 players, featuring thirty-three captains and seven one thousand-point scorers.

The largest representation of just right players from outside the New York metro area came from Los Angeles. Starting in 1985 with

---

[46] An Israeli sports organization that operates sporting teams in various Israeli cities.

the arrival of Lance Hirt, there have been twenty-one players, featuring twelve starters, six captains, and two thousand-point scorers.[47]

All the players who yelled *just right* accepted the double program because their need to compete trumped their hesitations about additional learning—and they recognized that only YU gave them the opportunity to compete without compromising their religious beliefs. Above all, they declared *just right* because they wanted the opportunity to represent the Jewish people.

Irrespective of why they chose YU, their all-star plaques, graduate school acceptance letters, or premium job offers confirmed what I had always preached; if you were willing to devote the time, *you really could have it all.*

D-I Mania

Recruiting against *too little, too much, and enough* was always challenging, but recruiting against the fantasy of a Division I basketball scholarship was almost impossible. The lure of D-I did not happen often, but when it did, it was ignited by man-bites-dog newspaper stories heralding a yeshiva high school player's multiple twenty-five points-a-game scoring performances. The story invariably generated D-I recruiting calls that were interpreted as scholarship offers, which created a "did-you-hear" frenzy within the Orthodox Jewish community.

Once the frenzy went viral, fantasy took hold—and all perspective, even among parents, was lost. Any inference on my part that the player would only be a reserve at the D-I level bred resentment and any concerns about continued Sabbath observance were rebuffed by vague assurances that either accommodations would be made or a *heter* (rabbinic permission) would be granted. During the days of frenzy, I had no option but to sit helplessly and wait for a return to reality,

---

[47]   Jeff Katz, David Gottlieb, Mark Galeck, Elisha Rothman, Erez Ben-Ami, Moshe Abehsera, Yoni Zadok, Michael Bernstein, Matt Rosenblatt, Eli Hami, Abe Malkin, Adam Misery, Zev Hendeles, Eli Hendeles, Mike Pollack, Dan Wizenfeld, Simon Brookhim, Aryeh Magilnick, Dovie Hoffman, Ben Silver.
Mark Levy, Manager, Effie Braun, Manager. See chapter 11 for player milestones.

which would eventually be restored by an offer to try out rather than a scholarship to play. Liberated from the lure of a D-I scholarship, parental and player perspective was restored, and YU once again became *just right.*

Although the majority of players ultimately rejected D-I mania, there have been recruits, who—with the encouragement of parents, coaches, and supporters—continued to pursue their D-I fantasy. Tamir Goodman is the most noted example because his odyssey included a scholarship offer. Although the offer fed his fantasy, it simultaneously blinded his entourage to the reality that scholarship offers guarantee a place on the team—not playing time on the court. I believed that Tamir was a D-III all-star who could have led YU to a berth in the NCAA D-III post-season tournament. Unfortunately, that was not enough for his entourage, and my repeated requests for an audience with Tamir were met with an incredulous, "Come on, Johnny, there is no point in talking; he's too good for Yeshiva." Even my cautionary advice to give consideration to the possibility that he might not succeed at the D-I level was dismissed out of hand. "Are you joking? He is the Jewish Jordan."

Entourages never like to confront reality. They have too much to lose. In the end, all the recruits, including Tamir, were left with scrapbooks of high school accomplishments rather than stories of college heroics.

What I found most intriguing about "D-I Mania" was why so many Yeshiva University basketball fans actively rooted for Tamir and other players to bypass YU and take their skills to the D-I world. I certainly understood why the players wanted to compete under the bright lights of big-time ESPN basketball. What I found puzzling was why so many YU supporters were blinded by the same bright lights.

The answer comes from the noted professor of American Jewish history and my former assistant coach, Dr. Jeffrey Gurock, who posited, "The chance to be chosen in is among the surest signs of an individual's or group's acceptance in a society."[48] Perhaps, upon reflection, the entire Goodman hysteria was nothing more than the Jewish community's need "to be chosen in."

---

[48] *Judaism's Encounter With American Sports,* Indiana University Press, Bloomington, 2005, p. 8.

When the Stars All Lined Up

In 2008, Martin Leibovich walked away from the fame of a D-II scholarship and declared Yeshiva *just right*. Martin had played his high school basketball in the public schools of Buenos Aires and his college ball at Southwestern State Junior College and Division II, Barry University. He was not scouted at a game or referred by his high school coach; he was discovered by Steve Savitsky, then president of the Orthodox Union (OU), at a chance meeting at the OU's annual National Council of Synagogue Youth's (NCSY) South American convention.

Steve listened as Martin related that although he was non-observant, he was becoming increasingly uncomfortable with playing on the Sabbath. His increased sense of Jewish identity was the combined product of his involvement with NCSY programs and the overt anti-Semitism he had experienced in the world of Argentina basketball. By the end of their conversation, Martin, who had never heard of Yeshiva before he met Steve, knew that it was possible to play at Yeshiva and still observe the Sabbath.

Within an hour of their conversation, my cell phone was ringing. "Hi, Johnny. This is Steve. I'm calling from Argentina, and I have a player for you."

Following a month of phone calls, Martin gave up his D-II basketball scholarship and accepted the challenge to have it all at Yeshiva. Three months after their chance meeting, Steve was transporting Martin from Kennedy Airport to Yeshiva University. As they approached the campus, Martin took a yarmulke from his pocket and said, "Now I can wear this, and no one will call me dirty Jew."

I knew that Martin was coming to Yeshiva with great basketball skills and an intense desire to embrace his Jewish faith. I didn't know that he was also bringing a perspective that everyone was anti-Semitic. Martin's adjustment to Yeshiva was immediate. It would take more time, however, for him to moderate his perspective on anti-Semitism in America.

With five minutes remaining and Yeshiva down by five, Martin was whistled for a foul, sending Mount St. Vincent to the line to complete a possible three-point play. Martin's reaction to the close call crossed the officiating line of conduct, and he was whistled for a technical foul. When the smoke cleared, Martin found himself on the bench for the remainder of the game, and Mount St. Vincent found themselves up by ten. We got no closer and lost 73-53.

Following the locker room postmortem, I started for home. When I got to the lobby, Martin was waiting for me. His distraught look forced me to violate my longstanding rule of never talking to an upset player until the next day.

"How could you do that to me?" Martin implored.

"What are you talking about?"

Martin's responses came in rapid gunfire order. "You didn't stick up for me. You didn't fight for me when the ref called that technical foul. You know that it was a terrible call. Why did you take me out of the game? Didn't you want to win?" With each question, Martin grew more emotional. "You know all the referees are anti-Semites. You know they only call those fouls on us because we're Jewish."

I didn't know which question to address first. What I did know was that this was the wrong time and place to try to answer any questions. I chose to respond to the basketball question only. "I took you out because I always remove a player when he commits a technical."

My answer did nothing to calm him down and only reaffirmed my belief that it is impossible to talk rationally to an angry player after a loss. We ended the conversation with the promise that we would continue the conversation the next day.

The next day, despite all my attempts to explain that the ref's "T" was not an act of anti-Semitism, Martin refused to concede.

In total exasperation, I offered my final rebuttal. "Martin, the ref is not anti-Semitic. He is Jewish."

After many discussions, I came to better understand what Martin's life was like in Argentina—and Martin came to better understand that America was not Argentina. Martin learned many things at Yeshiva, but perhaps the most important was that Jewish identity is grounded and sustained by the teachings of Torah and not by feelings of persecution— regardless how justified those feelings may be.

Martin, with the support of the entire Savitsky family, became Sabbath-observant, and in July 2012 married his high school girlfriend who also embraced Orthodox practice. Along the way, he majored in business management, earning a 3.53 grade index and a position at a commodities trading firm. He also found time to average seventeen points per game for his career and be named to the 2010 New York Metropolitan Basketball Writer's Association all-star team.

On May 11, 2012, hundreds of former players who believed that Yeshiva was "just right" returned to celebrate my floor-naming tribute. Their participation and words of appreciation were affirmations that we had all chosen well.

The Hod Towers

When fellow coaches ask me about my recruiting budget, I always respond, "I have no budget, but I do have hundreds of recruiters across the country." My personal recruiters included communal rabbis, high school basketball coaches, and most importantly YU's basketball alumni and fans.

In 1984, through a series of coincidences, a fan from the fifties and a player from the seventies came together to recruit the ultimate "just right" player who became YU's poster boy.

In 1955 Bill Gris graduated from YU, married, and—after serving in the army—moved to Atlanta. Although he never shot a basket for YU, Bill was an avid fan who had spent four years cheering the Blumenreich-Schlussel-Sodden teams of 1954-5. He went on to convince his neighbor, Willie Goldstein, to give up his all-night milk route and play the point on the victorious Ader-Bader-Badian-Baum teams of 1957-59. Bill's recruiting efforts lay dormant until 1976 when I received the first of many subsequent calls.

"Hi, Johnny. This is Bill Gris. I am a YU alumnus living in Atlanta, and I have some players for you." Although his recruits of the seventies had varying degrees of success, his efforts continued—and he hit the jackpot in 1984.

In 1972, six-six Paul Merlis was among my first recruits to yell "just right." He played, studied, went on to medical school at Penn and set up practice in Atlanta in 1984. He joined Rabbi Feldman's Congregation, Beth Jacob, and was immediately befriended by Bill Gris, a fellow congregant.

In 1980, Dov and Rivi Hod and their three children, Lior (fourteen), Ayal (thirteen), and Asaf (five) arrived in America in search of financial security. By chance, they settled in Atlanta where they invested their life savings in a restaurant and enrolled Lior and Ayal in public school.

The boys' athleticism enabled them to integrate easily into the American culture and despite being only five-six guards, they were selected to the Cross Keys High school junior varsity as the last two players on a team of eighteen. While Lior and Ayal were thriving, the family restaurant was failing and after eighteen months, it was forced to close. The family, left with no viable options, returned to Israel. Lior and Ayal, however, who had lobbied to remain in Atlanta under the watchful eyes of neighbors, remained on their own, studying and playing ball during the day and working nights and weekends at every available job from pumping gas to flipping pancakes. By their senior year, the two five-six guards had grown into six-five big men who led their Cross Keys High School team to its first winning season.

That same year, they managed to save enough money to buy a small truck, which Lior used to launch his landscaping company. Lior and Ayal cut and maintained lawns and cleaned dog kennels in Atlanta's ninety-five-degree heat and humidity. By chance, Rabbi Feldman was among their first landscaping customers, and he quickly recommended them to his congregants Bill Gris and Paul Merlis.

By the spring of 1984, all the stars had lined up. Bill and Paul knew that Lior could not only cut grass but could also shoot jump shots thus setting the scene for another Bill Gris phone call. "Johnny," the call began, "I have a six-foot-five player who can shoot, scored 750 on his math SATs, and reads Hebrew fluently. The only problem is that he has received a basketball scholarship to Emmanuel Junior College, an NAIA Catholic school."

With numerous recruiting pitches by Bill and Paul, followed by several phone calls from me, three months later I was at La Guardia Airport picking up Lior Hod. What was so extraordinary about Lior's arrival at Yeshiva was that I had never seen him play. This sight-unseen recruitment process was not the result of any philosophical theory; it came from the reality that beggars cannot be choosy. In the spring of 1984, I was a recruiting beggar; a recommendation from a fan and former player was more than sufficient.

It was easy to pick Lior out from the other passengers on the Delta flight. After all, how many six-five kids wear a red basketball jacket on a hot August night? I had tried to prepare for Lior's arrival by handpicking a roommate with whom he would be comfortable despite his limited knowledge of religious practice. I left him in the hands of a dorm counselor and returned home, confident that his transition to Yeshiva would go smoothly.

Lior's next-day phone call proved that even the best laid plans can go awry. "Coach, I woke up this morning, and there was a guy in my room with a big black yarmulke and long beard. I thought I was on Mars. Worse than that, when I left the room, there were three other guys outside who looked just like him." By the time I got to YU, Lior had regained the self-confidence and poise that had carried him through the previous four years and had made friends with everyone on the floor, from guys with big black yarmulkes and black beards to guys wearing crocheted yarmulkes and no beards.

Lior's first semester was a great success—both on and off the court—so I was taken aback by his anxious request to speak with me during intersession. I entered his dorm room, fearing he would say, "I am returning to Atlanta."

Instead, he said, "Coach, I just want to tell you that I love everything about Yeshiva."

His assertion of love only raised my anxiety level, and I waited for the "but." After all, why would he bring me to his room just to profess his love for Yeshiva? Fortunately for everyone, he finished his sentence with an *and*. "And I have a six-six younger brother who dunks and wants to come to Yeshiva."

It took me a few seconds to regain my heartbeat before I asked Lior how soon his brother could call me. "Immediately," he responded as he opened the door to his closet. "This is my brother Ayal. He was waiting and hoping you would say yes."

In March 1988, Lior and Ayal Hod combined with Yudi Teichman, Benjy Reichel, point guard Jeff Baum, and the supporting cast of Jonathan Ehrman, Donny Furer, David Gottlieb, Elliot Kramer, Jan Levine, Heshy Muehlgay, Sam Reichel, Marty Shlakman, David Weinreb, Zev Weiss, and Asher Wolmark to lead the Yeshiva Maccabees to their sixteenth victory of the season and the first-ever post-season tournament appearance against number one-seeded Jersey City State.

YU fans celebrated the ECAC invitation by filling the Jersey City gym and turning the March 5 opening-round contest into a home game. Yeshiva did not disappoint the fans and played nationally ranked

Jersey City State even for thirty-three minutes before fatiguing and succumbing 89-77. Lior, Ayal, Yudi, and the 1987-8 team had put YU back on the map and returned YU basketball to the glory days of the fifties.[49]

Although Lior's arrival at Yeshiva was without fanfare, his post-college successes have made him the poster boy for YU. He came from Atlanta with little money and even less background in Judaism. Today he is the owner of ELLKAY, a nationwide healthcare connectivity software company, his four children attended Yeshiva Day school, he and his wife Janet are prominent members of the Orthodox Teaneck community, and his son Jordan will be playing for YU in the fall of 2013. When Lior broke the all-time scoring record, Rabbi Miller and Rabbi Fulda, his Gemara teacher, were there to hug him and present the ceremonial basketball.[50]

In 1989, Ayal shattered his brother's scoring record to become YU's all-time leading scorer, a distinction he held until 2002. Not to be outdone off the court, Ayal went into partnership with former Knickerbocker great Allan Houston. Together they launched Top Gun, a chain of leather goods stores located throughout the New York metropolitan area. Ayal lives in Great Neck with his wife Janet and their six children.

In 2009 when Aviva and I took our granddaughters to a performance of The Nutcracker at Lincoln center we were thrilled to discover that Ashley Hod was performing that evening as part of the troupe. It was apparent that Ayal's three daughters had channeled his athletic skills into the world of ballet.

---

[49]   To listen to WYUR's audio broadcast of the March 5, 1988, ECAC game, go to www.backdoorhoops.com/audio.

[50]   To view Lior's record-breaking shot versus Vassar College on February 24, 1988, go to www.backdoorhoops.com.

Photo Courtesy Of Yeshiva University
Dr. Israel Miller, Senior Vice President Yeshiva University, Presenting the
Ceremonial Basketball to Lior Hod on the Occasion of Breaking Yeshiva
University's All-Time Scoring Record. February 24, 1988.

The Israelis Are Coming

On February 17, 1977, Maccabi Tel Aviv defeated CSKA Moscow 91-79
in the semi-finals of the European Cup. Tal Brody, Israel's basketball
hero, declared, "We are on the map, and we are staying on the map."

Two months later, on April 7, 1977, Maccabi Tel Aviv backed up
Tal Brody's declaration by defeating Mobilgirgi Varese of Italy 78-77
to win its first European Cup championship. In the ensuing years,
Maccabi would dominate European Cup play by winning four more
championships and finishing second nine times.

In 1977, everyone expected that the victories of Maccabi Tel Aviv would spur the growth of Israeli basketball. What no one predicted was the impact these victories would have on the Maccabees of New York who had just finished their season with a 4-17 record.

Within seconds of the 1977 Maccabi triumph, Israeli fans and supporters poured into the streets to celebrate Israel's entrance into the elite world of European basketball. With each successive triumph, the popularity of basketball in Israel soared. Soccer no longer enjoyed a monopoly on the sporting dreams of Israeli youth as evidenced by the development of such outstanding Israeli players as Nadav Henefeld, Oded Katash, Motti Daniel, Doron Jamchi, and Doron Scheffer.

It wasn't long before American college coaches, always on the lookout for new sources of recruits, found their way to Israel. In 1989, Nadav Henefeld was recruited to the University of Connecticut where he helped them reach the NCAA Elite Eight. The Henefeld experience generated such excitement that when Doron Scheffer chose to follow Nadav to UConn, all his games were televised on Israeli television. Israeli basketball players dreamed not only of playing for Maccabi but also about finding fame in American basketball programs.

If America's basketball youth in 1992 wanted to "Be like Mike," then Israeli kids wanted to "Be like Nadav." Fortunately for YU, many of the Israeli dreamers recognized that they could not succeed on the large stage of the Big East but needed a Division II or Division III venue to achieve their "Nadav" moments. Yeshiva's new Max Stern Athletic Center provided Yeshiva with the opportunity to be chosen as one of those venues.

Maccabi Tel Aviv had created the dreamers, and Max Stern's money had built the venue. All that was needed was permission to bring the dreamers to the venue.

I was the *shadchan* (matchmaker) who sought the permission, but Rabbi Israel Miller sealed the deal.

"Will the university permit me to recruit traditional but non-observant Israeli basketball players?" I asked nervously.

Rabbi Miller's response was direct. "Our students do not have to be rabbis before they come, and they don't have to become rabbis when they leave. They just have to pursue their Jewish studies seriously and be respectful of our traditions."

I thought I had my marching orders, but before I could salute and leave, he said,

"But you may not recruit them until they have finished their army service. They can't use Yeshiva to dodge their Israeli army obligations."

Before I could give my assurance, he stopped me and said, "You are going to be here a lot longer than I am. I need your promise that as long as you are coaching, you will never recruit an Israeli who has not completed his army service."

I gave my promise with a handshake. As I got up to leave, he sealed my handshake by invoking his connection to my parents. "Remember, Johnny, in 1938, your father and I were college classmates."

His reminder has never faded. To this day, my first question to all Israeli recruits is "Have you completed your army service?"

With Dr. Miller's approval, I went global and took my recruiting search to Israel. My challenge changed from identifying players with sufficient Jewish background and Hebrew language skills to succeed in the Jewish Studies program to finding Israeli players with the English language competency to succeed in college. A more immediate—but no less important—challenge was finding sites where I could meet the players and their parents. Aviva always accompanied me because beyond having insight into player character, she spoke Hebrew fluently. Although a gym or café was the preferred site, sometimes the Q&A venues took us to such exotic locations as a watermelon stand in the Ramla shuk, the hundred-degree heat of a Ra'anana playground, the Tel Aviv diamond exchange, and the beaches of Netanya.

In 1990, thanks to the efforts of Eli Friedman, the well-respected Israeli coach, Miko Danan of Ramla became the first Yeshiva basketball recruit to come directly from Israel. My friendship with Eli began when we worked together to organize the 1988 Elitzuria games, an international sports competition for Orthodox youth. In order to promote the games, Eli brought an Israeli high school all-star basketball team, featuring Miko Danan, to tour the US.

For the past twenty-five years, Eli has served as my eyes in the recruitment of Israelis to Yeshiva. Without his tireless efforts, the Israeli experiment could not have succeeded. Miko's outside shooting and engaging smile gained him instant popularity, but what permanently solidified Miko's place within Yeshiva basketball lore was his decision to rejoin his Israeli Defense Force's (IDF) unit at the outbreak of the first

Gulf War. His demonstration of loyalty to Israel brought him and Yeshiva instant acclaim in the national and local media. CNN, ESPN, and Russ Salzberg of local Channel 9 all descended on the Yeshiva campus to interview Miko and his classmates. Miko's action also served as Rabbi Miller's ultimate rebuttal to the claims that the recruitment of Israeli players could serve as a mechanism to avoid IDF service or lead to a diminution of loyalty to Israel.

After the war Miko returned to his studies and helped lead Yeshiva to a 15-10 record and a second ECAC postseason tournament appearance in Harrisburg, Pennsylvania. When we arrived in Harrisburg, we were met by television station WHTM and interviewed like conquering champions. The Yeshiva basketball team was no longer a beggar—thanks to Rabbi Miller's decision and Eli's friendship.

Today, Miko is director of sports for Yeshivat Hadarom, a prominent modern Orthodox elementary and high school in Rechovot, Israel. Miko draws some members of his teams from the non-Orthodox community in Rechovot and occasionally hosts the players for the Sabbath where they pray, eat, and sing together. Although Miko never heard Rabbi Miller's words, he certainly absorbed his message of outreach.

In 1998, Yossy Gev arrived from Rechovot, compliments of Marvin Hershkowitz, an all-time-great Yeshiva player. Yossy went on to break the Yeshiva scoring record and became the only player in YU history to be named to the Metropolitan Basketball Writer's Association D-III all-star team four consecutive years.[51] Following graduation, he served as my assistant coach for three seasons before returning to Israel.

In 2001, he created a new milestone by becoming my first married basketball player. His move to the *Chupah*[52] was followed by another Israeli recruit, Jack Yulzary from Ramla. Together they formed an outstanding backcourt combination and the only NCAA married backcourt twosome. Later that year, Shmuel "Pilly" Pilosoff, of Rishon Lezion, entered YU and became our third married player. The tradition of married players continued in 2003 with the addition of Ben Golbert who was MOA—married on arrival. The presence of married couples left me no alternative but to allow wives to accompany their husbands on

---

[51]   To view Yossy's record-breaking shot versus Stevens Tech on February 11, 2002, go to www.backdoorhoops.com.

[52]   Marriage canopy

weekend road trips. I could say no to the players, but I was not going to fight the wives. At Yeshiva, *shalom bayit* (family harmony) trumps all.

Ben arrived at YU courtesy of Ron Ganulin, coach of D-I St. Francis College and former coach of Gan Shmuel.[53]

"I would have tried to recruit him to St. Francis," Ronnie said, "but I thought an Israeli kid from Jerusalem would be a better fit at YU."

Ben proved to be the perfect fit. When he wasn't rebounding, passing, and defending, he was making 35 percent of his threes, placing him fourth among all YU players in three-point field goal percentage.

Six-five Harel Vatavu from Tel Aviv also arrived in 2003. His recruitment was not based on a recommendation from a D-1 coach—but on the enthusiastic approval of Nachshon, my then eight-year-old grandson, who listened to the entire recruiting Q&A from the top of the stairs of his home in Beit Shemesh. Harel went on to score 1,114 career points and handed out 333 career assists, including 136 in the 2003-4 season, the second-most assists earned in a single season. Before returning to Israel, he went on to serve as my assistant coach in 2004.[54]

Chen Biron arrived in 2008 with a reputation as a three-point shooter. In February 2010, his nine consecutive three point field goals and twenty-nine points on the road against Mount St. Mary propelled us into the Skyline Conference playoffs.[55] He finished his career shooting 37.6 percent from three, the third best in YU history.

In 2009, point guard Omer Haim of Rechovot transferred from D-II Bridgeport to Yeshiva. His arrival was the direct result of the tragic passing of his mother in 2008 after which he realized that he wanted more from college than just basketball. Omer graduated from YU with honors in both his secular and religious studies, impressing all his teachers and *rebbeim*[56] with his desire to learn more about religious practice and his tireless work on behalf of the developmentally disabled and food bank programs for the poor. In between his classes and charity

---

[53]   Ron Ganulin coached Gan Shmuel from 1976 to 1979, winning the Israel League two championships in 1979.

[54]   To view Harel and Ben versus Farmingdale on February 2, 2005, go to www.backdoorhoops.com.

[55]   To view Chen's three-point shooting performance versus Mount St. Mary on February 18, 2010, go to www.backdoorhoops.com.

[56]   Gemara teachers, singular rebbe.

work, Omer handed out 392 assists to become YU's all-time career assist leader.

In the summer of 2009, Gil Bash was accompanied by his parents on his recruiting visit to Yeshiva University. Despite their initial reservations about attending an Orthodox institution, Gil began a journey that would exceed all his expectations. In his senior year, Gil became the twenty-sixth player in YU history to score a thousand points while handing out 149 assists to tie Joe Eaves' record for all-time-assists in a single season.[57] He achieved a 3.7 cumulative grade index, earned a paid summer accounting internship at PricewaterhouseCooper, was accepted with a scholarship to YU's master's program in accounting, and most importantly came to understand that he has far more in common with YU's modern Orthodox community than he could have ever imagined.

Between 1990 and 2011, twenty-six Israeli recruits featuring ten captains, four one-thousand-point scorers, an all-time leader in assists, an all-time leader in steals for a single season, and seven players named to various all-star teams chose YU. The recruits graduated with a cumulative 3.5 grade index, and only two have not as yet returned to Israel.[58]

Although none of the recruits came to Yeshiva as rabbis, they all left with an enhanced respect and appreciation for Yeshiva University's religious practices and traditions. Among my great pleasures is to visit with my Israeli players and their families and witness how they have been touched by their exposure to the YU *Rebbeim* and students. Rabbi Miller would have been very proud of his recruits.

---

[57] To view Benjy Ritholtz' last-second shot and Gil's fifteen assists versus Brooklyn College on December 29, 2012, go to www.backdoorhoops.com.

[58] Miko Danan, Jose Jayinski, Igal Malul, Alon Zaibart, Yossy Gev, Asaf Hod, Jack Yulzary, Shmuel (Pilly) Pilosoff, Avi Tetro, Shai Musberg, Ben Golbert, Harel Vatavu, Matan Cohen, Daniel Vardi, Roy Goldstein, Ohad Babo, Daniel Somach, Chen Biron, Gil Bash, Omer Chaim, Chen Sina, Uri Volkov, Niv Zinder, Arman Davitian, Adam Levine, Netanel Weinstein. See chapter 11 for milestones.

The Sarachek Tournament

In March 2009 with five seconds remaining and the score tied, basketball fans around the country watched Scotty Reynolds, the star point guard for Villanova University, drive the length of the court and score the winning basket to propel Villanova into the NCAA Final Four.

Barely twenty-four hours later, with five seconds remaining and the game tied, six hundred fans watched Isaac Krupp, point guard for Yeshiva High School of Memphis, drive the length of the court and score the winning basket to propel Memphis into the Tier II championship game of the Red Sarachek Basketball Tournament.

Each drive took only five seconds, but the memory of those five seconds reinforces that dreams really can come true. The Sarachek Tournament provides the venue where every year more than 250 Yeshiva high school players can have an Isaac Krupp moment.

My dream to organize a national yeshiva high school tournament under the auspices of MTA, Yeshiva University High School, started in 1978, continued through 1983 and was put on hold until 1992 when it was revived and named for Red Sarachek. The 1978 tournament featured eight teams and was played during mid-year intercession with YU students lending their dorm rooms to the out-of-town participants.

Both the tournament and my coaching career, however, almost ended before they started. The tournament was played from Thursday night through Sunday, necessitating Sabbath observance and synagogue participation. In my naïveté, I entered the synagogue Friday night, expecting to see fully observant yeshiva high school students, but was rudely awakened by the sight and sound of transistor radios being played by some of the tournament participants. I visualized the headlines of the *Commentator*, the college student newspaper, "Halpert fired for holding a non-Sabbath observant high school basketball tournament."

I sat frozen with fear. It must have been the look of horror on my face that induced Yaakov Neuberger, a Yeshiva University rabbinic student, to ask, "Do you need some help?"

"Oh my G-D, yes," I answered.

Within a few minutes the future Rabbi Neuberger, along with Rabbi Blau took charge. Rabbi Blau's message to all the participants convinced them to respect the Sabbath and Rabbi Neuberger's after-dinner discussions turned Sabbath observance into a positive experience.

A few weeks after the tournament, I received letters from the high school principals expressing how wonderful the entire tournament had been, with special mention of how the less observant participants had enjoyed speaking with the future Rabbi Neuberger.

In 1979, the tournament inaugurated a two-tiered format that allowed teams that lost in the opening round to continue competing in a parallel championship tournament, providing championship opportunities to all players at all skill levels. In 1981, the tournament grew to twelve teams with the championship game in Madison Square Garden as a preliminary to the New York Knicks. Although 1981 witnessed an increase in the tournament's popularity, logistical difficulties were also increasing. There were not enough dorm rooms to house the additional participants and there were even fewer venues to play the additional games. Out-of-town players were now forced to sleep in dormitory lounges on mattresses. Unfortunately, the tournament had become a victim of its own success. On the final day of the 1983 tournament, four games were played simultaneously in four different sites, stretching from upper Manhattan to New Jersey and culminating in Madison Square Garden. At the conclusion of the 1983 championship game it was apparent that this would be the last tournament until Yeshiva University had its own facility. The logistics of the tournament had finally overwhelmed its good intentions.[59]

Despite the fact that Yeshiva opened its new gym in 1985, it took phone calls in 1991 from Sandy Ader, a former Yeshiva captain, and John Bandler, a participant in the 1983 tournament, to reawaken the tournament dream from its nine-year slumber. The time elapsed between the initial phone calls and submission of the tournament proposal was short. The desire to honor Red and give kids a chance to dream quickly turned into an obsession. All that was needed now was funding. The game plan was simple. Raise enough private money to cover the costs of the initial tournaments and then hope that the high school would assume the financing for future tournaments.

Dreams and prayers are powerful forces. Alvin Schwartz, a longtime fundraiser for Yeshiva, identified Bernard Mann, a part-owner of the New Jersey Nets, as a possible donor. Mr. Mann agreed to fund the

---

[59]   See Appendix C for a listing of teams that participated in the original 1978-1983 Yeshiva University National Basketball Tournament.

initial tournaments, provided that Yeshiva University high school would commit to funding future tournaments. His commitment was not only a testimony to his generosity but to his character as he gave the naming honor to Red. With Mr. Mann's commitment in hand, final approval was given. The date of the tournament was changed from January to March, and players were housed in a local hotel with all games played in the new Yeshiva University Max Stern Athletic Center.

In 1999, the tournament grew to eighteen teams with three championship tiers—and in 2009, it grew to twenty teams with four championships. Tournament Sunday was like a Jewish homecoming with over three thousand fans from across the United States and Canada passing through the gym. Dr. Lamm, past president of Yeshiva University, often complained that he was receiving more pressure from donors regarding acceptance of their team to the tournament than regarding admission to Yeshiva University's Albert Einstein School of Medicine. In the past twenty-two years, over 4,000 yeshiva high school students have participated in the Sarachek Tournament.

Each year as the tip-off to the championship game approaches, you can watch a thousand fans stand and cheer as yeshiva high school players from all over the United States and Canada pursue their dreams of championships. In 2011, I had the special privilege of watching my son Rafi coach SAR Academy to a 43-36 championship victory, becoming the first tournament participant to win as a player and a coach.

It all started with knocks on dormitory doors, dragging mattresses, and two phone calls. I am grateful that Yeshiva University high school provided the opportunity and am thankful that I had the passion to pursue my dream.

Chapter 7

ON THE COURT

Time-Out—I Am Having an Epiphany

G-D and the NCAA both recognized the need for rest. G-D got there first and gave man the seventh day. The NCAA, not to be outdone, followed G-D's example and allotted coaches five time-outs per game. Most coaches use the time allotted to refuel and refocus their players. In one fateful game, the use of the time-out took a novel twist.

November 29, 1976, started very poorly and only got worse. Due to traffic, we arrived at 7:45 for our 8:00 game and had only nine players available to play first-place Stony Brook University. They pressed us at every opportunity while continually substituting rested players. Their game plan was obvious—run us until we dropped. At halftime the players limped back to the locker room and due to fatigue returned to the gym using the elevator rather than the stairs.

The second half opened with a 14-0 run fueled by our opponent's continued full-court press. I called a time-out, hoping to find insights that would stop the press but soon recognized that no strategy could overcome their skill and tenacity. With eight minutes left, we were losing by thirty points. My only hope was that the opposing coach would abide by coaching protocol and call off the press. As they returned to the court with their press intact, all hope appeared lost. My moment of ultimate helplessness had arrived. We could not beat his press, and he would not stop pressing.

Hoping for an inspiration, I called my final time-out. I stood motionless in the huddle, searching helplessly for something to say. Finally, in desperation, I said, "If they press you, give them the ball! Just give it to them!"

My players looked at me incredulously, but before they could utter a word of protest, I said, "If they need it so badly, let them have it!" I had no idea what the consequences of my instructions would be, but I felt relieved that I had at least thought of something.

We returned to the court, and they pressed with the intensity of a one-point game with ten seconds remaining rather than a thirty-point rout with eight minutes left. Following instructions my in-bounder took the ball and handed it to his defender, who in disbelief, kicked it out of bounds.

My in-bounder repeated the play and shouted, "Shoot the ball."

I am not sure if it was the idea of being handed the ball or the taunt to shoot but the defender committed a traveling violation. On the next two successive possessions, they easily scored. My time-out decision had accomplished nothing but deepening my feelings of helplessness. Suddenly, like the cavalry coming to the rescue, the lead referee, Don Landolphi, started blowing his whistle at each attempt to press. It was as if he had declared martial law.

After another questionable call, the pressing coach jumped up to complain. Like a tiger waiting to pounce, Donnie issued a warning, "Coach, if you don't sit down, I'm going to 'T' you up."

The coach sat down and finally stopped pressing. Don returned to a more objective performance; we scored a few baskets and lost 136-81. After the game, the sports editor of the school's newspaper found me downstairs. "I have never seen a player just give the ball to the defender. What made you do it?"

I said, "If you cannot beat the press, accept the inevitable and just give them the ball."

The next day, Red Sarachek, Yeshiva's athletic director, wrote a letter of complaint to the opposing school's president. Red's letter created a counter letter of complaint because an athletic director lacks the status to write to a university president. Apparently, the 1976 Stonybrook basketball program had an institutional protocol for correspondence but none for sportsmanship.

A few weeks after the time-out, the hand of fate would strike the pressing coach. Larry Jacobowitz, my business partner, won significant money in his weekly poker game. The next day at lunch, Larry announced, "I had a big night last night; lunch is on me." In the process of regaling me with stories of his poker victories, he mentioned that the big loser was my pressing coach. One never knows how the hand of fate will strike.

The story of the time-out was resurrected for the last time thirty-two years later at the final home game of the 2008 season. Don Landolphi, the martial law referee, took me aside and said, "Johnny, this is my final college game and I have waited a long time to ask you this question. What made you give them the ball?"

Without a second's hesitation I responded, "What made you start calling those fouls?"

Neither one of us said a word. No explanations for our actions were necessary. We hugged each other for our thirty-three years of shared memories—but mostly for the memory of our shared epiphany.

I'm Begging You to Swallow Your Whistle

The often-contentious relationship between coaches and referees usually arises because coaches want every call. That was the case until the January 7, 1980, John Jay game. In the 70s and 80s, Yeshiva's roster was limited in size, and we continually suffered from late-game syndrome, a malady characterized by Yeshiva leading in the second half only to falter in the last minutes due to fatigue. Fatigue, which is never more evident than at the foul line, was on full display on January 7. With two minutes left and leading by six, we began to run out the clock and John Jay began to foul. It was at this point that the coach-referee dialogue took a dramatic twist.

Each John Jay foul produced a Yeshiva miss that led to a John Jay basket. Two consecutive missed one-and-one opportunities saw our six-point lead dwindle to two. Once again, late-game syndrome was spoiling thirty-eight minutes of good basketball.

With fifteen seconds remaining in regulation, Yeshiva was marching to the foul line. The opportunity produced another miss that allowed John Jay to score and send the game into overtime. We regrouped in the first overtime and jumped out to a four-point lead—only to watch a repeat of the regulation scenario where John Jay would foul, Yeshiva would miss, and John Jay would score.

With nine seconds left in the first overtime and Yeshiva winning by two points, we stepped to the line. One made foul shot would secure the victory and save us from the agony of another late-game loss.

Out of time-outs, I stood up and yelled, "No fouls."

As we stepped to the foul line, the gym grew quiet, which wasn't hard because there were only seventeen fans in attendance. We missed. The players—following directions to a fault—did not foul John Jay's point guard as he began his last-second sprint up the court, and did not even attempt to guard him. Like Moses parting the Red Sea, he dribbled the length of the court untouched and made the layup that sent the game into a second overtime.

Although Yeshiva grabbed the lead in the second overtime, I recognized that something had to be done to prevent a replay of the foul-line fiasco. A John Jay foul against Yeshiva provided that opportunity. Seizing the moment, I walked directly in front of lead referee Phil Lospitalier and uttered words never before heard by a referee. "Stop calling fouls on them; you're killing us."

Phil looked at me in disbelief and answered, "What are you complaining about? The foul is on John Jay."

Not hesitating, I countered, "That's how you're killing us; I am begging you to stop calling fouls."

Phil smiled and handed the ball to my scorer who, too tired to walk let alone bend his knees, added to our foul shooting woes when he missed. All my desperate pleas to the referees to stop calling fouls went unheeded and the game mercifully ended in a 77-65 double overtime loss.

Players, referees, and coaches shook hands and went home. The only thing left undone was to submit referee-rating cards. Although the refs had done an excellent job, I did not rate them but instead wrote the following complaint in the comment section. "Did a great job, but called too many fouls for Yeshiva."

A few days later, I received a phone call from the supervisor of officials. "Is this a serious complaint that they called too many fouls for Yeshiva?"

"Absolutely," I responded. "They cost me the game."

The supervisor laughed and assured me that he would speak to the refs.

One month later, we defeated Stevens Tech on a last-second basket 69-68. I rated the referees ten and wrote, "Refs were great; they never gave us a call all night."

Going Backdoor with the FBI

The start of the Gulf War on January 17, 1991, impacted everyone. American military personnel and their families lived with the constant fear of the death of a loved one, and Israeli citizens lived in sealed rooms with the fear of exposure to poisonous gas. Most American citizens experienced these same fears, but from the safe distance of their living rooms. It was not until the Barry University game on January 26 that the Yeshiva basketball team experienced these fears firsthand.

The build-up and start of the Gulf War brought heightened security to the Yeshiva University campus, and the usual laid-back college atmosphere gave way to an air of anxiety. Suddenly all students and faculty could not enter a building without displaying identification cards and offering all bags for inspections. The on-campus interviews by CNN prompted by the Israeli army recall of Miko Danan, our star Israeli forward, added to the anxious atmosphere. We looked forward to our Florida trip, hoping it would provide a pleasant escape from ID cards and book bag inspections. Practicing during daylight hours in warm weather was also a pleasant change from our usual snowy night practices. After three days of practice, we arrived at the Barry game expecting our usual pre-game regimen of warm-ups and taping.

Barry University's athletic director brought me back to New York reality. He said, "Hi, Coach. This is FBI Agent Jones. He needs to talk with you."

"Good evening, Coach," he began. "We have received a credible threat against your team, and we need to provide security for your players and the spectators."

It took a few minutes to absorb what I had just heard. We had come to Florida for an escape and suddenly were under threat.

The players completed their warm-ups and returned to the locker room where I emphasized our need to go backdoor. I then introduced Agent Jones, who informed the players about the reported threat and the security procedures that had been implemented. He finished by emphasizing that if an attack should suddenly occur, the players should immediately exit through the gym's backdoor where a bus would be waiting to transport them to a secure location. His instructions to use the back door gave our backdoor play a new perspective.

Fortunately, the Yeshiva players did not have to use the backdoor, but unfortunately, we did not run our own backdoor play either and lost 80-69. We returned to New York the next day, having experienced in a very small measure the anxiety of a possible terrorist attack. The next night, we sat glued to our televisions, watching as more SCUD missiles fell on Israel. Unfortunately, our families and friends in Israel did not possess the luxury of a back door to escape the threat of mass destruction.

Scouting, Scheduling, and Stereotyping

Until the advent of video exchanges, scouting an opponent was a standard aspect of game preparation. Although a no-brainer at other programs, scouting was a luxury at Yeshiva. I had neither the personnel to scout nor the practice time to review the report. For every problem, however there is a solution and coaching at Yeshiva has taught me to be creative.

It is a custom at pre-game introductions for players to shake hands with the opposing coach, a routine I initially found annoying. I quickly realized, however, that by combining the politically correct gesture of handshaking with the politically incorrect technique of stereotyping, I could simultaneously demonstrate sportsmanship and scout opposing players.

If you grew up in the pre-electric dishwasher era, you will remember the Ivory Snow commercial that profiled all human dishwashers as possessing either "Ivory snow" or "dishpan" hands. Housewives who used Ivory Snow were promised a life of smooth, soft hands, while their non-Ivory snow counterparts were destined to live a life with rough, dishpan hands. Since I grew up washing dishes for my mother, I immediately recognized that all ballplayers' hands were not created equal and could easily be stereotyped.

Players with dishpan hands were profiled as tough hard-nosed rebounders that dominated inside but could not shoot. After all have you ever seen a player who could crush your hands like a piece of matzoh shoot soft jump shots? Players with Ivory Snow hands were categorized as shooters and finesse players. When was the last time you saw a player with soft violin hands bang bodies inside?

Growing up in a religious world where tattoos were forbidden, my only encounter with them came from Popeye, the cartoon character known for his bulging muscles and tattoos. If ever there was a stereotype for an inside rebounder, it was Popeye. However, as tattooing became more prevalent, many players with "Ivory Snow hands" suddenly sported tattoos, proving that stereotyping can be complicated. Nevertheless, I continued to utilize hand-profiling to provide pre-game scouting reports. Typical reports were "Three dishpan hands, two Ivory Snows, play zone and box out" or "Four Ivory Snows and one dishpan, play man and guard the shooters."

With the increased success of my stereotyping technique I waited for the opportunity to apply its use to stereotype entire teams. My chance came in 1997 when I received a phone call from Cazzie Russell, the former New York Knicks all-star player. He had just assumed the coaching position at Savannah Arts and Design and was looking to schedule games in New York. After a brief discussion, I determined that Savannah's students were on their way to interior design careers in the fashion industry. I immediately scheduled the game, believing that there were very few interior decorators with dishpan hands.

On Saturday night, January 31, 1998, the Savannah Arts and Design interior decorators broke every stereotype ever applied to the fashion industry. At the pre-game handshake, I shook hands with five players who had never used Ivory Snow. They ran, jumped, and shot us out of the gym for an 81-51 victory. At the post-game handshake ceremony, Cazzie Russell further undermined my Ivory Snow stereotype as the great NBA shooter displayed the strongest dishpan hands I had ever experienced. I congratulated him for being able to find the only interior decorators in America who could dunk. He thanked me and went on to win eighteen games. His story never appeared in *Women's Wear Daily*.

Despite my 1997 stereotyping debacle, I continued to employ the technique until the fall of 2000 when my technique collided with the world of the political correctness and suffered its demise. At the weekly Metropolitan Basketball Writers luncheon, I made the mistake of publicly discussing my scouting routine. In reporting to the assembled sportswriters and coaches about my previous night's loss, I said, "All those kids had tattoos, so I knew we were in trouble."

The writers thought my insights were amusing and gave me four lines in the next day's tabloids. The following week, I was summoned to President Lamm's office to discuss an outraged letter from the athletic director of Tattoo University, asserting that my tattoo remarks had stereotyped his entire student body.

President Lamm wrote a sincere letter of apology, claiming that I certainly meant no harm and strongly suggested that in the future I show more sensitivity to the feelings of our opponents.

I obeyed the president's suggestion, and to this day, when I give my scouting report, I never mention tattoos or dishpan hands. I simply say, "Box out the three dermatologically challenged and guard the two violin players."

Danny Halpert, Belle Harbor, New York, July 1950

Irving Bader (1956-60), January 1960

Shelly Rokach (1962-66) driving for two on his way to his
record-breaking forty-eight-point single-game scoring record
versus Queens College, December 7, 1964

Johnny Halpert, December 1966
Photo courtesy of Yeshiva University

Stu Poloner (67-71) leading Yeshiva to an 81-72 upset victory
versus Brandeis, December 1967.
Photo courtesy of Yeshiva University

Johnny Halpert, December 1983
Photo courtesy of Yeshiva University

Joe Eaves (1982-86) shooting his patented jump shot, December 1985.
Photo courtesy of Yeshiva University

Johnny and Aviva Halpert, 1988

YU fans and players celebrating Yeshiva University's first post-season appearance versus Jersey City State. ECAC, March 5, 1988.

Robert Shotten "The Rabbi" standing and waving, Sam Reichel, Jan Levine, Jeff Baum, Ben Reichel, Donny Furer, Ayal Hod, David Weinreb, and Lior Hod.

Photo courtesy of Yeshiva University

First annual Red Sarachek Yeshiva University High School National Basketball Tournament Awards Dinner, March 30, 1992.

Willis Reed, all-time NY Knickerbocker, Red Sarachek, Bernie Mann, Tournament chairman and sponsor, Spencer Ross, radio and TV sports broadcaster, Lou Carnesecca, St. John's University Hall of Fame coach and Moshe Kranzler, Yeshiva University Director of Admissions.

Photo courtesy of Yeshiva University

Johnny Halpert, Miko Danan, Daniel Aaron, and Assistant
Coach Steve Podias, December 1994.
Photo courtesy of Yeshiva University

Yeshiva University versus NJIT, Madison Square Garden, preliminary to
Villanova-St. John's, February 1, 1995.
Kneeling: Alan Levy and Or Rose, co-captains
First row: Yehuda Halpert, Barry Aranoff, David Ruditsky, Ira Landsman
Back row: Steven Kupferman, Mark Saada, Joel Jacobson
Photo courtesy of Yeshiva University

Rafi, Yehuda, Aviva, Tzofit, and I celebrating my 200th career win versus St. Joseph's, Brooklyn, January 3, 1995.
Photo courtesy of Yeshiva University

Yehuda and me at halftime of YU versus Maritime College, preliminary to Georgetown-St. John's, Madison Square Garden, January 31, 1996.
Photo courtesy of Yeshiva University

Dr. Norman Lamm, president of Yeshiva University, presenting a plaque on the occasion of my 300th career win versus Mount St. Vincent, December 2003.
Photo courtesy of Yeshiva University

Rafi Halpert versus Manhattanville, February 2005.
Photo courtesy of Yeshiva University

Herb Schlussel (1953-7), Marvin Hershkowitz (1950-3), Abe Sodden (1952-6),
Elihu Levine (1950-4), at the ceremony honoring YU's thousand-point scorers,
December 16, 2007.
Photo courtesy of Yeshiva University

Back row: Ayal Hod (1985-9), Yossy Gev (1998-2002), Lior Hod (1984-8),
Harvey Sheff (1978-82), Red Blumenreich (1954-7)
Front row: Johnny Halpert, Jody King assistant coach, at the ceremony honoring
YU's thousand-point scorers. December 16, 2007
Photo courtesy of Yeshiva University

Yeshiva College and Stern College basketball teams with Speaker of the Assembly, the Honorable Sheldon Silver, New York State Assembly, February 7, 2009.

First row: Raphy Abergel, Udi Volkov, Omer Haim, Dovie Hoffman, Assistant Coach Carlos Morales, Assistant Coach Ron Rozenblat, Chen Biron.

Second row: Avi Varnai, Johnny Halpert, Honorable Sheldon Silver, Eli Goldenberg, Stern College Coach Karen Green, Jaclyn Ramras, Ricki Katz, Mercedes Cohen (behind Ricki Katz), Shir Fuchs, Lauren Kempin (behind Shir Fuchs), Littal Kravitz.

Third row: Martin Leibovich, Ohad Babo, Simon Brookhim, David Gilboa, Aryeh Magilnick, Daniel Somach, Chen Sina, Jeremy Pressman (captain).

Johnny Halpert, 2010
Photo by Brian Derballa

Johnny Halpert floor-naming ceremony, May 11, 2012.
Photo courtesy of Yeshiva University

The Halpert Team, May 2012

On floor (first row): Avigayil Halpert, Yael Baratz, Ezra Halpert.

On floor (second row): Aliza Butler, Shimona Shriki, Michelle Halpert (with Alyssa Halpert on lap), Rafi Halpert (with Ari Halpert on lap).

First row: Eytan Baratz, Joe Smith, Tamar Smith, Danny Halpert, Shoshana Halpert, Leora Halpert, Aviva Halpert, Johnny Halpert, Ariella Kaszovitz, Yedida Kaszovitz, Naomi Butler.

Back row: Elie Goldfarb, Jason Goldfarb, Tzofit Goldfarb, Dani Goldfarb, Tzippora Baratz, David Baratz, Yehuda Halpert, Aryeh Halpert, Talia Baratz, Daniella Baratz, Avital Kaszovitz, Yair Kaszovitz, Jonah Kaszovitz, Nachshon Kaszovitz.

Photo by Tamar Smith

Presentation of banner on the occasion of my 400th career victory December 6, 2012

First row: Co-Captain Dovie Hoffman, Arman Davtian, Co-Captain David Schmelzer, Eitan Selevan, Jack Beda, Johnny Halpert, Aviva Halpert, Raphy Abergel, Adam Levine, Shaye Weiss, and Rafi Halpert, assistant coach.

Second row: Yoni Eckman, Yosef Rosenthal, Ben Silver, Ben Ritholtz, Co-Captain Gil Bash, Shlomo Weissberg, Shelby Rosenberg, Netanel Weinstein (partially hidden behind Shelby Rosenberg), Aaron Kinderlehrer.

(Holding the banner) Toby Shapiro on the left and Lior Hod on the right.

Photo courtesy of Yeshiva University

Chapter 8

IT'S NOT ALL ROSES

If you are not careful, it is easy to fall into the trap of remembering the past as either all good or all bad. I have had the great fortune to coach the greatest kids in the world and work with incredibly dedicated people. It has not, however, been all roses.

Pride Goeth Before a Fall

We poured into our locker room with high-fives and chants of "Championship!" ringing in our ears. On the path to a 16-8 record, we had just secured a hard-fought team victory that should have been cherished by all.

The hugs and back slaps had barely ended when I suddenly heard a player say, "You're not giving me enough control. I am going to quit." Mr. "Control," consumed with self rather than team, walked out of the locker room. He was not the first or last player to utter the words, "I quit," but he was the only one to say it during a victory celebration. This memory is a constant reminder of just how egocentric some players have been.

No Good Deed Goes Unpunished

It is my custom to announce captains for the next year at the last game of the season. It starts the transition process. Since my current captain was only a junior, the announcement lacked all suspense. The only question was whether another player had earned the honor of being named co-captain. After some deliberation, I decided to stay with my returning leader.

A few days later, the captain asked me to reconsider. He pleaded his candidate's case by bearing witness to his dedication to the team.

I admired his willingness to share his honor, but I thought his insights were blinded by kindness to a friend who was more devoted to resume than to team. Despite my reservations, I yielded.

Three days after Mr. Co-captain was accepted to graduate school, his devotion suddenly dissipated. He quit, proving again that no good deed goes unpunished.

Substance versus Gesture

> "Letters, we get letters, lots and lots of letters.
> —Perry Como, *Dear Perry*"[60]

I opened the senior's letter with anticipation and closed it in disbelief.

It is traditional on Senior Night to honor seniors by introducing them prior to the start of their final home game. For seniors who regularly receive playing time, the ceremony ends with introductions. For reserves, the night includes the gesture of a cameo appearance.

Since I believe that giving an opportunity to play is a better way to say thank you than dispensing gestures, I start reserves and give them playing time on Senior Night.

The year of the letter featured three senior reserves. In anticipation of the difficulty of giving each senior his due I held a team meeting and announced that each senior would *start and play* in one of the last three home games. I therefore opened the letter with the anticipation of a thank you.

The senior began his letter by expressing the "humiliation and embarrassment that he suffered in front of family and friends" because unlike the seniors of Coach K, he did not receive a cameo in the last game of the season. The letter went on to proclaim that unlike my action, Coach K's gesture demonstrated "genuine love and appreciation."

The gap between the anticipated thank you and the accusation of disrespect was startling and left me questioning whether honor and affection can only be demonstrated in a last-game cameo.

---

[60] Perry Como's theme song from his popular 1957 television show, "The Perry Como Show."

I reflected a long time on the feelings expressed in the letter because its author was a young man of high character. I questioned whether my choice of substance over gesture was correct since the player had assigned it a value of zero. The experience confirmed that twenty-year-olds value what's currently *in* rather than what will be important in the future.

Despite my new understanding, I still believe substance that stands the test of time is more important than the fleeting gestures of now. I continue, therefore, to give seniors the opportunity to play—even if it's not in their final home game.

Fire the Coach! This Too Is for the Best

Coaches at every level have endured the chants of "Fire the coach." This demand, however, is never hurled with the same rage as when it is screamed by the parents of a player. Little-League-parent syndrome is a disorder fueled by not enough shots or not enough playing time, two sins that many parents equate with a public humiliation of themselves as well as of their child.

My personal episode occurred in 1990 when the sports editor of the *Yeshiva College Commentator* authored a back-page column supporting a "Fire-the-coach" letter to the editor. My coaching sin was emphasizing that "players should compete and have fun because winning was not the most important thing." According to the editor, that philosophy "created a lack of confidence and losing attitude among the players." The claim seemed to be contradicted by the accompanying back page story, "Macs win four straight."

Do not expect rationality when Little League parents go wild. The real impetus for the column was a single parent complaining that his son was not receiving sufficient playing time. His complaints fell on sympathetic ears as the sports editor was the aggrieved player's roommate. The parent's actions were especially disheartening because he was my former college teammate—and I had always passed him the ball. What ingratitude!

Although my coaching soap opera occurred in a Division III setting, it had all the trappings of any big-time fire-the-coach rant. There was a back-page school newspaper story and even fire-the-coach signs. The only difference was that the school newspaper did not have the same circulation as the *New York Post,* and my signs were not flying over Giants Stadium. All that was missing was sports talk radio. Fortunately at that time, WYUR was devoted to playing Chasidic music.

I made no attempts to mount my own defense, believing that the best response was to let my past actions bear witness and hope that others would testify on my behalf. Accusations cannot convict; only the absence of witnesses for the defense can result in that verdict. I did nothing but wait for witnesses to come forward. Fortunately, I did not have to wait long as the next edition of the *Commentator* contained letters of support from players, fans, and administrators—something for which I've always been grateful. Their statements were more powerful than any words that I could have summoned.

Most people only receive public praise at their funerals when they are unable to enjoy the adulation. I was fortunate because I survived the attempted assassination, and I got to read my eulogies.

As Jewish tradition teaches, "This too is for the best."[61]

The Rantings of a Losing Coach

While winning creates a great high, losing can cause temporary insanity. The following piece gives a little insight into the mindset of a coach during the highs and lows of a typical season.

The fourth-consecutive loss due to especially poor team play sent me home to vent with the following rant:

Since coaching is all about changing player's behaviors, it is a futile exercise filled only occasionally with a few small triumphs. These random triumphs serve no purpose other than to randomly reinforce the foolish notion that you are able to change the natural egocentrism of young adults. The coaching odyssey parallels an abusive relationship where the coach is the abused and the players are the abusers.

In the desperate desire to fulfill your own needs, you expend all your energy waiting for the crumbs that players occasionally toss at

---

[61] Babylonian Talmud, Ta'anit, 21a.

you in their fleeting moments of honesty. Each crumb gives you the toxic reinforcement to continue on a journey that may reward you in your years of dementia when you cannot even remember the players' names.

In truth, I am no better than my players because—like my players— all I really want is to fulfill my own egotistical needs. I deceive myself that I coach because I want to help others, but all I really want is personal triumph. How much more worthwhile would my life have been if I had spent my time just sitting alone all curled up in a dark corner reading books? At least at the end of those pursuits, I would have acquired knowledge rather than the empty feelings born of the realization that no one was listening to my babbling. Even if the books were bad, I could at least proclaim their completion as a victory and have something to show for my time spent besides a legacy of hundreds of failures.

Three nights later, the greatest kids in the world upset the first-place team on a perfectly executed play.

I love these kids. I love coaching.

Head, Shoulder, Knees, Knees, Knees, and . . .

Head

I picked up the phone and heard, "Hi Johnny. It's Tom Penders.[62] Tufts is coming down to play Fordham next year, and I am trying to find them a second game. Are you interested?"

The challenge of playing Tufts made my choice easy. I also believed that the 1981-2 team had the potential to score an upset victory.

On January 7, 1982 Fordham's Coach Penders watched as we led Tufts by four points with four minutes left. On the threshold of a big upset, Tuft's six-six center's left elbow collided with six-one Sol Krevsky's forehead.

---

[62]   Tom Penders had coached Tufts University from 1971 to 1974 and was coaching Fordham University at the time.

The two-inch cut ended Sol's night—and our chances for an upset. Tufts came back to earn a 49-47 victory. As we shook hands after the disappointing loss, Coach Penders consoled me with the following words, "Your team played great. My former assistant will never forgive me for booking the game."

Shoulder

On Saturday night, February 22, 2000, Yeshiva was poised to gain its fifteenth win. David Neiss, our starting center, was hit on the shoulder. The foul, which appeared insignificant at first, proved bad enough to keep him out of our three remaining games.

Despite the injury, we entered the Skyline playoffs sporting a 16-7 record, a second-place finish in the conference, and a realistic chance for a first-ever NCAA post-season bid. David was the glue that held us together. He rebounded, scored, and was the consummate unselfish player.

Every player, however, needs two arms. In our opening round playoff game, David had only one to give. We lost to eighth-seeded Mount St. Vincent on a last-second shot 54-53. It was the most disappointing loss in my forty-one-year career.

Knees

Prior to 1989, typical player injuries affected noses, fingers and ankles, were cared for in doctors' offices and healed in weeks. All that changed in the third game of the 1989 season when six-foot-eight junior Tzvi Himber tore the ACL of his right knee while attempting to secure a routine defensive rebound.

The injury, which occurred against Centenary College, required reconstructive surgery and a year of intensive rehabilitation. Despite the season-ending injury, Tzvi attended every practice and cheered the loudest at every game, home or away. In between cheering and attending classes, he dedicated himself to returning to the starting lineup for his senior year. The decision to honor his determination by naming him tri-captain was easy. The decision to honor his medical clearance to play, however, was much more difficult.

His preseason individual workout sessions only served to reinforce my fear that his surgically repaired knee would be at grave risk from a full-season bearing the weight of his six-foot-eight frame. Tzvi was persistent, and after great debate, I relented and accepted his medical clearance, but only on the condition that I would limit his playing time to short segments.

On Senior Night 1991, after a year of holding my breath, Tzvi started, scored, and exited to the loud cheers and high-fives of his parents, friends, and teammates. As he returned to the sidelines, we hugged and exhaled. It had been a very exhausting year for both of us.

Knees

On January 6, 1992, sophomore Daniel Aaron elevated and scored the 224th point of his young college career. The basket against Baruch put us up by thirteen and raised our hopes for a ninth win in eleven games. Visions of a twenty-win season danced in my mind.

The first indication of trouble was the discomfort he exhibited as he landed on his right foot and limped back on defense. A simple sprained ankle ran through my mind as I took him out of the game. There was no contact with his defender. It was just a small misstep; there was no need to worry.

By game's end, the simple sprained ankle was traveling to Englewood Hospital for a knee X-ray; by six AM there was a preliminary diagnosis of a torn meniscus and by four PM that afternoon he was out of surgery with a repaired ACL. He finished the year with 224 points.

YU went from an 8-2 start to a 13-9 finish. It was just one small misstep, but I have never forgotten the play.

Knees

On January 27, 1994, down by four (57-53) and with the ball, the standing-room-only crowd rose as we came out of our time-out.

Momentum is ephemeral; you can't touch it and you can't quantify it. All you can do is feel it.

Five minutes away from a possible upset victory over top-ranked NYU, Yeshiva fans and players were feeling it. The time-out play was executed perfectly, and Miko Danan drove baseline to the basket. He arrived at the basket half a second before his defender, and both players crashed to the floor. The referee whistled a two-shot foul against NYU.

The cheers of the crowd were silenced, and my vision of cutting the lead to two was dimmed by the sights and sounds coming from the gym floor. It is impossible to know if it was the seven-minute injury delay or simply the loss of a star player, but our momentum disappeared as quickly as it had arrived. Our bid for an upset victory dissolved into a 69-63 loss, leaving us one step from glory.

Knees

The five-second emotional rollercoaster ride of November 29, 2007, included a pinpoint pass from David Schaulewicz to Shuki Merlis, a missed layup, a stolen outlet pass, and a return pass back to Shuki.

Taking no chances, Shuki stretched his full six-foot-seven frame to the top of the rim and dropped the ball into the basket. Unfortunately, as he came down, his left knee gave out—and he crashed to the floor. In the fifth game of what had promised to be a season full of highs, Shuki's college career and our championship dreams came to a sudden end. When I was finished feeling sorry for myself, all I could think about was how in the span of five seconds, a miss and a steal had ended Shuki's senior season, leaving us again one small step from glory.[63]

AND . . .

Although the 1990-91 season featured a 15-10 record and selection to the ECAC post-season tournament, I spent the long ride home from Harrisburg pondering what could have been. At the inter-session break, we stood at eight wins and three losses and dreaming about sixteen wins

---

[63] To see Shuki score forty-one points in a double overtime victory versus City College on December 20, 2006, go to www.backdoorhoops.com.

and an NCAA selection. The dreaming stopped and the "what ifs" began with the start of the 1991 Gulf War and subsequent IDF[64] recall of Miko Danan.

When Miko resumed play in February, our record was 8-7; although his return was more than welcome, it did not stop the what ifs. In the sixteenth game of the season, our all-star point guard, Eric Davis, broke his hand. In the next game, Greg Rhine, our starting two guard, tore his ACL. When the smoke cleared from the emergency room, we were 9-8.

Despite the loss of our entire backcourt, we regrouped and went on to win six of our last seven games before falling in the ECAC 76-63 to top-seeded Lebanon Valley.

The 1990-91season taught me a valuable lesson about coaching at Yeshiva. Although the year was great, it wasn't all roses. Coaching is never all anything.

---

[64]   Israel Defense Forces

Chapter 9

NO ONE ASKED ME, BUT . . .

Cartoon by Jennifer Sohnen

Team Building—You Can Lose with Him, and You Can
Lose without Him

> *Give me a "T."*
> *"T"*
> *Give me an "E."*
> *"E"*
> *Give me an "A."*
> *"A"*
> *Give me an "M."*
> *"M"*
> *What do you get?*
> *A nice cheer.*

There is a tradition that after time-outs, players come together, clasp hands, and yell, "Team." We came out of our time-out trailing Emmanuel College by two with nine seconds remaining, enough time to execute two passes and a pick. It was a play that would require teamwork from all five players.

As we broke the huddle, five hands clasped in a symbolic gesture of teamwork. The inbounds pass was perfectly executed as our shooting guard came off the double pick. The point guard, in his need to play hero, had a different idea. He took one dribble left and hoisted up a jump shot that clanged off the backboard. Final score: Emmanuel 78, Yeshiva 75. So much for handclasps and fancy cheers.

All players and coaches believe in the concept of team, but what does the term mean—and what is it exactly that we are trying to build? Team play is often defined as taking good shots and making the extra pass. But is a good shot merely an attempt that results in scoring—and is the same shot always good?

We had fought from behind the entire night and with forty-five seconds left, Yeshiva held a two-point lead and possession of the ball. A basket would seal the victory. The time-out discussion was simple. Run the shot clock down to fifteen seconds and go inside to the big man. What we couldn't afford was a quick shot and miss.

Five seconds after the inbound pass, the ball landed in the hands of our 19 percent three-point shooter, who by fate, found himself unguarded in the corner. As the ball left his hands, my arms shot into the air, accompanied by a scream of "No!" Before my arms came down, we were up by five. Lehman missed the next shot and fouled. We won by seven. Mr. 19 Percent received high-fives from his teammates. I ranted for two minutes about his poor decision-making.

Everyone can intuitively identify a bad shot, but why do players persist in taking them? Why are some teams able to share one ball, and other teams need one ball for each player? The dilemma is that team play is one of those concepts that we recognize when we see it but have difficulty articulating. Belief in team requires more than wearing T-shirts with catchy slogans about teamwork. It goes beyond team meetings that turn into revival sessions where players build themselves into an emotional frenzy by chanting the word "Team." This emotional high lasts through warm-ups, but it dissipates with the opening jump ball and it disappears completely in the last possession when the game's outcome is decided. At that moment, team play is not fueled by emotion, but it is predicated upon good decision-making. The question is what exactly are the factors that create good decision-making—and what obstacles prevent players from making good decisions?

Coaches do not live in the make-believe world of computerized video games but interact with people who are egocentric by nature.

"I scored eighteen points a game in high school—let me shoot," is the mumbling of first-year players when I say, "Bad shot, too quick."

Athletes are competitors who pursue athletics because they enjoy the accolades that accrue from being victorious. Without entering into a long Freudian discussion on ego (after all, how many games did he ever win?), it is not a natural tendency for athletes to subjugate their own ego needs to some vague concept that we call the team. This is especially true if you have been the main man your entire life and a coach starts demanding that you share the spotlight.

If you want to know the true character of a person watch him play basketball. In most interpersonal interactions people have the opportunity to think before reacting and therefore can disguise their real feelings. Basketball games provide no such luxury. When the moment of decision arrives players have only a split second to decide whether to pass or shoot. It is therefore obvious when you have a player who believes in shoot first and pass never. The only question is whether you are willing to confront the problem, especially when your best player may be your biggest problem.

The rules of basketball are very simple. The team that scores the most points wins the game. Although players pay lip service to the skills of passing, rebounding, and defending, scoring is the fuel that feeds their fire. When players talk up the importance of those other skills, they are talking about what is important for their teammates—not for themselves. The natural emphasis on scoring results in the creation of the star player whose presence creates the most significant challenge to team building.

At first glance, it appears that there are innate contradictions in having a star player exist within a team context. After all, don't all coaches pray at the shrine of "There is no I in the word team?" Although the concept of equality is a noble idea, the reality is that players are not equal and individual stars will emerge in every group. You do not want to ignore the star but rather nurture his talent within the context of the team. It is impossible to win with only a star, but it is also impossible to win without the go-to player. The building of the team is not accomplished by dumbing down your best performer to the level of the group but by allowing the star to excel while not trampling on his teammates' opportunities to perform.

Successful team play is achieved when players make decisions based on their strengths and weaknesses—and when the star accepts the principle that the privilege of taking the most shots brings the responsibility of not taking every shot. Good decision-making is an ongoing learning process that evolves into spontaneous decisions. Just as there are fundamental physical skills that determine if a player will be a successful shooter, there is fundamental information that enables a player to be a good decision maker. It is far more difficult to convince a player to pass the ball than it is to teach the skill of how to pass the ball.

Every year, even with all my emphasis on team play, the current star and I suffer occasional disconnects that invariably result in the following fractured dialogue.

Star: "I've only gotten one shot in ten minutes."
Coach: "You shoot the ball every time you touch it. No one wants to pass you the ball."
Star: "Nobody is looking for me."
Coach: "You have to work harder without the ball."
Star: "Okay. I'll stop shooting."
Coach: "No one is telling you to stop shooting. Just stop shooting every time you touch the ball."

The partnership with the star is a never-ending balancing act between the need for his talent and the need to maintain team concepts. Nothing is always black and white, and the star often operates in the gray area. Although this struggle remains the most demanding aspect of coaching, if you remain focused on your principles no one has to fall off the wire. I have been very fortunate that my star players always wanted to win more than they wanted to score; therefore, together we have produced nineteen thousand-point scorers and twenty winning seasons.

Unfortunately, at some point, every coach confronts a selfish star. Seduced by the player's talent, coaches convince themselves that—as a result of maturity or a religious awakening—the selfish star will suddenly see the light and transform his personality. More often than not, the reawakening does not occur, and the coach finds himself continuing to compromise at the expense of his other players.

As soon as my captains entered the athletic office, I knew exactly why they had come. "Playing is not fun anymore," they began. "We are thinking about quitting."

Their feelings were justified and not based on any hidden agendas for more shots or playing time. What they didn't realize was that I was not having any fun either. Most fans and players think that the ongoing challenge that a coach faces is the game against the opponent. In reality, the real contest is between your passion for wins and your principles, between the need to accommodate the selfish star and the need to preserve the team. How much can you tolerate? What is your line in the sand? The resolution of this struggle ultimately determines who you are and what your priorities are.

I assured my captains that I would take care of the problem. The next day, I sat down with my star player, not to coax and coddle, but to explain why I was taking away his starting position. I assured him that he could earn it back if his attitude changed. Two games later, I reduced his playing time further. In the last two games of the season, he never got off the bench. That spring, I cut him. I had been guilty of the three great sins of coaching: arrogance that I could fix all problems, seduction by his skill, and an overriding desire to win.

The source of the difficulty is that the selfish star's individual playing needs are incompatible with the concept of Team. Preaching team to him is the equivalent of preaching humility to movie stars who perpetually seek adulation from their adoring fans. The star player devolves into a selfish star because, more than anything, he craves the entire stage for himself as his need to be recognized overwhelms the needs of the team.

The power of this need is displayed daily by highly paid professional athletes who, not satisfied with their ability to dunk a basketball or run for a touchdown, will follow their accomplishments by pounding their chest and uttering a primal scream, which says "Look at me, look at me, I am great." In reality, these screaming athletes have no self-confidence. If you need to scream, "I am great," you don't really believe you are. As the legendary football coach Tom Landry told his star running back after a touchdown celebration, "Next time you get to the end zone, make believe you've been there before."

Unfortunately, the selfish star defines himself by only one criterion—the number of points he has scored. He prefers that his team win rather than lose—but not if it has to come at the expense of his moment in the sun. The coach can never build a successful partnership with this player, and even if he can achieve periodic successes, the unfortunate reality is that in the crucial point of the game when all eyes are focused on the moment of triumph or defeat, the Selfish Star will revert to his ingrained needs and will neither share the spotlight nor the ball. To paraphrase *The Ethics of Our Fathers*, "He who needs to score will never have enough shots."

At some point, you have to face reality. Inevitably, you will lose the game *with* him—and you will lose the game *without* him. I have tried it both ways, and from experience, I can attest that you feel a hell of a lot better losing without him than losing with him.

Beware the Arrogance of "I"

Leaders come in all sizes and shapes. Some are executive directors, some are fortune 500 CEOs and some are even basketball coaches. The bestowal by a higher authority of the mantle of leadership, however, does not a leader make.[65] Successful leadership requires not just a title but followers, which explains why it is far easier to be appointed a leader than it is to lead. Considering the importance of followers I suggest that before any coach blows his first whistle he consider why some coaches succeed in creating devoted players while others fail to connect. The goal of a coach is to win, but even the great coaches lose. The measure of a successful coach, therefore, cannot be victories alone. It must measure the number of followers who remain loyal even after losses. Loyalty is not generated by style, speeches, or fear; it is born when a coach earns the respect of his players by demonstrating knowledge, integrity in his decision-making, and the courage to act on those decisions. Knowing what to do is easy; having the integrity and courage to act on that knowledge is what sets leaders apart.

There is a perception that since everyone loves a winner, it is winning that produces followers. Devotion born of victories alone,

---

[65] With apologies to Richard Lovelace, "To Althea from Prison."

however, is short lived and dissipates with the first loss when the Kool-Aid drinkers jump off the bandwagon. Many supporters are attracted by coaching style, even though it does not appear that any style has a monopoly on success. For every successful coach who screams there is another who displays a more understated approach. When the screamer wins, his supporters chant hallelujahs for his no-nonsense demeanor; when the same screamer loses, however, the same fans and players jump ship yelling, "The coach doesn't relate." Fear of the coach and the thrill of the win can create short-term player devotion, but when the fear inevitably dulls and the victories become random, the coach is left with fickle fate to sustain player loyalty. Knowledge, integrity, and courage are intrinsic values that command respect across time and enable a leader to survive the inevitable bumps. Respect derived from values is only forfeited if the leader allows himself to be seduced by the power of his position and forgets that leadership is about service to the group—not elevation above the group. All coaches preach "team" and rail against the "I" mentality, but coaches often fall victim to the arrogance of "I" and come to believe that the group exists to serve the leader.

The front and back pages of today's newspapers are filled with stories of what happens when the coach's need to win becomes an obsession that ultimately compromises his integrity.

Coaching should not be about winning; it should be about imparting knowledge and building character in the pursuit of winning. Many coaches win in the absence of character, and many coaches lose despite teaching values. Who do you want to be? What are your priorities? Everyone wants to win—but at what cost? Although integrity alone does not guarantee victories, it does create the respect that motivates your players to fight another day.

Shabbos Tryouts to the Intifada

I am always eager to dispel the belief that Yeshiva's players are frequently subject to anti-Semitic acts. Although during my coaching career, there have been occasional episodes, they were isolated events committed by individuals that were quickly addressed by the school's coaching or administrative staff. The only example of institutionalized discrimination against a YU player occurred in 1985 when the United

States Committee Sports for Israel conducted tryouts for the Maccabiah teams on the Sabbath.

The committee, which evolved into Maccabi USA/Sports for Israel (MUSA), was founded in 1948. According to the mission statement, the organization—through the Maccabiah Games and similar sports projects—attempts "to increase Jewish identity, encourage Jewish pride, and create a heightened awareness of Israel."

Although the committee has done an excellent job of building the Maccabiah Games, its performance in the 1985 Maccabiah was certainly not its finest hour.

Yeshiva's 1984-85 season began with the construction of its new gymnasium (scheduled to open in 1985) and featured an eleven-win campaign, the first winning season since 1959. The season was also highlighted by the exciting performance of junior guards Joe Eaves and Ronnie Schwartz who averaged twenty-one and seventeen points respectively. Their dream was to participate in the Maccabiah Games, and their selection to the twelfth Maccabiah basketball team would have represented a realization of those dreams. Unfortunately, decisions by the committee would not only deny them the fulfillment of their dreams but also disappoint members of the Jewish community.

The players and Yeshiva fans were extremely disappointed when they learned that Ronnie and Joey would not be able to participate in the Maccabiah Games because tryouts were being held on the Sabbath.

I called the basketball committee's co-chairman and explained that holding tryouts on the Sabbath would effectively deny Joe and Ronnie—as well as all Sabbath observers—the equal opportunity to be selected.[66]

The co-chairman, although sympathetic, stated that logistics made it impossible to change the tryout dates because it would "inconvenience the many to please the few." The committee's use of "inconvenience" as a rationale was shocking because it was the same rationalization used by businesses in the fifties and sixties to deny access to Jewish job applicants. Since Jews were the few among the many and Sabbath observers were the fewest of the few, Sabbath observers would always be

---

[66]   Karen Green, an all-star point guard from the Hebrew Institute of Long Island and Yeshiva University Stern College for Women's past coach, was also denied an opportunity to try out due to her Sabbath observance.

excluded. The committee's position was especially painful because it was a Jewish communal organization—financially supported by the Jewish community—that was discriminating against Jewish youth.

After repeated conversations, the basketball co-chairman conceded that not participating in Sabbath tryouts would unfairly exclude the athletes and, therefore, promised to waive the Friday/Saturday tryouts for Sabbath observers. Unfortunately, although the co-chairman intended to fulfill his promise, fellow members of the sports committee had no such intention. Approximately one week prior to the tryouts, parents and players were informed that there was no guarantee of a waiver, and players should make every attempt to participate in the Sabbath tryouts. The Yeshiva players resisted the pressure to participate and after prolonged discussions with the basketball committee were finally waived to the final tryouts on Sunday.

Neither Joey nor Ronnie earned a spot on the Maccabiah team, and although it is impossible to prove that their failure to participate in the Sabbath tryouts precluded their selection, by the committee's own admission, their limited opportunity to participate did "hurt their chances." It is interesting to note that following graduation from YU Joey moved to Israel and enjoyed a successful seventeen-year professional basketball career playing against the top Israeli and European professional players. Although discrimination was not purposely intended, Jewish youth, because of their religious beliefs, were subjected to discrimination by a Jewish organization.

In the wake of the Sabbath tryouts, Jewish newspapers published numerous articles and letters to the editor. The committee responded to the criticism by stating that they were not a "religious organization" and therefore were justified in holding tryouts on the Sabbath.[67] In a letter to *The Jewish Week* I responded that, "Although it is accurate that the Sports Committee for Israel is not mandated to be a religious organization, it still has a responsibility to be Jewish. When it totally denies central Jewish ideals, it has violated that responsibility." I concluded my letter by challenging the committee to be "more than a trivial sports federation attempting to emulate their secular counterparts

---

[67] "Maccabiah Sabbath Violation scored," *The Jewish Week*, May 17, 1985.

but to fulfill their own mission statement to be a positive force in the development of Jewish identity."[68] My letter was never answered.

The 1985 Maccabiah tryouts faded into memory until the 2001 sixteenth Maccabiah when the second intifada threatened to cancel the games. One month prior to the opening ceremony, the men's basketball coach and many of his players announced that they would not participate in the coming games. Under pressure from the Israeli government to send a delegation, the American committee turned to Hubie Brown to assemble a team.

Coach Brown called me in search of players, and I recommended my starting star point guard, Eli Hami. My only condition was that he would not be pressured to practice on the Sabbath and would be provided with kosher food. Based on Coach Brown's personal assurances, Eli became the third player in YU history to be selected to the Maccabiah team, joining Irwin "Red" Blumenreich who was selected to the fourth Maccabiah in 1953 and Sam Grossman who was selected to the sixth Maccabiah in 1961. To Coach Brown's great credit, he honored all his commitments and personally drove Eli to kosher restaurants, demonstrating that Sabbath-observing players can be accommodated without "inconveniencing the many." The intriguing question is why Coach Brown's 1985 counterparts did not feel compelled to do the same for Joey and Ronnie.

The error of the 1985 Sports Committee—all sincere, dedicated individuals—was their failure to internalize the principle that with the right to sponsor Jewish games comes the responsibility to respect Jewish traditions. Unfortunately, the disconnect between rights and responsibility that caused the 1985 decisions continues to this day among other Jewish communal organizations and individual athletes.

I am always saddened when leaders of Jewish sports organizations or individual athletes do not hesitate to publicly parade their Jewishness when it serves their interests but do not demonstrate an equal zeal to publicly respect the traditions that make their Jewishness distinct. You cannot have it both ways. You cannot stand victorious on the mountaintop, trophy held high, proclaiming your Jewishness when your accomplishments are achieved by trampling on the institutions that created your Jewishness.

---

[68]   *The Jewish Week*, Letters, Affront to Jews, May 31, 1985.

The Great Decade (1972-1984)

From 1972-84, seventy-four Yeshiva basketball players studied ten hours a day, practiced six hours a week in eight different gyms, and played home games on seven different courts. They also competed every night against the new reality of open admissions, a policy designed to give minority students advancement opportunities in the classroom, but produced the unintended consequence of providing opportunities to excel on the basketball court as well.

Although educators can debate the impact of open admissions on educational advancement, there is no debate that open admissions revolutionized college and professional basketball. The 74 players of the great decade had the additional burden of studying, practicing, and playing against the backdrop of Yeshiva University's ongoing attempts to stave off bank foreclosure. Despite the challenges, twelve teams collectively won forty games while twenty-eight of the players gained admission to medical, dental, or law school and forty-six players began careers as accountants, business owners, finance managers, IT programmers, principals, psychologists, rabbis, and teachers. Their determination to compete and willingness to sacrifice sustained the basketball program during these challenging years and made it possible for future Yeshiva basketball players to play in the yet-to-be-built Max Stern Athletic Center.

The Monday, Wednesday, and Thursday practices were always constant; although class schedules caused many players to come late, everyone always came. Where we practiced, however, was often a surprise and ranged from a walk to George Washington High School, Junior High School 143, and the MTA gym, to car rides to JFK High School, the Riverdale Jewish center, Barnard High School, the JCC of the Palisades, and our most unusual practice site, St. Helena's High School (currently St. Joseph School for the Deaf).

What always amazed me about the players' dedication was their willingness to drive to practices and games with my brother Danny or Mark's father, Harold Hoenig.

As Robert Rosenbloom said, "The toughest part of playing in the seventies was worrying if we would arrive safely in Danny's car."

We made a rule that starters couldn't go with him because his car often broke down. In addition, his defroster never worked, forcing him to hold the steering wheel with his right hand while he was reaching outside with his left to wipe the windshield. The only thing that compared to it was driving with Mr. Hoenig.

In January 1975, eleven players, one manager, and six basketballs piled into a caravan of cars driven by Danny, Mr. Hoenig, and me, and traveled to St. Helena's High School, a mile from the Bronx-Whitestone Bridge. An elderly priest ushered us through a maze of darkened hallways until we arrived at a pitch-black open area. Our fatherly guide flipped on the light switches, revealing a junior-high-sized-court that had originally served as an auditorium stage. The court was elevated above auditorium seats with one sideline abutting a six-foot drop to the floor. During games, the scoring table and team benches served as guardrails, preventing diving players and flying basketballs from falling into the abyss.

With only ten bodies, we had no guardrails and therefore chasing loose balls became a definite no-no. Players who missed shots or threw errant passes bore the extra consequence of having to search the auditorium seats to retrieve the ball. We practiced for ninety minutes, navigated the dark maze back to our cars, and returned to Yeshiva with eleven players—but only five basketballs. The next night, we defeated New Paltz 60-58 to earn our second win of the season. We didn't throw a pass out of bounds the entire night.

In February 1977, nine players, two managers, and twenty-two soggy tuna fish sandwiches traveled eighty miles by school bus to New Paltz, New York, to play the State University at New Paltz.

Down by six with less than twenty seconds remaining, Robert Rosenbloom scored to cut the lead to four. We pressed, New Paltz turned it over giving Robert the opportunity to go back door and cut the lead to two. New Paltz called time-out to regroup. My memory told me it was their last time-out. The scorer's table confirmed my memory. Their ensuing inbounds pass was deflected, bouncing off two New Paltz players before going out of bounds.

With three seconds on the clock and down by two, Robert faked back door, but took the conventional path through the front door to tie the game. Stunned by the sudden turn of events, New Paltz lost focus and called time-out. As the players started toward their benches, I jumped up and called to the refs, "Who called the time-out? Who called the time-out?

"Sit down and relax, Coach. It's New Paltz's time-out."

"I just wanted to make sure because they don't have any time-outs!"

The refs confirmed the violation. Robert made the technical, giving him seven points in twenty seconds and twenty-nine points for the game. His foul shot also gave us a 74-73 victory and our fourth win of the season. As soon as the buzzer sounded, we ran off the court without giving the refs a chance to change their minds. On the trip back to Yeshiva, the players celebrated with soggy tuna sandwiches while they studied for midterms. Mr. Parker's food never tasted so good.

On Friday, January 5, 1979, the Yeshiva basketball team embarked on a Sabbath weekend basketball trip to Baltimore. All that was missing as the bus left Yeshiva were the coach and assistant coach. The absence of the assistant coach was easy to explain; I had no assistant coach. As for me, I was sitting with my wife and son in the orthopedist's office waiting for a diagnosis. The all-clear evaluation came too late to beat the Sabbath siren, and I made plans to fly to Baltimore Saturday night, hoping to arrive before the 8:30 tip-off. Ice on the runway delayed my departure, and I arrived to the sound of the halftime buzzer.

Despite, or because of, my late arrival, the self-coached team handed me a four-point lead. In the locker room, I gathered my thoughts, gave the team a few reminders, and said, "Do not fall apart now that I am here."

With ten minutes to go, we were down by fifteen and ended up losing 80-53. The players were kind and attributed the loss to late-game fatigue. When I recently asked the players who coached the first half, no one could remember, proving what many have always believed, that coaching is very overrated. As for the John Hopkins coach, he thought that coaching was integral and thanked me for coming.

On Thursday, December 11, 1980, with nine seconds remaining, Harvey Sheff intercepted a crosscourt pass and drove the length of the court to give Yeshiva a last-second win over Northeastern Bible College. In the spring of 2009, when I started to compile background information for these stories, I wrote Northeastern in the hope that they could provide me with the score of the December 11 game.

A few weeks later, I received a call back. "Hi, Coach. The score of the game was 60-59. I know because I was the player who threw the crosscourt pass. Can you tell me which Yeshiva player made the basket? I'd like to contact him."

I paused, told him the player was Harvey Sheff, and asked, "Why do you want to talk to our last-second hero after all these years?"

"It's very strange, but I'll try to explain. My mother died last year, and I suddenly realized that I did not know anything about my father who had abandoned us when I was a little boy. So I researched my DNA and found that my father was Jewish. When N.E. Bible forwarded me your request, I thought it was destiny to reconnect."

I have often heard stories of coincidental events that create unexplainable endings. Hearing a story of how an errant basketball pass was motivation to connect gave new meaning to the Jewish concept of *Bashert* (pre-ordained).

In the spring of 1983, after a twelve-year hiatus, NYU resumed play as a Division III Program. Tempted by the opportunity to achieve a possible upset and be featured on MSG cable television, I scheduled the game. The arrival in 1981 of Joe Eaves, Sol Krevsky, and Shabsi Schreier—and the addition in 1982 of future thousand-point-scorer Ronnie Schwartz—made me believe that Yeshiva was competitive enough to dream about upsetting NYU. What I didn't know was that Joey was going to spend the 1983-4 season studying in Israel, and Sol Krevsky would be transferring. Despite their absences, we approached the TV game with dreams still intact. The game had all the feeling of big-time basketball, and it even featured a background discussion with Cal Ramsey, the former NYU All-American and color commentator for MSG. He said, "Tell me about your league-leading rebounder Shabsi Schreier."

Without thinking, I responded, "He can't jump, he can't run, but he always gets the job done."

Ramsey enjoyed my inadvertent rhyme, but I immediately regretted my phrasing. I had meant to praise Shabsi for his determination, but I had inadvertently implied that he lacked athleticism. I always regretted my flippant comment and hoped that my words would just fade away never to be heard again.

The game got off to a great start. Jeff Harris's rebound and put-back basket gave us a 12-4 lead, and Ronnie Schwartz's driving layup with 3:57 left in the half gave us a 21-21 tie. We entered halftime down only eight, 31-23.

While Mike Muzio, the NYU coach, refocused his team and I reinforced my players, Cal Ramsey was seizing the moment to tell his cable audience, "Shabsi Schrier is leading Yeshiva tonight. It's just like his coach said, 'He can't jump, he can't run, but he always gets the job done.'"

We came out of halftime fired up. We should never have come out. In the next twenty minutes, we scored only eleven points and went down in defeat 60-34.[69]

A year later, the season opened to a 3-1 start, our best in thirteen years. As I had done after every game, win or lose, I called the *New York Times* sports desk to report the score.

The intern manning the phones answered, *"New York Times* sports."

"Men's college basketball score," I responded.

"Go ahead."

"Yeshiva 63, New York Maritime 61."

Instead of hearing the usual thank you and a click, I heard, "Way to go, Yeshiva. That's three in a row."

"How did you know that?" I asked.

"I'm Jewish; I follow Yeshiva all the time."

I had always preached, but could never prove, that Yeshiva represented the Jewish people. Now a *New York Times* intern had provided confirmation that Yeshiva really was American Jewry's team.

Three months later, on February 25, the 84-85 team captained by Shabsi earned a 100-59 victory over Bard College, guaranteeing Yeshiva its first winning season in twenty-four years.

After the game, I thanked the team for their contributions and then addressed Shabsi. "Years from tonight, when you meet and reminisce with teammates, you will remember that you captained the team that renewed Yeshiva's winning tradition."

Twenty-six years later, on December 18, 2011, Shabsi stood in the lobby of the Melvin Furst Gymnasium, a gym in which he had never played, but which he and past Yeshiva players had made possible, and spoke about the new video interactive basketball display that he and his wife Julie had dedicated. His words were addressed to former captains, players, family, and friends who had gathered to honor Yeshiva's past captains. His speech was short but to the point.

He reminisced about Yeshiva basketball and then with exacting accuracy repeated Cal Ramsey's 1983 words "He can't jump, he can't

---

[69]   To view the NYU versus Yeshiva game, go to www.backdoorhoops.com.

run, but he always gets the job done." His words reflected his enormous pride at what he and all Yeshiva players had been able to accomplish through pure determination—and despite the challenges of the 72-84 decade.

In the world of NCAA basketball, teams that continually finish second are classified as losers. In the world of Yeshiva basketball where the pursuit of dreams is not diminished by losses, players who dare to dream are always winners. In basketball and in life, you cannot always control outcome, but you can always control its pursuit.

The players of the great decade exemplified the words of *Ethics of Our Fathers*. "It is not incumbent upon you to complete the work, but you are not exempt from starting it."[70]

---

[70] *Ethics of the Fathers*, Chapter 2, Verse 21.

Chapter 10

"BETTER TO LISTEN TO THE REBUKE OF A WISE MAN."
—ECCLESIASTES 7:5

I met Red in November 1960 when my high school coach Hy Wettstein introduced me following our victory in the prelim to the Yeshiva versus Hartwick game.

"Hey, Red. This is Johnny Halpert. He is going to be a great shooter for you in two years."

He looked me up and down, told me to follow through, and walked away.

My impression of Red was that he was the angriest person I had ever met. As I watched my first Yeshiva game, his every action confirmed my impression. He spent forty minutes yelling from the bench and during time-outs, he yelled even louder. Red's time-out performances were so famous that fans arrived early to get orchestra seats. Although fans came to see the yelling, coaches throughout New York came to absorb his basketball genius. Every practice from FIT to Power Memorial High School was a coaching clinic, and if you arrived early, you could catch the bonus of watching Red work with Power Memorial High School coach Jack Donohue and his star freshman Lew Alcindor (Kareem Abdul-Jabbar).

Coaches who couldn't get to Red's night practices came looking for plays at his store on Flatbush Avenue. On one occasion, I watched Red draw up an offensive scheme that we were using and hand it to the grateful coach.

"Here," he said. "Try it and see what you think."

As the coach was leaving, I whispered, "You only gave him half the play."

"I know. When he gives me the whole order, he will get the whole play."

Red gave coaches plays, but to Yeshiva he imparted a basketball philosophy that to this day has enabled YU players to compete against stronger, bigger, and quicker opponents. Red's emphasis on moving without the ball turned good players into college players and very good players into all-stars. Every team that played Yeshiva thought they should win, but they were all scared to death that Red's system could beat them. Red's legacy, which I have carried for forty-one years, was to give kids who were pursuing their dreams of winning a system that enabled them to win.

Although Red was universally respected for his basketball knowledge, his chair kicking, screaming, and berating of refs gave him his aura. Despite his very loud public persona, the real Red was very much a mass of contradictions.

Red was often the abrasive coach who told us that "You can't make chicken salad out of chicken___." Nonetheless, he never hesitated to express his admiration for our academic accomplishments and firm religious beliefs. He was an enormously proud Jew who lectured us on how fortunate we were to represent the Jewish people and how proud he was to be our coach.

The contrast between his words of reverence and his rants was startling. Red often chose the Brooklyn College game to deliver his Jewish pride speech because Brooklyn fielded many Jewish players who had rejected the opportunity to attend Yeshiva and represent their people. Although I had spent twelve years in a Yeshiva day and high school, I acquired my Jewish pride from the non-Orthodox, chair-kicking Red Sarachek.

Red was a basketball genius who could see scenarios three steps ahead of the opposing coach, but he could also become so obsessed with strategy that he once attempted to substitute a player for himself.

"Katz, get in the game."

"Who should I go in for?"

"Go in for Katz. He stinks."

"But, Coach, I'm Katz."

"Then sit down; you stink also."

He also became so crazed by the smallest mistake that he physically threw an eighteen-year-old freshman across the gym for not cutting to the up bucket.

Forty-two years later, in the middle of a scrimmage, I was reminded of that incident when my star Israeli player stood frozen in the corner despite my screams for him to cut to the up bucket. I suddenly realized that he, like I forty-two years earlier, had never before heard the term "up bucket." He stayed in the corner because there was a bucket under the water cooler. Now every year before we start practice, I make sure to explain, without any physical intervention, Red's lingo of "chest to chest," "mambo," and "up bucket."

Despite his angry demeanor, Red could also be very funny. During one halftime rant about our poor play execution, he screamed, "Every coach in New York is running my plays except Yeshiva."

In addition to criticism, halftime also featured a tray of oranges cut in quarters. While Red was criticizing our defense, Ken Jacobson, our star forward, was methodically devouring the oranges and leaving only a pile of peels. Suddenly, Red, in mid-sentence, stopped and asked, "Jacobson, did you come here to play or eat supper?"

Red was loyal to any player in need and served as a father figure for many. He stopped talking to one player for thirty years, however, because he had failed his loyalty test by not ordering his school's uniforms from him.

The more I interacted with Red, the more I understood that his contrasting behaviors were motivated by his innate need to speak the truth. He could not control this need any more than he could control his biological need for oxygen. It was why, despite the racial bias prevalent in 1947, he put three black Scranton Miner players on the court at the same time. It is also why he could cut his pro players if they didn't perform—but under the threat of firing, he joined them on the picket lines when they struck for raises. Red never meant to embarrass anyone, but a lie, an injustice, a bad shot, or a poorly executed play was a wrong that he felt compelled to reject. He just rejected these wrongs more vocally than others and without any inhibitions.

Red not only spoke the truth but respected anyone who told the truth—even when it was at his expense. In my first two years of coaching, I was 5-34 and struggling to earn the respect of my players. I sought help by inviting Red to practices, but that decision did nothing to enhance my standing. His personality was so dominating that I often found myself standing and watching like a player rather than a head coach, reinforcing the image of an inexperienced coach who was desperate for help.

Starting with the 1974-75 season, I began to acquire the self-confidence to develop my own offensive schemes, which I took to Red for approval.

"Try it," he said, "and let me know how it goes."

I introduced the scheme and shared the positive feedback with him.

A few days later he called and told me that he was coming to practice that night to work on the offense. To this day, I have no idea where I found the courage and I can actually remember my voice shaking as I responded to his unsolicited offer to attend practice. "Red, when you come you have to let me teach the offense. I need to show that I am the coach."

He neither responded nor showed up to the practice. Although relieved by his absence, I was afraid to call him, fearing that I had violated his loyalty commandment.

A few days later, he called as if nothing had happened. "So, Johnny, how is the offense going?"

I avoided the elephant in the room and just responded to his question, "It's going great. I'm just not sure what to do with the off guard."

"Think about it," he said. "You got a good head. Remember you learned from the best."

I got off the phone relieved. I was still okay. Red had accepted my rejection because he knew I was right. Although he respected my honesty, his ego would never allow him to play second fiddle to a twenty-nine-year-old "Pisher." He never came to another practice. I would like to tell you that with the new offense and my newfound assertiveness, the season ended happily ever after. Unfortunately, we finished the season 5-14, and it would take a lot more than new plays and renewed confidence to start winning consistently.

Red was not an easy coach to play for, and anyone who tells you differently is violating his dictum of "Thou shall not spin the truth." I believe that every player who played for him thought about quitting at least once; I know I did. My basketball transition from high school to college was very difficult. In two years of high school, I had scored 820 points; suddenly I was a bench player. Where Mr. Wettstein had praised, now Red screamed.

The low point came late in my freshman year against City College. Red often reacted to a player's mistake by subbing him. Being substituted after a mistake to face Red had the feel of a murderer being led to the electric chair. At City College, this feeling was magnified because the benches in the old gym were under the basket. Players had to walk the length of the court like models on a runway when subbed in or out. I had spent the first fifteen minutes of the game at the end of the bench until Red screamed, "Johnny."

At the next stoppage of play, I took the long walk to the offensive zone and tapped the teammate who Red had designated for execution. The game continued until a foul created another stoppage. I had not been in the game long enough to do anything right or wrong; when the buzzer sounded for a substitution, I assumed the call was for someone else. To my surprise, the very same player that I had just sent to the electric chair had come back from the dead to tap my shoulder. The good news was that there was nothing to yell at me about. The bad news was that I was back on the bench. However, I did not have to wait long for another player's mistake and for Red's call of, "Johnny!"

I dutifully obeyed and delivered another execution tap only to be retapped almost immediately by the same player. This game of tap and re-tap repeated itself two more times with two different players. In a little more than two minutes, Red had used me to execute the entire starting team. He had finally discovered a role for me. I was to be his tapper. To this day, I am sure I hold the NCAA record for most substitutions in two minutes.

The City College fans recognized my tapping skills; with each substitution walk, their cheers grew louder. Halftime ended my execution walks, and I spent the rest of the game at the end of the bench, alternating between staring aimlessly into space and thinking about a 1962 Yeshiva-St. Francis game where I had watched Sam Grossman, on his way back to the bench, punch Red in reaction to his substitution rant. At the time, I couldn't understand how a player could do that. Now I regretted not doing it.

After our post-game locker room lecture, I dressed and left, choosing to walk back to Washington Heights rather than take the train. As I walked up Amsterdam Avenue I debated with myself about quitting and by the time I arrived home I had decided to quit. Fortunately there was no practice the following night and after forty eight-hours my need to dream had replaced my need for revenge.

Although the mock cheers of the City fans had no lasting impact on my play, their memory accompanies me to every game I coach. To this day a player has to commit murder before I will sub him immediately after a mistake and although during time-outs I do yell with Red's intensity, the anger is always directed at the team rather than at an individual player. I save the targeted yelling for the privacy of practice.

I always encourage players to come to me with their complaints; some years, I spend more time with players off the court than on. "Tell me when you are upset or think that I am being unfair," I frequently remind them. "It will give me a chance to persuade you that I am right or apologize if you prove me wrong."

There is only one complaint that does not get a fair hearing.

"Coach, you embarrassed me the other night when you . . ."

I rarely let the player finish his sentence. "Embarrass you?" I respond. "You have no idea what embarrassment is."

The five remaining games of my freshman season were like a blur. I finished the season watching rather than playing. For the first time, I had finished the season as a sub, not a starter, and I approached my summer workout routine without goals.

My former high school opponents and current teammates told me, "Don't listen to his yelling, just shoot." My friends who had spent four years telling me how great I was, also told me, "He's killing your confidence. Ignore him." Even Rabbi Urivetsky, my high school *rebbe* joined my support group and counseled me to have more belief in myself. Although Red was certainly not giving me any confidence, my bigger, quicker opponents were not helping either. With no disrespect to my former yeshiva high school opponents, RJJ was not Fairfield, LIU, or Farleigh Dickinson.

After the season, I returned to Mr. Wettstein's high school practices to regain my confidence. Although I relived my glory days of shooting jump shots over passive high school zones, rather than convincing me "to shoot more and listen less," those shots only reminded me of the disparity in skill between high school and college players.

It was tempting to blame Red for my freshman failures, but I had learned from my games of fungo stickball that when you strike out, you have no one to blame but yourself. Besides, if my problem was Red, then why was my teammate Shelly Rokach able to score fifteen points a game. Red yelled at him even more than he yelled at me. It was undeniable that Red was a screamer, but it was also undeniable that embedded in his words of rebuke was knowledge that could make you a better player if you could only get past the screaming. It was all or nothing with Red. His style left you no options. If I was going to become a college player, I would have to listen more and shoot less.

As for my confidence, I knew that Red was not going to engage in any handholding and if that was what I needed to become a college player I was going to have to rely on my girlfriend. Fortunately, I had a girlfriend and in those days religious couples still held hands.

I returned to the sanctuary of my park but instead of shooting jump shots I practiced changing, spinning and picking. I practiced visualizing the game by placing the ball on the foul line and moving in relation to the ball. Players on the other courts tried to figure out what I was doing, but they eventually gave up and assumed that I had been out in the sun too long. In three-on-three park games, I never shot unless it came off a pick or a spin. Moving without the ball became my obsession, and a basket off a backdoor cut was my ultimate triumph.

I returned from the park a different player. In pre-season practices, I cut, passed, and never took a shot, making me the most popular guy on the team. Fewer shots created fewer scream opportunities; after three team defections and one injury, I earned a start against Marist College in the third game of my sophomore year.

With the game tied in overtime and time running out, I called Red's "C" play, making myself the second option. Fate interceded, however, and put the ball in my hands for the last shot. I executed to perfection every fundamental that I had practiced all summer. I caught, faced up, froze my defensive man, pump faked, jab stepped right, and drove left past my man for the winning basket. I finished the game with six points on three-for-three shooting, earning me four lines in the *New York Times* and a phone call from my hand-holder. The locker room was euphoric. I listened to every compliment.

Among the celebrants in the locker room was Midgie, a character right out of a Damon Runyon novel. He was one of Red's groupies who came to games and at every chance, he told anyone who would listen that Red was the greatest. We met at the bathroom sink. Out of the side of his mouth, he growled, "Hey, kid, you did a good job tonight, but you cost me a lot of money." I was a naïve, nineteen-year-old Yeshiva kid, and it would take years before I understood what he meant.

Red also had a post-game comment for me. "You were lucky; don't let it go to your head."

Although it was not your traditional "good game" coach comment, it was Red's best attempt at praise, and I gladly accepted it. Despite the grudging compliment, I knew he was thrilled because I had run his play, executed the fundamentals he had taught me, and he wasn't yelling. As for me, I had accomplished my summer goals. I had started, scored, and had a high school moment. Although it was not what I had envisioned for my college career, I was happy that I now actually had a college career. That being said, although I accepted my new role, having to do so angered me throughout college.

My decision to listen more and shoot less got me playing time (PT) in my sophomore year and a starting spot for the next two years. I had a few more high school moments, including scoring nineteen points in a triple overtime 100-96 win against Queens College. Along with a record-breaking forty-eight-point single-game scoring performance by Shelly Rokach, the game also featured my last-second tying basket in regulation and my last-second three-point play to force a second overtime. Despite a follow-up sixteen-point game against Bridgeport and six double-digit scoring games, my career was a five-point, four-shot experience.

In my last college practice, after four years of screams, disappointments, and a few high school moments, I did the impossible. It was a backdoor play that we ran all the time, but this time I "played against my man" as Red always preached and executed a variation that left my defensive man frozen in place. Unfortunately, I missed the layup. The play was a microcosm of my college career and represented the ultimate dilemma for Red. In one second, I had integrated everything he had taught me and created his perfect play, but at the same time, I failed to turn his knowledge into the ultimate goal of basketball: a successful basket. As Red would often say, "They don't give points for style."

The practice stopped for what seemed like an hour as I waited for Red's verbal explosion. Instead, there was a look of resignation and a shake of the head. For the first time in his entire coaching career, I had accomplished the impossible. I had left Red speechless.

It is very difficult to reflect back forty-five years and recall accurately how much Red's yelling affected my play. Without question, achievement requires confidence, but what creates confidence is not so clearly defined. After forty-one years of providing confidence to other Johnny Halperts, I have learned that, although handholding is important ultimately it is skill, not handholding that produces confidence.

I finished my college career very conflicted. My wife, who had experienced the four years with me, says I was just angry. I appreciated everything that Red had given me, but I was still angry enough not to invite him to our wedding.

After graduation, I got married, won a fellowship, and landed the MTA junior varsity coaching position. My interaction with Red during the next five years was random, and although I attended YU games, it was not to see him, but to cheer Stu Poloner and Harold Perl who I had coached in Camp Raleigh.

In 1971 I watched Stu, guarded by three Brandeis players, hit a jump shot off the dribble to break Irv Bader's Yeshiva University's all time scoring record. His record of 1,378 points in only three seasons would stand until 1982 when Harvey Sheff scored 1,500 points. Fans who had the opportunity to watch Stuie play were very fortunate.

In the spring of 1972, Mr. Wettstein announced his retirement from MTA and my former high school principal, Rabbi Weinbach, offered me the varsity position. Thrilled, I accepted immediately. The next week, I received the first in what would become a forty-year tradition of phone calls from Red.

"Sammy Stern is leaving to coach New York Tech. You can recruit the Yeshiva High School League and are the best man to replace him."

Given our past relationship, I was shocked by his offer. MTA had a long and fabled history of championships and a pool of outstanding players. The college team presented a far different picture. They were coming off ten consecutive losing seasons, including seven wins and fifty losses in the past three years.

I chose the challenge of college basketball rather than the lure of high school championships because Red had chosen me. I have never regretted my decision, although there were moments during forty-point losses that I considered going for therapy. Since I had learned from Red, I started my coaching career believing I knew everything and could control anything. Now after forty-one years, I realize that I learn something new every day, and I can control very little. Five hundred losses will do that to you.

Immediately upon assuming the coaching position, my relationship with Red changed. Praise replaced criticism, and post-game losses earned consolation rather than harangues. I received more confidence-building messages in one month of coaching than I received in four years of playing. Despite Red's support and confidence building, my six-year coaching record upon his retirement as AD in 1978 was twenty-two wins and ninety-eight losses. So much for the correlation between confidence and accomplishment; I was the most confident losing coach in New York City.

After his retirement from YU in 1978, Red devoted his basketball energies to Lou Carnesecca and St. John's University. Although his focus was on Lou, he still found time for me. I would meet him at St. John's to talk basketball and watch him work individually with future NBA stars Chris Mullen and Mark Jackson. Through Red, I developed a relationship with Lou that continues today. Every year before Rosh Hashanah, Lou still calls to wish me a happy New Year. There is a reason why everyone loves Lou Carnesecca.

In 1992, Red moved to Florida, and we started a twenty-year AT&T ritual. In the off-season, we would speak to each other twice a week, and in season, we would talk before and after every game. The ritual was always the same. If I called him after ten, he would answer the phone yelling, "How could you lose to those guys?"

"How do you know we lost?" I would ask sheepishly.

"When you win, you call me before ten."

The relationship also had a written component that was strictly one way. Phone strategy sessions were often followed by either a Rosh Hashanah or birthday card. The nature of the card had nothing to do with the calendar. Rosh Hashanah cards could appear in the spring, and birthday cards could appear in the fall even though my birthday was in the summer. The only thing the cards shared in common was illegibly scribbled Xs and Os that represented basketball players. If Red's offensive schemes were difficult to understand over the phone, they became impossible to decipher when scribbled on a Rosh Hashanah card.

Often, I would make the mistake of saying, "I can't understand the play. There is a player missing."

"Look under the R. Do you see him now?"

"I can't see anything under the R."

"Than look under the O."

"The only O I see is the O in the word Rosh."

Red finally ran out of patience and yelled, "If you can't find the fifth guy, then figure it out for yourself."

I found out later that Red was doing the same thing with Jack Alisi, the coach of Xaverian High School, except Jack's plays were scribbled on Christmas cards or paper napkins.

Red was an equal opportunity screamer; when Jack complained that he could not find the missing player, Red would yell, "Go find it for yourself."

Jack and I each shared a special relationship with Red, but he was able to do something I could never achieve. In 2005, Xaverian High School won the New York City Catholic High School Championship. The next day, Jack, Sal Ferrera (the president of Xaverian), and Lou Piccola flew to Florida and at 10:00 in the morning personally presented Red with the championship trophy. When people asked Jack why he had flown to Florida to personally present the trophy he answered simply, "I had promised Red that I would." Jack had obviously not only absorbed Red's basketball wisdom but the importance of loyalty as well.

Over time, our phone conversations evolved from calls dealing with outcome and consolation to "why" and "what" questions. "Why did you play zone?" he would ask. "What were you thinking about when they switched to man?"

Each of my answers was followed by more why questions. The why and what dialogue was eerily reminiscent of my days in Talmud class where the emphasis was centered on understanding the "why." Over time, I became the questioner. "Did you see the Bulls game last night? What was Jackson thinking? What would you have run in that last play?"

The phone dialogue slowly seeped into my coaching style. When a player would take a bad shot rather than just stopping to yell "Bad shot" I would ask "Why did you take that shot? What were you thinking? Do you know why that was a bad shot?"

The player's immediate response was to try to guess the answer that I was looking for. In the end, he would never find an answer because he didn't have one.

"You have no idea why you took that shot," I would respond. "That's the problem. You have to understand what you are doing on the court."

Talmudic method had moved from the study halls to the gym. Who would believe that I would be teaching basketball by employing the same technique used by my Rebbeim?

Our long-distance relationship also had a face-to-face aspect. I would try to schedule my Florida trips to visit my father on Tuesdays, which was the day for Red's old-timers' breakfast. Red would sit at the head of the table and hold court for former basketball players, coaches, and referees. The first time I attended the breakfast, I was struck by the similarity between the breakfast and a traditional Hasidic *Tisch*.[71] Just as the aged and respected *Rebbe* sat at the head of the table while his *Chasidim* sat as close as possible to hear his every word, Red sat at the head of the table, and his basketball fraternity sat around him in a semicircle. The only difference was that Red's *Chasidim* ate bagels, lox, and eggs. The seat next to the *Rebbe* was the most coveted, and only followers who were summoned by the Rebbe himself could sit there. Red treated me like his chief *Chasid*. When I came to the breakfast, Red would summon me to his side telling anyone who was sitting there, "This is Johnny Halpert. Move over."

The interaction between Red and the old-timers was fascinating. I listened to all the old stories, but I mostly sat back and watched the enormous respect they afforded him. It was the same old Red; only truth could be brought to the breakfast table.

Red served as the master of ceremonies and decided who could speak. If he didn't like what someone said, he would cut him off or just tell him, "You knew nothing about basketball thirty years ago, and you still don't know anything."

When Red's health began to deteriorate in 2000, our conversations turned more personal. We would share stories about our children and grandchildren, and in one phone call Red asked about my son Yehuda. "Which law firm is your son working for?"

"He is at Weil, Gotshal."

"How are they treating him?"

"He just started and seems to be doing okay."

---

[71] A *tisch* is literally a table and represents a gathering, usually on the Sabbath, when the Rebbe's disciples or Chassidim would gather to eat and listen to the Rebbe speak and preach.

The conversation moved on to other subjects and was completely forgotten until about a month later when Yehuda called me. "The craziest thing happened to me today. All of a sudden I was summoned to a senior partner's office. I was scared they were firing me. Brand new lawyers don't get called to a private meeting with a partner."

When I got there he asked me. 'Are you happy? Is everyone treating you okay?'

I answered yes, but I had no idea why I had been summoned for this personal little chitchat. Then everything became clear."

"Do you know who I am?"

"Of course. You are David Blittner, partner."

"Do you know who else I am?"

"No."

"I'm Red Sarachek's grandson. He called me and told me that if I did not take care of you, he would kick my ass. So please do me a favor. If you have any problems, come and see me right away because my grandfather really will kick my ass."

Red and I had come a long way together. In November 1960, he had treated me as an afterthought—and now he was taking care of my son. For four years he had screamed at me and for the next thirty-four he held my hand. He had taught me everything I knew about coaching, both substance and style. Although I employ his wisdom every day, I have chosen a very different teaching style. I fully understand that my measured approach often leads players to mistake kindness for weakness, but I cannot change my approach to coaching any more than I can abandon the wisdom of Red's knowledge.

Players and supporters often say, "Coach, you are not tough enough. You need to yell more."

Critics are never so kind. I listen, but I rarely respond because my coaching style is by design. In the quiet of post-game losses, I often wonder if yelling more would have gotten me the win. After the requisite self-flagellation, I reject the premise. Believing in yourself however can be very lonely and therefore when random reinforcement appears, it is very powerful.

After a hard-fought win against Bard College, the father of an opposing player stopped me as I was leaving the gym. "My son graduated a few years ago, but I still never miss the Yeshiva games. I love to watch the way your teams play and how you coach them."

I thanked him profusely for his kind words; you don't get many compliments like that. As we shook hands, he said, "You know, I played against Red in the fifties, and I think you're a soft Red." At first, I was taken aback by his characterization of me as soft. In sports lingo, being called soft is a big negative. However, when used as an adjective for Red, I took it as a great compliment.

In January 2005, I took the team to Florida to play Johnson and Wales and Palm Beach Atlantic. It was my hope that Red, who by this time was suffering from chronic heart failure and periodic hospitalizations, would be able to come watch us play. I wanted more than anything to show him that I was continuing his legacy and teaching the game the way he had taught me. I also wanted his seal of approval that I was doing a good coaching job. His opinion was the only one that mattered.

Unfortunately, Red was not strong enough to make the trip and after the Palm Beach Atlantic game I decided to bring the team to his home. We arrived after ten and it was obvious how much seeing the Yeshiva basketball team meant to him. Seventeen players plus my wife and I crowded into Red's living room where the players sat on the floor at his feet while he held court in his living room chair. The players sat quietly hanging on every word. They answered Red's questions, listened to his insights and got a chance to ask him some questions. He was the same old Red.

"You got big hands, but can you rebound?"

"You're a big guy," he said to my starting center, "but it looks like you're eating too many doughnuts."

"Can any of these guys shoot?" he asked.

"They all want to shoot," I answered.

We sat for an hour and talked until Red said he was tired. It was the first time I had ever heard Red say that he was tired. Every player shook his hand as they left. My wife and I lagged behind to say our good-byes.

As we got into the car I mumbled to myself the same words I said after each visit to my ailing father. "This could be the last time that I will ever see him."

A week later, an envelope-sized card arrived in the mail. I opened the envelope, fully expecting to see little Xs and Os scrolled across a greeting. Instead, I found a handwritten note on the back of a picture of Jerusalem.

Postcard from Red Sarachek to Johnny Halpert. January 2005

John
I felt like rambling
my hand shakes (excuse
Thank you for meeting
with your team—I was
very proud—
I wish I had more
time to spend with you and
them. They look good
to me They
show respect for you—
So important.
You're giving them your
knowledge.
Johnny you have proven
to me and to others
to be a good Coach &
Teacher

I listen when you
and I talk. Your smart
and willing to give your
utmost—
Your reputation is
growing—
Your intense and
you have the desire
to honestly give all—
Especially for YU
They should respect and
honor you for being
successful. You have been
an asset
Coaches know your good
And Red Sara✓ knows
Your good
Proud of you
Sincere Red Sara✓

I read the card slowly and then read it again, savoring every word. I read it all the time, especially after bad losses. Even coaches of forty-one years need periodic handholding.

On November 15, 2005, at the age of ninety-three, Bernard "Red" Sarachek, Benjamin Son of Yehuda Halevi, passed away. The family asked Lou and me to speak. I eulogized Red by emphasizing that he was a basketball genius, a proud Jew, a man of truth, and a loyal friend. I concluded by referring to Deuteronomy 31:7, when Moses upon transferring his leadership to Joshua charged Joshua to have "Strength and courage." The strength that accrues from truth and the courage to act on the truth. Red possessed both qualities.

I think of Red every day. I miss him very much.

Photo courtesy of Yeshiva University
Red Sarachek and Johnny Halpert, February 1966

Chapter 11

PLAYERS AND COACHES
(EIGHTY-THREE YEARS OF
YESHIVA UNIVERSITY BASKETBALL)

Why They Played

The nine members of the 1975-1976 varsity basketball team attended their Jewish studies classes from nine to one, their secular classes from two to seven, practiced until ten, and everyone became a doctor, dentist, or lawyer. The 1975 team's daily schedule and accomplishments were not unique, but rather representative of the approximately six hundred players who for eighty-three years have worn the Yeshiva University blue and white uniform. Their determination to compete was not fueled by victories or deterred by losses.

The players played—and the coaches coached—because competing gave them the opportunity to chase their dreams while representing the Jewish people. As soon as the players ran onto the court with the word Yeshiva emblazoned on their chests, they experienced the pride that accrues from representing a belief. The players never gave loud cheers proclaiming their heritage—they never had to because they knew that in the eyes of the world they were the "Jewish school and the Jewish players."

This chapter is dedicated to the players, managers, coaches, and assistant coaches who represented the values and traditions of Yeshiva University with pride and distinction.

The Players (1930-1972)[72]

1930-1931	
Eisenberg, J	Captain
Engleberg, L	
Guterman, A	
Izenberg, L	
Steinberg, H	
Troy, Al	
1931-1932	
No Records	
1932–1933	
Aranoff, Hy	
Brown, Tzvi	
Fallek, Dave	
Friedman, Israel	
Gordon, Morris	
Green, Sid	Captain
Kasten, Eliyahu (Red)	
Muss, Louis	
Troy, Al	
1933–1934	
Aranoff, Hy	Captain
Brown, Tzvi	
Goodman, Joe	
Greenberg, Abraham	
Hurewitz, Marvin	
Kasten, Eliyahu (Red)	
Krieger, Morris	

---

[72] Pictures of individual teams can be found by going to www.backdoorhoops. com/teams.

Levy, Max	
Muss, Louis	
1934–1935	
Aranoff, Hy	
Eisenberg, Isaiah	
Feuerstein, Moses	
Goldklang, Norman	
Goodman, Joe	Captain
Greenberg, Abraham	
Kasten, Eliyahu (Red)	
Koshar, Herbert	
Krieger, Morris	
Levy, Max	
Mager, Jules	
Muss, Louis	
Zolt, Erwin	
1935–1936	
Aranoff, Hy	Captain
Cohen, Artie	
Eisenberg, Isaiah	
Friedberg, Arthur	
Goldklang, Norman	
Goodman, Joe	
Kasten, Eliyahu (Red)	
Kolatch, Alan	
Krieger, Morris	
Krischewsky, Manny	
Levy, Max	
Mager, Jules	
Muss, Louis	
Tittlebaum, Milton	

1936–1937	
Avrech, Abe	
Eisenberg, Isaiah	
Goldklang, Norman	
Goodman, Joe	
Koslovsky (Koslowe), Irving	
Levy, Max	Captain
Lipschitz, Nathan	
Mager, Jules	
Pauker, Norman	
Ribner, Herbert	
Rosenblum, Jack	
Rubinroth, Emanuel	
Schwartz, Robert	
Sklaren, Morton	
Stern, Irving	
1937–1938	
Avrech, Abraham	
Eisenberg, Isaiah	
Goldkrang, Norman	Captain
Koslovsky (Koslowe), Irving	Captain
Lipschitz, Nathan	
Mager, Jules	
Rosenblum, Jack	
Schwartz, Robert	
Sklaren, Morton	
1938–1939	
Avrech, Abraham	
Egelnick, Dave	
Esterson, Harold	
Jaret, Irving	

Koslovsky, (Koslowe) Irving	Captain
Maimon, Sol	
Meyer, Samuel	
Rosenblum, Jack	
Rosenblum, Sam	
Schwartz, Robert	
1939–1940	
Avrech, Abraham	
Brandwein, Unknown	
Egelnick, Dave	
Esterson, Harold	
Jaret, Irving	
Koslovsky, (Koslowe) Irving	Captain
Maimon, Sol	
Meyer, Samuel	
Rosenblum, Sam	
Schwartz, Robert	
1940–1941	
Egelnick, Dave	
Esterson, Harold	
Friedman, Marshall	
Meyer, Samuel	Captain
Rosenblum, Sam	
Steinberg, Irv	
1941–1942	
Block, Zelig	
Doppelt, Stan	
Elgart, Joseph	
Esterson, Harold	Captain
Hartstein, Abe	
Hartstein, Sam	

Jaret, Irving	
Kalb, Sam	
Kaplan, Sol	
Kramer, Milton	
Rosenblum, Sam	Captain
Susskind, David	
1942–1943	
Bloch, Zelig	Captain
Doppelt, Stan	
Friedman, Marshall	
Hartstein, Sam	Captain
Jaret, Irving	
Kalb, Sam	
Perlow, Blondy	
Rosen, Sam	
Scharfstein, Bedo	
Susskind, David	
1943–1944	
Beinhorn, Joe	
Doppelt, Stan	
Fredman, Marvin	
Friedman, Marshall	
Kalb, Sam	
Lieb, Julius	
Perlow, Blondy	
Pomerantz, Hyman	
Rosen, Sam	
Rosenbloom, Sam	
Scharfstein, Bedo	
Steinberg, Irv	
Susskind, David	Captain

1944–1945	
Abrams, Jerry	
Adler, Jacob	
Beinhorn, Joe	
Doppelt, Stan	Captain
Doppelt, Manny	
Fenster, Myron	
Fredman, Marvin	
Friedman, Marshall	
Friedman, Sy	
Jaret, Irving	
Pomerantz, Hyman	
Rosenbloom, Sam	
Scharfstein, Bedo	
1945–1946	
Abrams, Jerry	
Adler, Jacob	
Beinhorn, Joe	
Fredman, Marvin	
Geller, Donny	
Gewirtz, Arthur	
Kalb, Sam	
Pomerantz, Hyman	Captain
Rubin, Merrill	
Scharfstein, Bedo	
Wiesel, Irv	
1946-1947	
Abrams, Jerry	
Blumenfeld, Solomon	
Danzig, Howard	
Fredman, Aaron	
Fredman, Alvin	

Fredman, Mel	Captain
Friedman, Marvin	
Geller, Donny	
Hyatt, Isidore	
Poleyeff, Israel	
Rubin, Merrill	
Scharfstein, Bedo	
Shapiro, Abraham	
Simon, Yechiel	
Wiesel, Irv	
1947-1948	
Danzig, Howard	
Davidman, Ruby	
Dyen, Sam	
Fredman, Aaron	
Fredman, Alvin	
Fredman, Mel	
Geller, Donny	
Hyatt, Isidore	
Komsky, Daniel	
Poleyeff, Israel	
Rubin, Merrill	Captain
Simon, Yechiel	
1948-1949	
Bomstein, Leo	
Danzig, Howard	
Davidman, Ruby	
Dryspiel, Hillel	
Dyen, Samuel	
Fredman, Aaron	
Geller, Donny	Captain
Komsky, Daniel	

Krieger, Nate	
Kupchick, Abe	
Noveseller, Maurice	
Poleyeff, Israel	
Simon, Yechiel	
Stein, Arthur	
Tepper, William	
1949-1950	
Danzig, Howard	Captain
Davidman, Ruby	
Dryspiel, Hillel	
Eidman, Seymour	
Fingerhutt, Bernard	
Fredman, Aaron	
Hartman, David	
Komsky, Daniel	
Krieger, Nate	
Kupchick, Abe	
Mayer, Murray	
Noveseller, Maurice	
Shevrin, Howard	
Stein, Arthur	
Tepper, William	
Weinberg, Murray	
1950-1951	
Davidman, Ruby	
Dryspiel, Hillel	
Forman, Irving	
Hershkowitz, Marvin	
Kramer, Abraham	
Krieger, Nate	
Levine, Elihu	

Narrowe, Morty	
Staiman, Larry	
Stein, Arthur	Captain
1951-1952	
Citron, Jay	
Davidman, Ruby	Captain
Forman, Irving	
Freundlich, Charles	
Gewirtz, Allen	
Hershkowitz, Marvin	
Krieger, Nate	Captain
Levine, Elihu	
Morhaim, Abe	
Narrowe, Morty	
Orlian, Mitchel	
Schuchalter, Ralph	
Staiman, Larry	
Stein, Arthur	
1952-1953	
Anisfeld, Fred	
Citron, Jay	
Cohen, Sam	
Gewirtz, Allen	
Green, Leon	
Hershkowitz, Marvin	Captain
Kupietsky, Jonah	
Levine, Elihu	
Narrowe, Morty	
Orlian, Mitchel	
Schuchalter, Ralph	
Sodden, Abe	
Steinkoler, Alex	

Taragin, Josh	
1953-1954	
Anisfeld, Fred	
Charney, Herbert	
Citron, Jay	
Cohen, Sam	
Gewirtz, Allen	
Green, Leon	
Hochdorf, Barry	
Hulkower, William	Manager
Kupietsky, Jonah	
Levine, Elihu	Captain
Listowsky, Irving	
Orlian, Mitchel	
Pruzansky, Wallace	
Schuchalter, Ralph	
Schlussel, Herb	
Sodden, Abe	
Taragin, Josh	
Teicher, Marvin	
1954-1955	
Blumenreich, Irwin	
Citron, Jay	
Gewirtz, Allen	Captain
Green, Leon	
Hochdorf, Barry	
Leibowitz, Seymour	
Listowsky, Irving	
Orlian, Mitchel	
Palefski, Norman	
Schlussel, Herb	
Schuchalter, Ralph	

Sodden, Abe	
Teicher, Marvin	
1955-1956	
Berkstein, Leon	
Blumenreich, Irwin	Captain
Bursky, Herman	
Chaiken, Alfred	
Englard, Bernard	
Helfer, Alan	
Hochdorf, Barry	
Krieger, Morty	
Listowsky, Irving	
Mehlman, Danny	
Meiselman, Nat	
Schlussel, Herb	
Sodden, Abe	Captain
Steinmetz, Ira	
Teicher, Marvin	
1956-1957	
Ader, Sandy	
Bader, Irving	
Badian, Stu	
Blumenreich, Irwin	Captain
Bursky, Herman	
Chaiken, Alfred	
Charney, Leon	
Feinstein, Alex	
Goldstein, William	
Helfer, Alan	
Krieger, Morty	
Lebowitz, Sy	
Listowsky, Irving	

Mallet, Jerry	
Meiselman, Nat	
Paulan, Fred	
Schlussel, Herb	Captain
Steinmetz, Ira	
1957-1958	
Ader, Sandy	
Bader, Irv	
Badian, Stu	
Baum, Gary	
Goldstein, William	
Grossman, Herb	
Korngold, Louis	
Sarinsky, Gary	
Steinmetz, Ira	Captain
Wernick, Nissim	
1958-1959	
Ader, Sandy	Captain
Bader, Irv	Captain
Badian, Stu	
Baum, Gary	
Goldstein, Herb	
Goldstein, William	
Grossman, Herb	
Grossman, Sam	
Korngold, Louis	
Kramer, Sheldon	
Sarinsky, Gary	
Wieder, Sheldon	
1959-1960	
Bader, Irv	Captain
Badian, Stu	Captain

Baum, Gary	
Botnick, Victor	
Garmise, Mike	
Goldstein, Marvin	
Goldstein, William	Captain
Grossman, Herb	
Grossman, Sam	
Harris, Stuart	
Jacobson, Sam	
Korngold, Louis	
Wieder, Sheldon	
1960-1961	
Aaron, Arthur	
Baum, Gary	
Bergman, Norman	Manager
Burson, Phillip	
Cohen, Howard	
Garmise, Mike	
Goldstein, Marvin	
Grossman, Sam	
Jacobson, Ken	
Korngold, Louis	Captain
Kranes, Larry	
Pincus, Lenny	
Podhurst, Robert	
Silver, Sheldon	Manager
Wieder, Sheldon	
Wise, Mike	
1961-1962	
Aaronwald, Mike	
Aaron, Arthur	
Bromfeld, Sheldon	

Crane, Joel	
Garsman, Jay	
Gralla, Steve	
Grossman, Sam	Captain
Jacobson, Ken	
Katz, Neil	
Podhurst, Robert	
Silver, Sheldon	Manager
Wieder, Sheldon	
1962-1963	
Aaron, Arthur	Captain
Aaronwald, Mike	
Bergman, Norman	Manager
Garsman, Jay	
Gralla, Steve	
Halpert, Jonathan˙	
Jacobson, Ken	Captain
Katz, Neil	
Podhurst, Robert	Captain
Rokach, Sheldon	
Silver, Sheldon	Manager
Weiner, Hillel	
1963-1964	
Aaron, Arthur	Captain
Davis, Meyer	
Garsman, Jay	
Gralla, Steve	
Halpert, Jonathan	
Jacobson, Ken	Captain
Newman, Steve	
Ostreicher, Harvey	
Podhurst, Robert	Captain

Rokach, Sheldon	
Silver, Sheldon	Manager
Sherman, Charles	
Weiner, Hillel	
1964-1965	
Bernstein, Nathan	
Fine, Steven	
Goldschmidt, Eric	
Gralla, Steve	Captain
Halpert, Jonathan	
Korn, Gene	
Kurz, Irwin	
Pachter, Leon	
Palefski, Paul	
Rokach, Sheldon	
Sherman, Charles	
Shimansky, Henry	
Speiser, Abe	
Stern, Sam	
Weiner, Hillel	
1965-1966	
Aboff, Ray	
Halpert, Jonathan	Captain
Hershkovits, David	
Koenig, Mike	
Korn, Gene	
Kurz, Irwin	
Palefski, Paul	
Raphael, Stan	
Rokach, Sheldon	
Shimansky, Henry	
Stern, Sam	

Weiner, Hillel	
1966-1967	
Blumenthal, Alan	
Fischer, Joel	
Hershkovits, David	
Kaplow, David	
Koenig, Mike	
Kurz, Irwin	
Shimansky, Henry	
Singer, Steve	
Stern, Sam	Captain
Wien, Arthur	
Winderman, Harry	
Zuroff, Efrem	
1967-1968	
Aboff, Ray	
Blumenthal, Alan	
Fisher, Joel	
Friedman, Joel	
Hershkovits, David	
Kurz, Irwin	
Palefski, Paul	
Poloner, Stu	
Schiffman, Larry	
Shimansky, Henry	Captain
Stern, Norbert	
Waller, Abraham	
Weiner, Danny	
Zuroff, Efrem	
1968-1969	
Aboff, Ray	Captain
Blumenthal, Alan	

Hecht, Howard	
Hershkovits, David	Captain
Koenig, Mike	
Perl, Harold	
Poloner, Stu	
Reiss, Lawrence	
Salit, Richard	
Schoenfeld, Unknown	
Wiener, Danny	
Winderman, Harry	
1969-1970	
Blumenthal, Alan	Captain
Friedman, Joel	
Gettinger, David	
Hecht, Howard	
Perl, Harold	
Reiss, Lawrence	
Rich, Joel	
Salit, Richard	
Simon, Steve	
Smith, Michael	
Weiner, Danny	
Winderman, Harry	
Zuroff, Ephrem	
1970-1971	
Bertram, Josh	
Faber, Albie	
Hecht, Howard	
Perl, Harold	Captain
Poloner, Stuart	Captain
Reiss, Lawrence	
Rich, Joel	

Simon, Steve	
Strulowitz, Morris	
Tilson, Morris	
Weiner, Danny	
Wilzig, David	
Yammer, David	
1971-1972	
Amsel, Norman	Manager
Aron, Marc	
Bertram, Josh	
Cohen, Dov	Manager
Engel, Marc	
Faber, Albie	
Goldfinger, Mark	
Hecht, Howard	
Levner, Chuck	
Lockspeiser, Alan	
Perl, Harold	Captain
Rich, Joel	
Scharaga, Ira	
Wilzig, David	

The Players (1972-2013)[73]

1972-1973			
Beren, David	Denver	CO	
Bertram, Josh	Brooklyn	NY	
Cohen, Dov	Oceanside	NY	Manager
Faber, Albie	Queens	NY	
Glicksman, Howard	Woodmere	NY	Manager

---

[73] Pictures of individual teams can be found by going to www.backdoorhoops. com.

Goldfinger, Mendy	Brooklyn	NY	
Haber, Jimmy	Brooklyn	NY	
Levner, Chuck	Brooklyn	NY	Captain
Lockspeiser, Alan	Jersey City	NJ	
Mann, Morris	Brooklyn	NY	
Merlis, Paul	Brooklyn	NY	
Reisbaum, Steve	Bayside	NY	Manager
Rich, Joel	Queens	NY	Captain
Schachnow, Jack	North Bergen	NJ	Manager
Scharaga, Ira	Brooklyn	NY	
Wenig, Bruce	Fairlawn	NJ	
Wilzig, David	Brooklyn	NY	
Yarmush, Maish	Brooklyn	NY	
1973-1974			
Beren, David	Denver	CO	
Bertram, Josh	Brooklyn	NY	
Cohen, Dov	Oceanside	NY	Manager
Faber, Albie	Queens	NY	Captain
Joszef, Jerry	Brooklyn	NY	
Lockspeiser, Alan	Jersey City	NJ	
Reisbaum, Steve	Bayside	NY	Manager
Schachnow, Jack	North Bergen	NJ	Manager
Scharaga, Ira	Brooklyn	NY	
Wenig, Bruce	Fairlawn	NJ	
Wilzig, David	Brooklyn	NY	Captain
1974-1975			
Alter, Sandy	Bayonne	NJ	Manager
Behar, Leon	Brooklyn	NY	
Beren, David	Denver	CO	
Gittleman, Bob	Scranton	PA	Manager
Gold, Norman	Brooklyn	NY	Manager

Hoenig, Mark	Monsey	NY	
Joszef, Jerry	Brooklyn	NY	
Lockspeiser, Alan	Jersey City	NJ	Captain
Menche, David	Brooklyn	NY	
Merlis, Paul	Brooklyn	NY	
Reisbaum, Steve	Bayside	NY	Manager
Rosen, Phil	Brooklyn	NY	
Rosenbloom, Robert	Bronx	NY	
Schachnow, Jack	North Bergen	NJ	Manager
Scharaga, Ira	Brooklyn	NY	Captain
Schuchalter, Alan	New York	NY	
Wenig, Bruce	Fairlawn	NJ	
1975-1976			
Genuth, Sol	Brooklyn	NY	
Hoenig, Mark	Monsey	NY	
Joszef, Jerry	Brooklyn	NY	
Lerer, Paul	Lawrence	NY	
Mandel, David	Brooklyn	NY	
Merlis, Paul	Brooklyn	NY	
Rosenbloom, Robert	Bronx	NY	
Schwartzbaum, Len	Bayonne	NJ	
Wenig, Bruce	Fairlawn	NJ	Captain
1976-1977			
Genuth, Sol	Brooklyn	NY	Captain
Gittleman, Bob	Scranton	PA	Manager
Gomberg, Alan	Staten Island	NY	Manager
Hoenig, Mark	Monsey	NY	
Joszef, Jerry	Brooklyn	NY	Captain
Kramer, Jon	Cedarhurst	NY	
Kufeld, David	Great Neck	NY	
Rosenbloom, Robert	Bronx	NY	

Scheinfeld, Josh	Chicago	IL	
Schwartzbaum, Lenny	Bayonne	NJ	
Weinstock, Dov	Brooklyn	NY	
1977-1978			
Altholtz, Seth	Brooklyn	NY	
Cumsky, Frank	Scranton	PA	
Goldman, Sheldon	Brooklyn	NY	
Hartman, Danny	Brooklyn	NY	
Hirschberg, Mark	Atlanta	GA	
Hoenig, Mark	Monsey	NY	Captain
Kufeld, David	Great Neck	NY	
Nachimovsky, Yoram	Brooklyn	NY	
Rosenbloom, Robert	Bronx	NY	Captain
Scheinfeld, Josh	Chicago	IL	
Schwartzbaum, Lenny	Bayonne	NJ	
Small, Sheldon	Far Rockaway	NY	
Varon, Jack	Seattle	WA	
Weinstock, Dov	Brooklyn	NY	
Yaffa, Joel	Cherry Hill	NJ	
1978-1979			
Azose, Morris	Seattle	WA	
Cumsky, Frank	Scranton	PA	
Gettenberg, Chaim	Far Rockaway	NY	
Goldman, Sheldon	Brooklyn	NY	
Kirschblum, Joel	Unknown	Unk	
Klapper, Phillip	Flushing	NY	
Kufeld, David	Great Neck	NY	Captain
Livni, Isaac	Jerusalem	Israel	Manager
Rhode, Louis	Brooklyn	NY	
Savage, Eugene	Pittsburg	PA	Manager
Schwartzbaum, Lenny	Bayonne	NJ	

Seidman, Judah	Houston	TX	Manager
Sheff, Harvey	Far Rockaway	NY	
Stein, Lewis	Woodmere	NY	
Stern, David	Unknown	Unk	Manager
Thomas, Morris	Memphis	TN	
Varon, Jack	Seattle	WA	
Weinstock, Dov	Brooklyn	NY	
Weiss, Mitchel	Unknown	Unk	
Yaffa, Joel	Philadelphia	PA	
1979-1980			
Felder, Lou	Oceanside	NY	
Goldfeder, Chayim	Washington	DC	
Goldman, Sheldon	Brooklyn	NY	
Green, Sheldon	Long Beach	NY	
Gris, Samson	Atlanta	GA	
Klein, Barry	Atlanta	GA	
Kufeld, David	Great Neck	NY	Captain
Livni, Isaac	Queens	NY	Manager
Maslowe, Adam	Brooklyn	NY	
Sapadin, Allen	Woodmere	NY	
Seidman, Judah	Houston	TX	Manager
Sheff, Harvey	Far Rockaway	NY	
Sklare, Josh	Boston	MA	
Stern, David	Unknown	Unk	Manager
Varon, Jack	Seattle	WA	
Wiesenberg, Avi	Unknown	Unk	
1980-1981			
Brickman, Josh	Brooklyn	NY	
Goldman, Sheldon	Brooklyn	NY	Captain
Greenberg, Alan	Long Beach	NY	
Klein, Barry	Atlanta	GA	

Lazaros, David	Riverhead	NY	Manager
Marmorstein, Bernard	New York	NY	Manager
Reinhart, Hank	Montreal	Canada	
Rosenbloom, Michael	Bronx	NY	
Sapadin, Allen	Woodmere	NY	
Schondorf, Robert	Far Rockaway	NY	Manager
Sheff, Harvey	Far Rockaway	NY	
Sklare, Josh	Boston	MA	
Tilson, Neil	Monsey	NY	
Varon, Jack	Seattle	WA	Captain
1981-1982			
Eaves, Joe	Hartford	CT	
Greenberg, Alan	Long Beach	NY	
Krevsky, Sol	Harrisburg	PA	
Reinhart, Hank	Montreal	Canada	
Rosenbloom, Michael	Bronx	NY	
Sapadin, Allen	Woodmere	NY	
Schondorf, Robert	Far Rockaway	NY	Manager
Schreier, Shabsi	Brooklyn	NY	
Sheff, Harvey	Far Rockaway	NY	Captain
Tilson, Neil	Passaic	NJ	
Wertheimer, Aaron	Unknown	Unk	
1982-1983			
Appel, David	Queens	NY	
Eaves, Joe	Hartford	CT	
Franco, Joey	Huntington	WV	
Gellman, Aryeh	Brooklyn	NY	Manager
Klein, Barry	Atlanta	GA	
Korngold, Jay	Unknown	Unk	Manager
Krevsky, Sol	Harrisburg	PA	
Levine, Greg	Brooklyn	NY	

Menorah, Shalom	Chicago	IL	
Rosenbloom, Michael	Bronx	NY	Captain
Sapadin, Allen	Far Rockaway	NY	Captain
Schreier, Shabsi	Brooklyn	NY	
Schwartz, Ron	Pittsburgh	PA	
Skolnick, Zev	Oceanside	NY	Manager
Tamir, Eddie	Unknown	Unk	
Thomas, Beryl	Memphis	TN	
Tilson, Neil	Passaic	NJ	
1983-1984			
Davidoff, Eli	Woodmere	NY	
Frenkel, Steven	Westchester	NY	
Gellman, Aryeh	Brooklyn	NY	Manager
Grad, Michael	Philadelphia	PA	Manager
Harris, Jeff	Monsey	NY	
Herschman, Eric	Unknown	FL	
Katz, Jeff	Orange	CA	
Orlian, Moshe	Brooklyn	NY	
Schreier, Ben	Brooklyn	NY	
Schreier, Shabsi	Brooklyn	NY	Captain
Schwartz, Ron	Pittsburgh	PA	
Taragin, Michael	Monsey	NY	
1984-1985			
Davidoff, Eli	Woodmere	NY	
Eaves, Joe	Hatford	CT	
Frenkel, Steven	Westchester	NY	
Grad, Michael	Philadelphia	PA	Manager
Hod, Lior	Atlanta	GA	
Kreinberg, David	Far Rockaway	NY	Manager
Orlian, Moshe	Brooklyn	NY	
Schreier, Shabsi	Brooklyn	NY	Captain

Schwartz, Ron	Pittsburgh	PA	
Thomas, Beryl	Memphis	TN	
Weisman, Mark	Toronto	Canada	
1985-1986			
Davidoff, Eli	Woodmere	NY	
Eaves, Joe	Boston	MA	Captain
Frenkel, Steven	Westchester	NY	
Harris, Jeff	Monsey	NY	
Hirt, Lance	Los Angeles	CA	
Hod, Ayal	Atlanta	GA	
Hod, Lior	Atlanta	GA	
Kirsch, Richard	Bloomfield	NJ	
Lebowitz, Ira	Brooklyn	NY	
Levine, Jan	West New York	NJ	
Marcus, Izzy	Yonkers	NY	
Orlian, Moshe	Brooklyn	NY	
Richman, Judah	Boston	MA	
Schwartz, Ron	Pittsburgh	PA	Captain
Thomas, Beryl	Memphis	TN	
1986-1987			
Bandler, Jonathan	Silver Spring	MD	Manager
Baum, Jeff	Memphis	TN	
Furer, Donny	Hillside	NJ	
Harris, David	Monsey	NY	
Hirt, Lance	Los Angeles	CA	Captain
Hod, Ayal	Atlanta	GA	
Hod, Lior	Atlanta	GA	Captain
Kramer, Elliot	Montreal	Canada	
Lebowitz, Ira	Brooklyn	NY	
Levine, Jan	West New York	NJ	
Levy, Danny	Brooklyn	NY	

Lumerman, Jeff	Denver	CO	Manager
Marcus, Izzy	Yonkers	NY	
Reichel, Ben	Queens	NY	
Richman, Judah	Boston	MA	
Schlakman, Marty	Elizabeth	NJ	
Soble, Jay	Denver	CO	Manager
Teichman, Yudi	Queens	NY	
Weiss, Zev	Cleveland	OH	
Wolmark, Asher	Memphis	TN	
Zier, Gary	Miami Beach	FL	Manager
1987-1988			
Bandler, Jonathan	Silver Spring	MD	Manager
Baum, Jeff	Memphis	TN	
Chefitz, Danny	Boston	MA	
Cohen, Michael	Kfar Haroeh	Israel	Manager
Ehrman, Jonathan	New York	NY	
Furer, Donny	Hillside	NJ	
Gottlieb, David	Los Angeles	CA	
Hod, Ayal	Atlanta	GA	Captain
Hod, Lior	Atlanta	GA	Captain
Kramer, Elliot	Montreal	Canada	
Levine, Jan	West New York	NJ	
Lumerman, Jeff	Denver	CO	Manager
Muehlgay, Heshy	Brooklyn	NY	
Reichel, Ben	Queens	NY	Captain
Reichel, Sam	Queens	NY	
Schlakman, Marty	Elizabeth	NJ	
Sobel, Jay	Denver	CO	Manager
Teichman, Yudi	Queens	NY	Captain
Weinreb, David	Syracuse	NY	
Weiss, Zev	Cleveland	OH	

Wolmark, Asher	Memphis	TN	
1988-1989			
Aaron, Avrum	Teaneck	NJ	
Berger, Alan	Albany	NY	
Chefitz, Danny	Boston	MA	
Cohen, Michael	Kfar Haroeh	Israel	Manager
Davis, Eric	New York	NY	
Dayan, Joey	Unknown	Unk	Manager
Ehrman, Jonathan	Manhattan	NY	
Finkelstein, Barry	New York	NY	
Gottlieb, David	Los Angeles	CA	
Himber, Tzvi	Brooklyn	NY	
Hod, Ayal	Atlanta	GA	Captain
Levine, Jan	West New York	NY	Captain
Lumerman, Jeff	Denver	CO	Manager
Oz, Michael	Miami Beach	FL	
Reichel, Sam	Queens	NY	
Rhine, Greg	Brooklyn	NY	
Teichman, Yudi	Queens	NY	Captain
Wigler, Michael	Queens	NY	Manager
Yaish, Ilan	Cedarhurst	NY	Manager
1989-1990			
Aaron, Avrum	Teaneck	NJ	
Berger, Alan	Albany	NY	
Cohen, Seth	Teaneck	NJ	
Davis, Eric	New York	NY	
Dayan, Joey	Unknown	Unk	Manager
Ehrman, David	New York	NY	
Finkelstein, Barry	New York	NY	
Gottlieb, David	Los Angeles	CA	Captain
Himber, Tzvi	Brooklyn	NY	

Rhine, Gregory	Brooklyn	NY	
Rosner, Jonathan	Brooklyn	NY	
Rothman, Elisha	Los Angeles	CA	
Zabib, Eli	Unknown	Unk	Manager
1990-1991			
Aaron, Avrum	Teaneck	NJ	
Cohen, Baruki	Englewood	NJ	
Cohen, Dovid	Lawrence	NY	
Cohen, Seth	Teaneck	NJ	
Danan, Miko	Ramla	Israel	
Davis, Eric	New York	NY	
Dobin, Josh	Miami Beach	FL	
Ehrman, David	New York	NY	
Goldsheider, Hillel	North Bellmore	NY	
Himber, Tzvi	Brooklyn	NY	Captain
Kimmel, Shlomo	Monsey	NY	Manager
Klein, Mathew	Brooklyn	NY	
Kuttner, Ephraim	Memphis	TN	Manager
Rhine, Greg	Brooklyn	NY	Captain
Rosner, Jonathan	Brooklyn	NY	Captain
Rothman, Elisha	Los Angeles	CA	
Schiffman, David	Highland Park	NJ	Manager
Steiner, Josh	Hollywood	FL	Manager
1991-1992			
Aaron, Daniel	Monsey	NY	
Ben-Ami, Erez	Los Angeles	CA	
Cohen, Dovid	Lawrence	NY	
Cohen, Seth	Teaneck	NY	
Danan, Miko	Ramla	Israel	
Dobin, Josh	Miami Beach	FL	
Dube, Michael	Teaneck	NJ	

Furst, Donny	Englewood	NJ	
Galeck, Mark	Los Angeles	CA	
Jayinski, Jose	Givatayin	Israel	
Kolb, David	Sunny Isles	FL	Manager
Resnick, Binyamin	Elizabeth	NJ	
Rose, Or	Winnipeg	Canada	
Rothman, Elisha	Los Angeles	CA	Captain
Schiffman, David	Highland Park	NJ	Manager
Steiner, Josh	Hollywood	FL	Manager
Stepner, Saul	Hollywood	FL	
1992-1993			
Aaron, Daniel	Monsey	NY	
Ben-Ami, Erez	Los Angeles	CA	
Cohen, Dovid	Lawrence	NY	Captain
Danan, Miko	Ramla	Israel	
Davis, Donny	Hollywood	FL	Manager
Dobin, Josh	Miami Beach	FL	Captain
Dube, Michael	Teaneck	NJ	
Furst, Donny	Englewood	NJ	
Jayinski, Jose	Givatayin	Israel	
Levy, Alan	Brooklyn	NY	
Levy, Mark	Los Angeles	CA	
Melul, Igal	Ramla	Israel	
Neumann, Isaac	Brooklyn	NY	
Rose, Or	Winnipeg	Canada	
Schiffman, David	Highland Park	NJ	Manager
Stepner, Saul	Hollywood	FL	
Wallach, Israel	Brooklyn	NY	
1993-1994			
Aaron, Daniel	Monsey	NY	Captain
Bogdansky, Mark	Olny	MD	Manager

Danan, Miko	Ramla	Israel	Captain
Davis Donny	Hollywood	FL	Manager
Dube, Michael	Teaneck	NJ	
Frankel, Samson	New York	NY	Manager
Furst, Donny	Englewood	NJ	
Graber, Ezra	West Hempstead	NY	Manager
Grinshpun, Roman	Saddle Brook	NJ	Manager
Halpert, Yehuda	Queens	NY	
Jayinski, Jose	Givatayin	Israel	
Kofsky, Jay	Forest Hills	NY	Manager
Kupferman, Steven	Woodmere	NY	
Levy, Alan	Brooklyn	NY	
Neumann, Isaac	Brooklyn	NY	
Rosenberg, Jacob	Queens	NY	
Schiffman, David	Highland Park	NJ	Manager
Wallach, Israel	Brooklyn	NY	
1994-1995			
Aranoff, Barry	Teaneck	NJ	
Bronstein, Neil	Atlanta	GA	
Davis, Donny	Hollywood	FL	Manager
Halpert, Yehuda	Queens	NY	
Jacobson, Joel	Champaign	IL	
Jayinski, Jose	Givatayin	Israel	
Koffsky, Jay	Forest Hills	NY	Manager
Kupferman, Steven	Woodmere	NY	
Landsman, Ira	Chicago	IL	
Levy, Alan	Brooklyn	NY	Captain
Markowitz, Ron	Staten Island	NY	Manager
Neumann, Isaac	Brooklyn	NY	
Rose, Or	Winnipeg	Canada	Captain
Rosenberg, Jacob	Queens	NY	

Ruditsky, David	Teaneck	NJ	
Saada, Mark	Hollywood	FL	
1995-1996			
Aranoff, Barry	Teaneck	NJ	
Bronstein, Neil	Atlanta	GA	
Halpert, Yehuda	Queens	NY	
Jacobson, Joel	Champaign	IL	
Koffsky, Jay	Forest Hills	NY	Manager
Kupferman, Steven	Woodmere	NY	
Landsman, Ira	Chicago	IL	
Levy, Alan	Brooklyn	NY	Captain
Markowitz, Ron	Staten Island	NY	Manager
Neiss, David	Bronx	NY	
Neumann, Isaac	Brooklyn	NY	
Rosenberg, Jacob	Queens	NY	
Ruditsky, David	Teaneck	NJ	
Shakhmurov, Alex	Queens	NY	
Wein, Brian	Teaneck	NJ	
Weiner, Neil	Woodmere	NY	
Zaibert, Alon	Tel Aviv	Israel	
1996-1997			
Abehsera, Moshe	Los Angeles	CA	
Bronstein, Neil	Atlanta	GA	
Forman, Dovey	Edison	NJ	
Halpert, Yehuda	Queens	NY	Captain
Jacobson, Joel	Champaign	IL	Captain
Kruger, Joel	Ontario	Canada	
Kupferman, Steven	Woodmere	NY	Captain
Landsman, Ira	Chicago	IL	
Lasker, Gabe	Winnipeg	Canada	
Markowitz, Ron	Staten Island	NY	Manager

Nadritch, Marc	Staten Island	NY	
Posner, Mark	Brooklyn	NY	Manager
Renna, Jeremy	Colts Neck	NJ	Manager
Shakhmurov, Alex	Queens	NY	
Teitelbaum, Jonathan	Edison	NJ	Manager
Wein, Brian	Teaneck	NJ	
Zaibert, Alon	Tel Aviv	Israel	
1997-1998			
Bronstein, Neil	Atlanta	GA	
Garmai, Moshe	Be'er Sheva	Israel	
Gross, Carmi	North Miami Beach	FL	Manager
Jacobson, Joel	Champaign	IL	Captain
Karesh, Avi	Chicago	IL	
Kruger, Joel	Ontario	Canada	
Lasker, Gabe	Winnipeg	Canada	
Martinek, Steven	Toronto	Canada	
Nadritch, Marc	Staten Island	NY	
Neiss, David	Bronx	NY	
Posner, Mark	Brooklyn	NY	Manager
Rabin, Shane	Atlanta	GA	
Reichardt, Corey	Adventura	FL	Manager
Rosen, Ami	Philadelphia	PA	
Teitelbaum Jonathan	Edison	NJ	Manager
Walls, Eytan	Great Neck	NY	Manager
Wein, Brian	Teaneck	NJ	
Zadok, Yoni	Los Angeles	CA	
Zaibert, Alon	Tel Aviv	Israel	Captain
1998-1999			
Batalion, David	Boston	MA	
Gev, Yossy	Rechovot	Israel	
Hershman, Steven	Scarsdale	NY	

Hod, Asaf	Queens	NY	
Karesh, Avi	Chicago	IL	
Kruger, Joel	Ontario	Canada	
Meyer, Joseph	Woodmere	NY	
Nadritch, Marc	Staten Island	NY	Captain
Neiss, David	Bronx	NY	Captain
Palefski, Nachum	Boston	MA	
Rabin, Shane	Atlanta	GA	
Shakhmurov, Alex	Queens	NY	
Weiner, Dov	Woodmere	NY	
Yudewitz, Uri	North Miami Beach	FL	
Zadok, Yoni	Los Angeles	CA	
1999-2000			
Batalion, David	Boston	MA	
Bransdorfer, Joseph	Woodmere	NY	
Gev, Yossy	Rechovot	Israel	Captain
Hendeles, Zev	Los Angeles	CA	
Hershman, Steven	Scarsdale	NY	
Hod, Asaf	Queens	NY	
Karesh, Avi	Chicago	IL	
Martinek, Steven	Toronto	Canada	
Meyer, Joseph	Woodmere	NY	
Neiss, David	Bronx	NY	Captain
Palefski, Nachum	Boston	MA	
Rosenblatt, Matt	Los Angeles	CA	
Shakhmurov, Alex	Queens	NY	
Steinmetz, Elliot	Woodmere	NY	
Weiner, Dov	Woodmere	NY	
Yulzary, Jack	Ramla	Israel	
2000-2001			
Batalion, David	Boston	MA	

Bernstein, Michael	Los Angeles	CA	
Cohen, Natan	Teaneck	NJ	
Gev, Yossy	Rechovot	Israel	Captain
Hami, Eli	Los Angeles	CA	
Hendeles, Zev	Los Angeles	CA	
Hershman, Steven	Scarsdale	NY	
Hod, Asaf	Teaneck	NJ	
Lifshitz, Arik	Wesley Hills	NY	
Rosenblatt, Matt	Los Angeles	CA	
Steinmetz, Elliot	Woodmere	NY	
Strauss, Samuel	Skokie	IL	
Yulzary, Jack	Ramla	Israel	
Yunger, Simon	Montreal	Canada	
2001-2002			
Batalion, David	Boston	MA	
Bernstein, Michael	Los Angeles	CA	
Braun, Effie	Los Angeles	CA	Manager
Gev, Yossy	Rehovot	Israel	Captain
Halpert, Rafi	Queens	NY	
Hami, Eli	Los Angeles	CA	Captain
Hendeles, Zev	Los Angeles	CA	
Hod, Asaf	Teaneck	NJ	
Joszef, Yoni	Teaneck	NJ	
Lapidus, Alex	Toronto	Canada	
Lifshitz, Arik	Wesley Hills	NY	
Mazor, Netanel	Highland Park	NJ	
Pilossof, Shmuel	Rishon Le'zion	Israel	
Rosenblatt, Matt	Los Angeles	CA	
Steinmetz, Elliot	Woodmere	NY	
Strauss, Sam	Chicago	IL	
Tetro, Avi	Tel Aviv	Israel	

Yulzary, Jack	Ramla	Israel	Captain
Yunger, Simon	Montreal	Canada	
2002-2003			
Barak, Shmuel	Miami Beach	FL	Manager
Bensimon, Daniel	Boca Raton	FL	
Braun, Effie	Los Angeles	CA	Manager
Gottlieb, Josh	Elizabeth	NJ	
Halpert, Rafi	Queens	NY	
Hami, Eli	Los Angeles	CA	Captain
Heurizadeh, Sasha	Saddle River	NJ	
Hoffer, Benjamin	Springfield	NJ	
Joszef, Yoni	Teaneck	NJ	
Lapidus, Alex	Toronto	Canada	
Lifshitz, Arik	Wesley Hills	NY	
Missry, Adam	Los Angeles	CA	
Musberg, Shai	K Bialik	Israel	
Pilossof, Shmuel	Rishon Le'zion	Israel	
Pliner, Yishai	Pittsburgh	PA	
Rotenberg, Jonathan	Roma	Italy	
Sicherman, Max	Philadelphia	PA	
Yunger, Simon	Montreal	Canada	
2003-2004			
Cooper, Avi	Boston	MA	
Golbert, Ben	Jerusalem	Israel	
Gordon, Ross	Chicago	IL	
Gottlieb, Josh	Elizabeth	NJ	
Halpert, Rafi	Queens	NY	Captain
Lapidus, Alex	Toronto	Canada	
Lewis, Richard	Memphis	GA	
Malkin, Abe	Los Angeles	CA	
Missry, Adam	Los Angeles	CA	

Pilossof, Shmuel	Rishon Le'zion	Israel	
Pliner, Yishai	Pittsburgh	PA	
Ribald, Ian	Dallas	TX	
Rotenberg, Jonathan	Roma	Italy	
Vatavu, Harel	Ramat Gan	Israel	
Yulzary, Jack	Ramla	Israel	Captain
2004-2005			
Cohen, Matan	Jerusalem	Israel	
Golbert, Ben	Jerusalem	Israel	Captain
Goldstein, Roy	Bear Sheva	Israel	
Halpert, Rafi	Queens	NY	Captain
Kelson, Moshe	Teaneck	NJ	
Lewis, Richard	Memphis	GA	
Malkin, Abe	Los Angeles	CA	
Missry, Adam	Los Angeles	CA	
Moskowitz, Yehuda	Miami Beach	FL	
Pilosoff, Shmuel	Rishon Le'zion	Israel	Captain
Pollack, Michael	Los Angeles	CA	
Ribald, Ian	Dallas	TX	
Rotenberg, Jonathan	Roma	Italy	
Schwartzbaum, Tzvi	Miami Beach	FL	
Servi, Natan	Florence	Italy	
Vardi, Danny	Ashdod	Israel	
Vatavu, Harel	Ramat Gan	Israel	
Wolk, Gavi	Dallas	TX	
2005-2006			
Cohen, Matan	Jerusalem	Israel	
Golbert, Ben	Jerusalem	Israel	
Goldstein, Roy	Bear Sheva	Israel	
Hendeles, Eli	Los Angeles	CA	
Himmelfarb, Eli	Silver Spring	MD	

Lewis, Richard	Memphis	GA	
Merlis, Shuki	Atlanta	GA	
Moskowitz, Yehuda	Miami Beach	FL	
Pollack, Michael	Los Angeles	CA	
Ribald, Ian	Dallas	TX	
Rotenberg, Jonathan	Roma	Italy	Captain
Schaulewicz, David	East Brunswick	NJ	
Schiffman, Josh	Highland Park	NJ	
Schwartzbaum, Tzvi	Miami Beach	FL	
Vardi, Danny	Ashdod	Israel	
Vatavu, Harel	Ramat Gan	Israel	Captain
Wolk, Gavi	Dallas	TX	
Zakaim, Michael	Paramus	NJ	Manager
Zimmern, Zack	Merrick	NY	Manager
2006-2007			
Block, Noam	Teaneck	NJ	
Claster, Alex	Oakland park	KS	
Cohen, Matan	Jerusalem	Israel	
Ephron, Moshe	Houston	TX	
Glustein, Zvi	Toronto	Canada	
Lewis, Richard	Memphis	GA	
Lockspeiser, Ben	Highland Park	NJ	
Merlis, Shuki	Atlanta	GA	
Pollack, Michael	Los Angeles	CA	
Ribald, Ian	Dallas	TX	Captain
Saraf, Yoel	Great Neck	NY	
Schaulewicz, David	East Brunswick	NJ	
Schwartzbaum, Tzvi	Miami Beach	FL	
Vatavu, Harel	Ramat Gan	Israel	Captain
Wolk, Gavi	Dallas	TX	

2007-2008			
Babo, Ohad	Kiryat Ono	Israel	
Block, Noam	Teaneck	NJ	
Brookhim, Simon	Los Angeles	CA	
Claster, Alex	Oakland Park	KS	
Genet, Josh	Miami Beach	FL	
Glustein, Zvi	Toronto	Canada	
Gordon, Zak	Miami Beach	FL	
Ladenheim, Mark	Bala Cynwyd	PA	
Lockspeiser, Ben	Highland Park	NJ	
Lolai, Daniel	Great Neck	NY	
Magilnick, Aryeh	Los Angeles	CA	
Merlis, Shuki	Atlanta	GA	Captain
Pollack, Michael	Los Angeles	CA	Captain
Pressman, Jeremy	Bala Cynwyd	PA	
Saraf, Yoel	Great Neck	NY	
Schaulewicz, David	East Brunswick	NJ	Captain
Somach, Daniel	Jerusalem	Israel	
Wizenfeld, Dani	Los Angeles	CA	
2008-2009			
Babo, Ohad	Kiryat Ono	Israel	
Biron, Chen	Tel Aviv	Israel	
Block, Noam	Teaneck	NJ	
Boussi, Yechiel	Fairlawn	NJ	
Brookhim, Simon	Los Angeles	CA	
Claster, Alex	Oakland Park	KS	Captain
Cohen, Joseph	Bronx	NY	
Genet, Josh	Miami Beach	FL	
Gilboa, David	Tenefly	NJ	
Glustein, Zvi	Toronto	Canada	
Hakak, Ron	Toronto	Canada	
Ladenheim, Mark	Bala Cynwyd	PA	

Leibovich Martin	Buenos Aires	Argentina	
Lockspeiser, Ben	Highland Park	NJ	Captain
Magilnick, Aryeh	Los Angeles	CA	
Pressman, Jeremy	Bala Cynwyd	PA	
Somach, Daniel	Jerusalem	Israel	
Wizenfeld, Dani	Los Angeles	Ca	
2009-2010			
Aberjel, Raphy	Montreal	Canada	
Babo, Ohad	Kiryat Ono	Israel	
Bash, Gil	Tel Aviv	Israel	
Biron, Chen	Tel Aviv	Israel	
Boussi, Yechiel	Fairlawn	NJ	
Brookhim, Simon	Los Angeles	CA	
Claster, Alex	Oakland Park	KS	
Gilboa, David	Tenefly	NJ	
Haim, Omer	Rishon Le'zion	Israel	
Hoffman, Dovie	Los Angeles	CA	
Kinderlehrer, Baruch	Queens	NY	
Leibovich Martin	Buenos Aires	Argentina	
Magilnick, Aryeh	Los Angeles	CA	
Offenbacher, Richard	Brooklyn	NY	
Pressman, Jeremy	Bala Cynwyd	PA	Captain
Schmelzer, David	Columbus	OH	
Sina, Chen	Rishon Le'zion	Israel	
Somach, Daniel	Jerusalem	Israel	
Volkov, Uldi	Nordiya	Israel	
2010-2011			
Aberjel, Raphy	Montreal	Canada	
Babo, Ohad	Kiryat Ono	Israel	
Bash, Gil	Tel Aviv	Israel	
Biron, Chen	Tel Aviv	Israel	Captain

Botwinick, Noah	New York	NY	
Brookhim, Simon	Los Angeles	CA	
Eckman, Yoni	Philadelphia	PA	
Furer, Jonathan	Teaneck	NJ	
Haim, Omer	Rishon Le'zion	Israel	Captain
Hoffman, Dovie	Los Angeles	CA	
Kashani, Mazyar	Great Neck	MD	
Offenbacher, Richard	Teaneck	NJ	
Pressman, Jeremy	Bala Cynwyd	NY	Captain
Schmelzer, David	Columbus	OH	
Selevan, Eitan	Teaneck	NJ	
Sina, Chen	Rishon Le'zion	Israel	
Somach, Daniel	Jerusalem	Israel	
Weissberg, Shlomo	Chicago	IL	
Zinder, Niv	Tel Aviv	Israel	
2011-2012			
Aberjel, Raphy	Montreal	Canada	
Babo, Ohad	Kiryat Ono	Israel	
Bash, Gil	Tel Aviv	Israel	
Beda, Jack	Miami Beach	FL	
Biron, Chen	Tel Aviv	Israel	Captain
Botwinick, Noah	New York	NY	
Davtian, Arman	Haifa	Israel	
Eckman, Yoni	Philadelphia	PA	
Furer, Jonathan	Teaneck	NJ	
Haim, Omer	Rishon Le'zion	Israel	Captain
Hoffman, Dovie	Los Angeles	CA	
Levine, Adam	Jerusalem	Israel	
Ritholtz, Ben	West Hempstead	NY	
Schmelzer, David	Columbus	OH	
Selevan, Eitan	Teaneck	NJ	

Silver, Ben	Los Angeles	CA	
Weinstein, Netanel	Jerusalem	Israel	
Weissberg, Shlomo	Chicago	IL	
Zinder, Niv	Tel Aviv	Israel	
2012-2013			
Abergel, Raphy	Montreal	Canada	
Bash, Gil	Tel Aviv	Israel	Captain
Beda, Jack	Miami Beach	FL	
Davtian, Arman	Haifa	Israel	
Eckman, Yoni	Philadelphia	PA	
Hoffman, Dovie	Los Angeles	CA	Captain
Levine, Adam	Jerusalem	Israel	
Ritholtz, Ben	West Hempstead	NY	
Rosenberg, Shelby	Woodmere	NY	
Rosenthal, Yosef	West Hempstead	NY	
Schmelzer, David	Columbus	OH	Captain
Selevan, Eitan	Teaneck	NJ	
Silver, Ben	Los Angeles	CA	
Weinstein, Netanel	Jerusalem	Israel	
Weiss, Shaye	Elizabeth	NJ	
Weissberg, Shlomo	Chicago	IL	

Captains (1930-1972)

1930-1931 Judah Izenberg
1931-1932 No Record
1932-1933 Sid Green
1933-1934 Hy Aranoff
1934-1935 Joe Goodman
1935-1936 Hy Aranoff
1936-1937 Max Levy
1937-1938 Norman Goldklang, Irving Koslowe
1938-1939 Irving Koslowe

1939-1940 Irving Koslowe
1940-1941 Samuel Meyer
1941-1942 Harold Esterson, Sam Rosenblum
1942-1943 Zelig Bloch, Sam Hartstein
1943-1944 David Susskind
1944-1945 Stan Doppelt
1945-1946 Hyman Pomerantz
1946-1947 Mel Fredman
1947-1948 Merrill Rubin
1948-1949 Donny Geller
1949-1950 Howard Danzig
1950-1951 Arthur Stein
1951-1952 Ruby Davidman, Nate Krieger
1952-1953 Marvin Hershkowitz
1953-1954 Elihu Levine
1954-1955 Allen Gewirtz
1955-1956 Irwin Blumenreich, Abe Sodden
1956-1957 Irwin Blumenreich, Herb Schlussel
1957-1958 Ira Steinmetz
1958-1959 Sandy Ader, Irv Bader
1959-1960 Irving Bader, Stu Badian, William Goldstein
1960-1961 Louis Korngold
1961-1962 Sam Grossman
1962-1963 Arthur Aaron, Ken Jacobson, Bob Podhurst
1963-1964 Arthur Aaron, Ken Jacobson, Bob Podhurst
1964-1965 Steve Gralla
1965-1966 Jonathan Halpert
1966-1967 Sam Stern
1967-1968 Henry Shimansky
1968-1969 Ray Aboff, David Hershkovits
1969-1970 Alan Blumenthal
1970-1971 Harold Perl, Stu Poloner
1971-1972 Harold Perl

Captains (1972-2013)

1972-1973 Chuck Levner, Joel Rich
1973-1974 Albie Faber, David Wilzig
1974-1975 Alan Lockspeiser, Ira Scharaga
1975-1976 Bruce Wenig
1976-1977 Sol Genuth, Jerry Joszef
1977-1978 Mark Hoenig, Robert Rosenbloom
1978-1979 David Kufeld
1979-1980 David Kufeld
1980-1981 Sheldon Goldman, Jack Varon
1981-1982 Harvey Sheff
1982-1983 Michael Rosenbloom, Allen Sapadin
1983-1984 Shabsi Schreier
1984-1985 Shabsi Schreier
1985-1986 Joe Eaves, Ron Schwartz
1986-1987 Lance Hirt, Lior Hod
1987-1988 Ayal Hod, Lior Hod, Ben Reichel, Yudi Teichman
1988-1989 Ayal Hod, Jan Levine, Yudi Teichman
1989-1990 David Gottlieb
1990-1991 Tzvi Himber, Greg Rhine, Jonathan Rosner
1991-1992 Elisha Rothman
1992-1993 Dovid Cohen, Josh Dobin
1993-1994 Daniel Aaron, Miko Danan
1994-1995 Alan Levy, Or Rose
1995-1996 Alan Levy
1996-1997 Yehuda Halpert, Joel Jacobson, Steven Kupferman
1997-1998 Joel Jacobson, Alon Zaibert
1998-1999 Marc Nadritch, David Neiss
1999-2000 David Neiss, Yossy Gev
2000-2001 Yossy Gev
2001-2002 Yossy Gev, Eli Hami, Jack Yulzary
2002-2003 Eli Hami
2003-2004 Rafi Halpert, Jack Yulzary
2004-2005 Rafi Halpert, Shmuel Pilossof
2005-2006 Ben Golbert, Jonathan Rotenberg, Harel Vatavu
2006-2007 Ian Ribald, Harel Vatavu
2007-2008 Shuki Merlis, Mike Pollack, David Schaulewicz

| 2008-2009 Alex Claster, Ben Lockspeiser |
| 2009-2010 Jeremy Pressman |
| 2010-2011 Chen Biron, Omer Haim, Jeremy Pressman |
| 2011-2012 Chen Biron, Omer Haim |
| 2012-2013 Gil Bash, Dovie Hoffman, David Schmelzer |

Coaches
Career Won-Lost Records

Years	Coach	Record	Comments
1930-1931	None	3-1	Club Team
1931-1932	None	2-2	Club Team
1932-1933	Hy Litman	7-5	
1933-1934	None	8-5	
1934-1935	None	Unknown	
1935-1936	Milt Trupin	5-4	
1936-1937	Milt Trupin	7-4	
1937-1938	Irving Koslowe	11-5	
1938-1939	Irving Koslowe	10-5	
1939-1940	Hy Wettstein	11-8	
1940-1941	Hy Wettstein	9-10	
1941-1942	Al Goldstein	8-13	
1942-1943	Bernard "Red" Sarachek	10-5	
1943-1944	Mike Pincus	9-6	
1944-1945	Nat Kraditor	12-8	
1945-1969	Bernard "Red" Sarachek	191-259	
1969-1972	Sam Stern	7-50	
1972-2013	Jonathan Halpert	409-531	

Assistant Coaches

1935-1936	Manny Krischewsky
1936-1950	None
1950-1951	Chili Edelstein
1952-1954	Arthur Stein
1954-1956	Marvin Hershkowitz
1956-1960	Manny Greenblum
1960-1964	Manny Greenblum, Irv Bader
1964-1969	Manny Greenblum
1969-1973	None
1973-1975	Stu Poloner
1975-1979	None
1979-1988	Jeff Gurock
1988-1994	Steve Podias
1994-1995	Steve Post
1995-1996	Steve Post, Evan Goldstein
1996-2000	Evan Goldstein
2000-2002	Jodi King, Tzvi Himber
2002-2005	Yossy Gev
2005-2006	Jodi King
2006—2007	Yishai Pliner
2007-2008	Harel Vatavu
2008-2009	Ron Rozenblat, Robert Hoenig
2009-2011	Ron Rozenblat, Carlos Morales
2011-2012	Ron Rozenblat
2012-2013	Rafi Halpert

Individual and Team Records

Points

Career[74]

- 1,871, Yossy Gev, 1998-2002, 4 years, 95 games
- 1,807, Ayal Hod, 1985-1989, 4 years, 94 games
- 1,541, Lior Hod, 1984-1988, 4 years, 90 games
- 1,500, Harvey Sheff, 1978-1982, 4 years, 84 games
- 1,378, Stu Poloner, 1967-1969; 1970-1971, 3 years, 61 games
- 1,374, Irving Bader, 1956-1960, 4, years, 78 games
- 1,360, Irwin "Red" Blumenreich, 1954-1957, 3 years, 55 games
- 1,330, Joel Jacobson, 1994-1998, 4 years, 91 games
- 1,324, Joe Eaves, 1981-1983; 1984-1986, 4 years, 83 games
- 1,287, Miko Danan, 1990-1994, 4 years, 79 games
- 1,287, Ian Ribald, 2003-2007, 4 years, 99 games
- 1,266, Eli Hami, 2000-2003, 3 years, 70 games
- 1,250, David Kufeld, 1976-1980, 4 years, 81 games
- 1,247, Robert Rosenbloom, 1974-1978, 4 years, 81 games
- 1,223, Sheldon Rokach. 1962-1966, 4 years, 79 games
- 1,207, Abe Sodden, 1952-1956, 4 years, 79 games
- 1,195, Dovie Hoffman 2009-2013, 4 years, 95 games
- 1,176, Ronnie Schwartz, 1982-1986 4 years, 81 games
- 1,117, Sam Grossman, 1958-1962, 4 years, 75 games
- 1,115, Harel Vatavu, 2003-2007, 4 years, 96 games
- 1,109, Yudi Teichman, 1986-1989, 3 years, 68 games
- 1,095, Marvin Hershkowitz, 1950-1953, 3 years 54 games
- 1,088, Gil Bash, 2009-2013, 4 years 90 games
- 1,054, Daniel Aaron, 1991-1994, 3 years, 54 games
- 1,052, David Wilzig, 1970-1974, 4 years, 76 games
- 1,008, Eric Davis, 1988-1991, 3 years, 55 games

Season

- 548, Eli Hami, 2002-2003, 25 games
- 534, Stu Poloner, 1970-1971, 19 games

---

[74] Pictures of Yeshiva University's thousand-point scorers can be found by going to www.backdoorhoops.com.

- 525, Zach Gordon, 2007-2008, 26 games
- 514, Ayal Hod, 1988-1989, 23 games
- 513, Irwin Blumenreich, 1954-1955, 21 games
- 511, Yossy Gev, 2001-2002, 26 games

Freshman Season
- 525, Zach Gordon, 2007-2008, 26 games
- 443, Stu Poloner, 1967-1968, 21 games
- 380, Richie Salit, 1968-1969, 21 games
- 357, Harvey Sheff, 1978-1979, 20 games
- 325, Jonathan Rosner 1989-1990, 22 games

Game
- 48, Sheldon Rokach vs. Queens College, December 7, 1964
- 47, Stu Poloner vs. Pratt, January 9, 1971
- 44, Irwin Blumenreich vs. Patterson State, March 1,1955
- 41, Marvin Hershkowitz vs. Cathedral, February 6, 1952
- 41, David Kufeld vs. Hunter, February 15, 1979
- 41, Roy Goldstein vs. Centenary, January 25, 2005
- 41, Shuki Merlis vs. City College, December 20, 2006
- 41, Zach Gordon vs. Old Westbury, February 26, 2008
- 40, Sam Grossman vs. Brooklyn Poly Tech, January 27,1962
- 40, Harvey Sheff vs. Dominican College, December 15, 1980
- 39. Marvin Hershkowitz vs. Patterson State. February 11, 1952
- 39, Sandy Ader vs. Brooklyn Poly Tech, February 17, 1959
- 39, Stu Poloner vs. Hunter, February 20, 1971
- 39, Yitz Ribald vs. Mount St. Vincent, February 21, 2004
- 38, Marvin Hershkowitz vs. Montclair State, February 1952
- 38, Sheldon Rokach vs. Marist, February 24, 1965
- 38, Joe Eaves vs. Pratt, February 23, 1985
- 38, Joel Jacobson vs. Pratt February 5, 1998
- 37, Sheldon Rokach vs. Hartford, February 3, 1966
- 37, Stu Poloner vs. Stony Brook February 24, 1971
- 37, Richie Salit vs. Pace February 8, 1969
- 37, Robert Rosenbloom vs. Concordia December 1, 1977
- 36, Marvin Hershkowitz, Farleigh Dickinson University, February 16, 1952
- 36, Allen Gewirtz vs. Patterson State March 1, 1955

- 36, Robert Rosenbloom vs. Mercy College December 6, 1975
- 35, Irving Bader vs. Kings College February 10, 1958
- 35, Sheldon Rokach vs. Patterson State, February 24, 1966
- 35, Harvey Sheff vs. Dominican College, February 21, 1980
- 35, Eric Davis vs. City College, December 4, 1989
- 35, Daniel Aaron vs. Stevens Tech, December 6, 1992
- 35, Daniel Aaron vs. City College, December 12, 1992
- 35, Gil Bash vs. Sage College, February 13, 2011
- 34, Stu Poloner vs. Sacred Heart, February 18, 1971
- 34, Stu Poloner vs. Drew February 10, 1971
- 34, Ayal Hod vs. Mount St. Vincent, December 21, 1987
- 34, Yossy Gev vs. Brooklyn Poly Tech, February 17, 2000
- 34, Eli Hami vs. Manhattanville, February 2, 2003
- 34, Yitz Ribald vs. Centenary, February 7, 2007
- 33, Arthur Stein vs. Cooper Union, March 18,1950
- 33, Sheldon Rokach vs. Bridgeport, January 5, 1965
- 33, Sam Stern vs. Brooklyn Poly Tech January, 1967
- 33, Richard Salit vs. Marist, December 1,1969
- 33, David Wilzig vs. Newark State College February 5, 1972
- 33, Harvey Sheff vs. Beaver College December 12, 1981
- 33, Ayal Hod vs. Barry January 24, 1987
- 33, Ayal Hod vs. Pratt, March 1, 1988
- 33, Yossy Gev vs. Mount St. Mary November 28, 2000
- 33, Shuki Merlis vs. Old Westbury January 20, 2007
- 33, Dovie Hoffman vs. Old Westbury February 2, 2012
- 32, Marvin Hershkowitz vs. Hunter February 11,1950
- 32, Irwin Blumenreich vs. Pace December 21, 1955
- 32, Arthur Aaron vs. Adelphi, February 9,1963
- 32, Stu Poloner vs. City College January 6,1968
- 32, David Wilzig vs. Lehman, February 3, 1974
- 32, Harvey Sheff vs. Maritime College, February 15, 1982
- 32, Ayal Hod vs. St. Joseph's Brooklyn, February 24, 1987
- 32, Lior Hod vs. Western Connecticut, February 1, 1988
- 32, Eric Davis vs. Maritime, November 30, 1989
- 32, Eric Davis vs. Brooklyn Poly Tech, February 15,1990
- 32, Miko Danan vs. Kings Point, February 15,1992
- 32, Yossy Gev vs. Mount St. Vincent, February 22, 2000
- 32, Yossy Gev vs. Manhattanville, February 3, 2002

- 32, Eli Hami vs. Brooklyn College, January 30, 2003
- 31, Sam Grossman vs. Danbury State, February 7, 1962
- 31, Richie Salit vs. C.W. Post, December 3, 1969
- 31, David Gettinger vs. Sacred Heart, February 18, 1971
- 31, Richard Salit vs. Brooklyn Poly Tech, December 12, 1970
- 31, Stu Poloner vs. Jersey City State, December 9, 1970
- 31, Stu Poloner vs. Pace, December 7, 1970
- 31, Harvey Sheff vs. Drew, February 11, 1981
- 31, Daniel Aaron vs. Stevens Tech, February 10, 1992
- 31, Miko Danan vs. Mount St. Vincent, January 30,1993
- 31, Yossy Gev vs. Brooklyn College, January 31, 2002
- 31, Eli Hami vs. Manhattanville, February 3, 2002
- 31, Eli Hami vs. Brooklyn Poly Tech, January 25, 2003
- 31, Zach Gordon vs. Mount St. Vincent, February 20, 2008
- 30, Gary Baum vs. Patterson State, December 10, 1960
- 30, Sam Grossman vs. NYU, February 25, 1961
- 30, Sam Grossman vs. New Paltz, December, 1961
- 30, Sheldon Rokach vs. Drew, December 12, 1964
- 30, Ray Aboff vs. Adelphi, December 19, 1967
- 30, Stu Poloner vs. Queens, December 17, 1970
- 30, Stu Poloner vs. Brandeis, February 28, 1971
- 30, Harvey Sheff vs. Pace, December 14, 1978
- 30, Harvey Sheff vs. New Jersey Institute Technology, February 13, 1980
- 30, Harvey Sheff vs. Bard, November 29, 1981
- 30, Joe Eaves vs. New Jersey Institute Technology, December 8, 1982
- 30, Ron Schwartz vs. Vassar, February 27, 1984
- 30, Ayal Hod vs. Pratt, January 29, 1987
- 30, Lior Hod vs. St. Joseph's Brooklyn, February 6, 1988
- 30, Eric Davis vs. Mount St. Vincent, February 3, 1990
- 30, Miko Danan vs. Brooklyn Poly Tech, December 15, 1991
- 30, Miko Danan vs. St. Joseph's, Brooklyn, February 16, 1992
- 30, Joel Jacobson vs. Massachusetts College of Pharmacy, November 23, 1996
- 30, Yossy Gev vs. Stevens Tech, November 26, 2000
- 30, Eli Hami vs. Mount St. Vincent, December 18, 2002
- 30, Martin Leibovich vs. Mount St. Vincent, February 12, 2009

Average per Game—Career
- 24.7, Irwin Blumenreich, 1954-1957, 3 years, 55 games
- 22.5, Stu Poloner 1967-1969; 1970-1971, 3 years, 61 games
- 20.0, Marvin Hershkowitz, 1950-1953, 3 years, 54 games
- 19.6, Yossy Gev, 1998-2002. 4 years, 95 games
- 19.5, Daniel Aaron, 1991-1994, 3 years, 54 games
- 19.2. Ayal Hod, 1985-1989, 4 years, 94 games
- 18.3, Eric Davis, 1988-1991, 3 years, 55 games
- 18.1, Eli Hami, 2000-2003, 3 years 70 games
- 17.8, Harvey Sheff, 1978-1982, 4 years, 84 games
- 17.6, Irving Bader, 1956-1960, 4 years, 78 games
- 17.1, Lior Hod, 1984-1988, 4 years, 90 games
- 16.3, Miko Danan, 1990-1994, 4 years, 79 games
- 16.3, Yudi Teichman, 1986-1989, 3 years, 68 games
- 15.9, Joe Eaves, 1981-1983; 1984-1986, 4 years, 83 games
- 15.5, Sheldon Rokach, 1962-1966, 4 years, 79 games
- 15.4, David Kufeld, 1976-1980, 4 years, 81 games
- 15.3, Robert Rosenbloom, 1974-1978, 4 years, 81 games
- 15.3, Abe Sodden, 1952-1956, 4 years, 79 games
- 14.9, Sam Grossman, 1958-1962, 4 years, 75 games
- 14.6, Joel Jacobson, 1994-1998, 4 years, 91 games
- 14.5, Ron Schwartz, 1982-1986, 4 years, 81 games
- 13.9, David Wilzig, 1970-1974, 4 years, 76 games
- 13.0, Ian Ribald, 2003-2007, 4 years, 99 games
- 11.6, Harel Vatavu, 2003-2007, 4 years, 96 games

Average per Game—Season
- 28.1, Stu Poloner, 1970-1971
- 24.7, Irwin Blumenreich, 1955-1956
- 24.4, Irwin Blumenreich, 1954-1955
- 23.5, Sheldon Rokach, 1964-1965
- 22.6, Sheldon Rokach, 1965-1966
- 22.6, Eric Davis, 1990-1991
- 22.5, Eric Davis, 1989-1990
- 22.3, Ayal Hod, 1988-1989
- 21.2, Stu Poloner, 1967-1968
- 21.9, Eli Hami 2002-2003
- 21.6, Eric Davis 1989-1990

- 21.6, Roy Goldstein, 2004-2005
- 21.3, Sam Grossman, 1960-1961
- 21.1, Sam Grossman, 1961-1962
- 21.0, Yossy Gev 1999-2000
- 20.9, Harvey Sheff, 1981-1982
- 20.9, Joel Jacobson, 1997-1998
- 20.7, Robert Rosenbloom 1977-1978
- 20.6, Irv Bader, 1958-1959
- 20.5, Joe Eaves, 1984-1985
- 20.2, Irwin Blumenreich, 1956-1957
- 20.2, Zach Gordon, 2007-2008
- 20.1, Yossy Gev, 2001-2002

Three-Point Field Goal Percentage

Career
- 45.7%, 279/610, Yitz Ribald, 2003-2007
- 41.9%, 88/210, Jack Yulzary, 1999-2002; 2002-2004
- 37.6%, 188/499, Chen Biron, 2008-2012
- 35.0%, 159/453, Yossy Gev, 1998-2002
- 35.0%, 88/251, Ben Golbert, 2003-2006

Season
- 50.9%, 84/165, 2005-2006, Ian Ribald
- 47.8%, 43/90, 2012-2013, Dovie Hoffman
- 47.8%, 33/69, 2003-2004, Jack Yulzary
- 46.5%, 86/185, 2006-2007, Ian Ribald
- 42.6%, 52/122, 2004-2005, Ian Ribald
- 42.2%, 38/90, 1998-1999, Yossy Gev
- 41.3% 57/138, 2012-2013, Benjy Ritholtz
- 41.3%, 57/138, 2003-2004, Ian Ribald
- 40.8%, 60/147, 2009-2010, Chen Biron
- 39.6%, 63/159, 2004-2005, Roy Goldstein
- 39.4%, 28/71, 2008-2009, Chen Biron
- 39.1%, 29/74, 2001-2002, Jack Yulzary
- 38.8%, 33/85, 2009-2010, Martin Leibovich
- 38.7%, 24/62, 2004-2005, Jonathan Rotenberg
- 37.8%, 42/111,2009-2010, Omer Haim

- 37.0%, 43/116, 1999-2000, Yossy Gev
- 36.8%, 49/133, 2011-2012, Chen Biron
- 36.6%, 48/131, 1991-1992, Miko Danan
- 36.4%, 36/99, 2008-2009, Martin Leibovich

Free Throw Percentage

Career

- 84.8%, 280/330, Yudi Teichman, 1986-1989
- 84.7%, 195/230, Ian Ribald, 2003-2007
- 80.4%, 182/225, David Schaulewicz, 2005-2008
- 79.1%, 182/230, Jack Yulzary, 1999-2002; 2003-2004

Season

- 95.2%, 119/125, Yudi Teichman, 1988-1989
- 88.4%, 84/95, David Ehrman, 1990-1991
- 87.7%, 57/65, Ian Ribald, 2003-2004
- 82.8%, 82/99, David Schaulewicz, 2007-2008
- 81.9%, 72/88, Jack Yulzary, 2000-2001
- 80.3%, 53/66, David Schaulewicz, 2006-2007

Free Throws Attempted

Season

- 229, Ayal Hod, 1988-1989
- 218, Ayal Hod. 1987-1988
- 192, Ayal Hod, 1985-1986
- 172, Stu Poloner, 1970-1971
- 160, Stu Poloner 1967-1968
- 151, Sam Stern, 1966-1967
- 132, Sheldon Rokach, 1964-1965
- 131, Dovie Hoffman 2010-2011
- 125, Yudi Teichman, 1995-1996
- 121, Roy Goldstein 2004-2005
- 115, Dovie Hoffman 2011-2012

Rebounds

Career

- 1222, David Kufeld, 1976-1980, 4 years, 81 games
- 1109, Ayal Hod, 1985-1989, 4 years, 94 games
- 1020, Sheldon Rokach, 1962-1966, 4 years, 79 games

Season

- 411, Sheldon Rokach, 1964-1965, 20 games
- 410, Sheldon Rokach, 1965-1966, 20 games
- 355, David Kufeld, 1978-1979, 20 games
- 320, Ayal Hod, 1988-1989, 21 games
- 295, Jonathan Rosner, 1990-1991, 22 games
- 286, Irwin Blumenreich, 1954-1955, 21 games

Game:

- 33, Sheldon Rokach vs. Brooklyn College, January 8, 1966
- 33, David Kufeld vs. New Jersey Institute Technology, December 17, 1977
- 32, Sheldon Rokach vs. Drew, December 12, 1964
- 31, Marvin Hershkowitz vs. Cathedral February 7, 1952
- 30, Ayal Hod vs. Vassar, February 22, 1989
- 27, Paul Merlis vs. Pratt, January 4, 1973
- 25, David Kufeld vs. MIT, January 25, 1979
- 22, Ray Aboff vs. Brooklyn Poly Tech, February 26, 1966
- 22, Paul Merlis vs. John Jay, December 1, 1974
- 22, Harvey Sheff vs. Stevens Tech, February 22, 1982
- 22, Daniel Aaron vs. Purchase, January 31, 1994
- 22, Daniel Aaron vs. Maritime February 16, 1994
- 21, Bob Podhurst vs. C.W. Post, December, 1961
- 21, Ray Aboff vs. Brooklyn College, February 24, 1968
- 21, David Kufeld vs. Hunter, February 15, 1979
- 21, David Kufeld vs. Brooklyn Poly Tech, December 11, 1978
- 20, Joel Rich vs. St. Thomas Aquinas February 24, 1973

Average Per Game—Career

- 15.1, David Kufeld, 1976-1980, 4 years, 81 games
- 12.9, Sheldon Rokach, 1962-1966, 4 years, 79 games

- 11.8, Ayal Hod, 1985-1989, 4 years, 94 games

Average Per Game—Season
- 21.5, Sheldon Rokach, 1964-1965, 20 games
- 20.5, Sheldon Rokach, 1965-1966, 20 games
- 17.6, David Kufeld, 1978-1979, 20 games
- 13.9, Ayal Hod, 1988-1989, 21 games
- 13.4, Jonathan Rosner, 1990-1991, 22 games

Assists

Career
- 392, Omer Haim, 2009-2012, 3 years, 67 games
- 367, Jack Yulzary, 1999-2002; 2003-2004, 4 years, 94 games
- 348, Eric Davis, 1988-1991, 3 years, 55 games
- 333, Harel Vatavu, 2003-2007, 4 years, 96 games
- 312, Gil Bash, 2009-2013, 4 years, 90 games
- 263, David Schaulewicz, 2005-2008, 3 years, 73 games
- 214, Rafi Halpert, 2001-2005, 4 years, 96 games
- 203. Donny Furst, 1991-1994, 3 years, 69 games
- 192, Dovid Cohen, 1991-1993, 2 years, 45 games
- 141, Dov Weiner, 1998-2000, 2 years, 47 games

Season:
- 149, Joe Eaves, 1981-1982, 22 games
- 149, Gil Bash, 2012-2013, 26 games
- 136, Harel Vatavu, 2006-2007, 25 games
- 132, Omer Haim, 2009-2010, 25 games
- 131, Omer Haim, 2011-2012, 21 games
- 129, Eric Davis, 1989-1990, 21 games
- 129, Omer Haim, 2010-2011, 21 games
- 128, Jack Yulzary, 2000-2001, 23 games
- 115, Eric Davis, 1988-1989, 18 games
- 115, Dovid Cohen, 1991-1992, 22 games
- 111, Mike Pollack, 2007-2008, 26 games
- 104, Eric Davis, 1990-1991, 16 games
- 103, Jack Yulzary, 2001-2002, 23 games
- 100, David Schaulewicz, 2007-2008, 26 games

Game:

- 18, Dovid Cohen vs. Brooklyn Poly Tech, February 19, 1991
- 15, Allen Gewirtz vs. Patterson State, February 1955
- 15, Bruce Wenig vs. New Jersey Institute Technology, 1975-1976
- 15, Gil Bash vs. Brooklyn College, December 29, 2012
- 14, Joe Eaves vs. Bard, November 19 1985
- 14, Rafi Halpert vs. Brooklyn College, January 30, 2003
- 12, Eric Davis vs. Pratt, 1989-1990
- 12, Omer Haim vs. City College, November 18, 2010
- 11, Jack Yulzary vs. St. Joseph's, Patchogue, January 29, 2001
- 11, Harel Vatavu vs. Old Westbury, January 20, 2007
- 11, David Schaulewicz vs. Berkeley College, November 18, 2007
- 11, Omer Haim vs. Old Westbury, January 27, 2010
- 11. Omer Haim vs. Brooklyn College, February 16, 2011
- 10, Eric Davis vs. Stevens Tech, January 28, 1990
- 10, Dov Weiner vs. Mount St. Mary, January 25, 2000
- 10. Jack Yulzary vs. Brooklyn Poly Tech, January 27, 2001
- 10, Jack Yulzary vs. Baruch College, November 23, 2003
- 10, David Schaulewicz vs. City College, December 20, 2006
- 10, Mike Pollack vs. State University, Purchase, December 16, 2007
- 10, Omer Haim vs. Bard College, January 31, 2010
- 10, Omer Haim vs. Russell Sage, February 7, 2010
- 10, Omer Haim vs. St. Joseph's, Patchogue, February 28, 2011

Average per Game—Career

- 6.32, 348 Eric Davis, 1988-1991, 3 years, 55 games
- 5.85, 392 Omer Haim, 2009-2012, 3 years, 67 games
- 4.26, 192, Dovid Cohen, 1991-1993, 2 years, 45 games
- 3.90, 367, Jack Yulzary, 1999-2002; 2003-2004, 4 years, 94 games
- 3.60, 263, David Schaulewicz, 2005-2008, 3 years, 73 games
- 3.46, 333, Harel Vatavu, 2003-2007, 4 years, 96 games
- 3.46, 312, Gil Bash, 2009-2013, 4 years, 90 games
- 3.00, 141, Dov Weiner, 1998-2000, 2 years, 47 games
- 2.94, 203. Donny Furst, 1991-1994, 3 years, 69 games
- 2.21, 214, Rafi Halpert, 2001-2005, 4 years 96 games

Average per Game—Season:
- 6.7, 149, Joe Eaves, 1981-1982, 22 games
- 6.5, 104, Eric Davis, 1990-1991, 16 games
- 6.4, 115, Eric Davis, 1988-1989, 18 games
- 6.2, 131, Omer Haim, 2011-2012, 21 games
- 6.1, 129, Omer Haim, 2010-2011, 21 games
- 6.1, 129, Eric Davis, 1989-1990, 21 games
- 5.7, 149, Gil Bash, 2012-2013, 26 games
- 5.6, 128, Jack Yulzary, 2000-2001, 23 games
- 5.4, 136, Harel Vatavu, 2006-2007, 25 games
- 5.3, 132, Omer Haim, 2009-2010, 25 games
- 5.2, 115, Dovid Cohen, 1991-1992, 22 games
- 4.5, 103, Jack Yulzary, 2001-2002, 23 games
- 4.3, 98, Joe Eaves, 1985-1986, 23 games
- 4.3, 111, Mike Pollack, 2007-2008, 26 games
- 4.2, 92, David Schaulewicz, 2006-2007, 22 games
- 3.8, 100, David Schaulewicz, 2007-2008, 26 games
- 3.0, 60, Bruce Wenig, 1973-1974. 20 games

Assist records prior to 1986 are incomplete. The following players, however, have earned recognition as outstanding playmakers based on the testimonials of teammates

- Allen Gewirtz, 1951-1955
- Willie Goldstein, 1956-1959
- Sam Stern, 1966-1968.
- Bruce Wenig, 1972-1976
- Joe Eaves, 1981-1983; 1984-1985

Steals

Career:
- 258, Jack Yulzary, 1999-2002; 2003-2004, 94 games
- 235, Barry Aranoff, 1994-1996, 47 games
- 221, Eli Hami, 2000-2003, 70 games
- 201, Rafi Halpert, 2001-2005, 96 games

Season:
- 128, Jack Yulzary, 2000-2001, 23 games
- 121, Barry Aranoff, 1994-1995, 22 games
- 114, Barry Aranoff, 1995-1996, 25 games
- 91, Eli Hami, 2001-2002, 22 games

Game:
- 12, Barry Aranoff vs. SUNY Purchase, February 13, 1995
- 11, Eli Hami vs. City College, December 23, 2002

Average per Game—Career
- 5.0, 235, Barry Aranoff, 1994-1996, 47 games
- 3.2, 221, Eli Hami, 2000-2003, 70 games
- 2.7, 258, Jack Yulzary, 1999-2002; 2003-2004, 94 games
- 2.1, 201, Rafi Halpert, 2001-2005, 96 games

Average per Game—Season
- 5.5, Jack Yulzary, 2000-2001, 23 games
- 5.5, Barry Aranoff, 1994-1995, 22 games
- 4.6, Barry Aranoff, 1995-1996, 25 games
- 4.1, Eli Hami, 2001-2002, 22 games

All-Star Awardees

Macabbiah Team
- 1953, Irwin Blumenreich
- 1961, Sam Grossman
- 2003, Eli Hami

Small College All-American Awardees
- 1951, Marvin Hershkowitz
- 1951, Artie Stein
- 1953, Marvin Hershkowitz
- 1956, Abe Sodden
- 1957, Irwin Red Blumenreich
- 1959, Sandy Ader
- 1960, Irv Bader
- 1971, Stu Poloner

New York Metropolitan Basketball Writers Association D-III All-Star Awardees

- 1988, Lior Hod, first team
- 1989, Ayal Hod, first team
- 1991, Eric Davis, second team
- 1993, Miko Danan, second team
- 1994, Daniel Aaron, second team
- 1995, Alan Levy, third team
- 1999, Yossy Gev, third team
- 2000, Yossy Gev, second team
- 2001, Yossy Gev, first team
- 2002, Yossy Gev, first team
- 2003, Eli Hami, first team
- 2005, Roy Goldstein, third team
- 2007, Shuki Merlis, third team
- 2008, Zach Gordon, second team
- 2010, Martin Leibovich, second team

National Association Basketball Coaches (NABC) Division III Atlantic All-District All-Star Team:

- 2001, Yossy Gev, second team

ECAC Division III Men's Metro Basketball All-Star Team

- 2002, Yossy Gev, honorable mention
- 2003, Eli Hami, second team
- 2008, Zach Gordon, second team

Independent Athletic Conference (1974-1997) All-Star Team

- 1972, David Wilzig, first team
- 1975, Paul Merlis, first team
- 1976, Paul Merlis, second team
- 1977, Robert Rosenbloom, first team
- 1977, David Kufeld, second team
- 1977, Jerry Joszef, second team
- 1978, David Kufeld, first team
- 1979, David Kufeld, first team
- 1979, Harvey Sheff, second team

- 1980, David Kufeld, first team
- 1980, Harvey Sheff, second team
- 1980, Shelly Green, honorable mention
- 1981, Harvey Sheff, first team
- 1981, Sheldon Goldman, honorable mention
- 1982, Harvey Sheff, first team
- 1982, Joe Eaves, second team
- 1983, Joe Eaves, first team
- 1983, Ron Schwartz, honorable mention
- 1984, Ron Schwartz, first team
- 1985, Joe Eaves, second team
- 1986, Joe Eaves, second team
- 1986, Ayal Hod, rookie of the year
- 1987, Ayal Hod, first team
- 1987, Lior Hod, second team
- 1988, Lior Hod, MVP
- 1989, Ayal Hod, first team
- 1989, Yudi Teichman, second team
- 1990, Eric Davis, second team
- 1991, Miko Danan, rookie of the year
- 1991, Eric Davis, first team
- 1991, Jon Rosner, second team
- 1992, Daniel Aaron, first team, rookie of the year
- 1992, Miko Danan, first team
- 1992, Donny Furst, honorable mention
- 1992, Elisha Rothman, honorable mention
- 1993, Daniel Aaron, first team
- 1993, Miko Danan, first team
- 1993, Donny Furst, honorable mention
- 1994, Daniel Aaron, first team
- 1994, Miko Danan third team
- 1995, Barry Aranoff, rookie of the year
- 1995, Alan Levy, third team
- 1996, Alan Levy, second team
- 1996, Barry Aranoff, third team

IAC All-Decade Team (1983-1993)
- Joe Eaves
- David Kufeld
- Robert Rosenbloom, honorable mention
- Harvey Sheff

1997-1999 (No League Affiliation)[75]

Skyline Conference (1999-Present)
Player of the Year
- 2003, Eli Hami

Rookie of the Year
- 2008, Zach Gordon

All-Star Team
- 2000, Yossy Gev, first team
- 2000, David Neiss, honorable mention
- 2001, Yossy Gev, first team
- 2002, Yossy Gev, first team
- 2002, Jack Yulzary, second team
- 2003, Eli Hami, first team
- 2004, Ben Golbert, honorable mention
- 2004, Jack Yulzary, honorable mention
- 2005, Roy Goldstein, first team
- 2006, Ian Ribald, second team
- 2007, Shuki Merlis, second team
- 2007, Ian Ribald, honorable mention
- 2008, Zach Gordon, first team
- 2009, Martin Leibovich, second team
- 2010, Martin Leibovich, first team
- 2012, Dovie Hoffman, second team
- 2013, Gil Bash, first team

---

[75] I wish to express my appreciation to Mr. John Lyons, former IAC public relations director, for providing the IAC's all-star selections.

Team Scoring Offense

Game:

- 116 vs. Brooklyn Poly Tech 80, 1958-1959
- 110 vs. Patterson State 96, 1954-1955
- 110 vs. Pratt 89, 1984-1985
- 110 vs. St. Joseph's Brooklyn 75, 1987-1988
- 109 vs. C.W. Post 66, 1957-1958
- 108 vs. Stevens Tech 82, 1990-1991
- 107 vs. Massachusetts School of Pharmacy 76, 1999-2000
- 105 vs. Molloy 53, 1985-1986
- 104 vs. St. Thomas Acquinas 90, 1972-1973
- 104 vs. Molloy 66, 1987-1988
- 104 vs. Bard 50, 1998-1999
- 104 vs. Purchase 79, 1999-2000
- 103 vs. Northeastern Bible 58, 1985-1986
- 101 vs. Vassar 84, 1988-1989
- 101 vs. City College 98, 2006-2007
- 100 vs. Pace 57, 1957-1958
- 100 vs. Queens College 96 (3OT), 1964-1965
- 100 vs. Bard 59, 1984-1985
- 100 vs. Stevens Tech 79, 1990-1991
- 100 vs. New York Maritime 80, 1991-1992

Individual Game Results (1930-1972)

Individual game results and scores organized by season and opponent can be found by going to www.backdoorhoops.com/gameresults.

Individual Game Results (1972-2013)

Individual game results and scores organized by season and opponent can be found by going to www.backdoorhoops.com/gameresults.

Conference Playoff Results

Season	Conference	Record	Playoff Result
1972-1973	Knickerbocker	0-8	No League Playoffs
1973-1974	Knickerbocker	1-7	No League Playoffs
1974-1975	Knickerbocker	0-8	No League Playoffs
1974-1975	IAC[75]	3-2	No League Playoffs
1975-1976	Knickerbocker	0-8	No League Playoffs
1975-1976	IAC	2-3	No League Playoffs
1976-1977	Knickerbocker	0-3	Loss vs. Pace; Loss vs. Pratt (consolation)
1976-1977	IAC	2-3	No League Playoffs
1977-1978	IAC	3-5	No League Playoffs
1978-1979	IAC	1-7	No League Playoffs
1979-1980	IAC	4-4	No League Playoffs
1980-1981	IAC	1-6	No League Playoffs
1981-1982	IAC	4-4	Loss vs. Maritime
1982-1983	IAC	2-5	No League Playoffs
1983-1984	IAC	3-4	No League Playoffs
1984-1985	IAC	3-5	No League Playoffs
1985-1986	IAC	3-7	No League Playoffs
1986-1987	IAC	5-5	No League Playoffs
1987-1988	IAC	5-5	No League Playoffs
1988-1989	IAC	6-4	No League Playoffs
1989-1990	IAC	3-6	No League Playoffs
1990-1991	IAC	4-5	Win vs. Stevens Tech; Loss vs. Western Connecticut
1991-1992	IAC	7-2	Win vs. Stevens Tech; Loss vs. Mount St. Vincent.

---

[76] Independent Athletic Conference

1992-1993	IAC	5-4	Win vs. Brooklyn Poly Tech; Win vs. Mount St. Vincent; Loss vs. NJIT, finals
1993-1994	IAC	5-4	Win vs. Stevens Tech; Loss vs. NJIT, Semi-Finals
1994-1995	IAC	6-3	Win vs. Bard; Loss vs. Mount St. Vincent, Semi-Finals
1995-1996	IAC	5-4	Win vs. Maritime; Loss vs. Mount St. Vincent, Semi-Finals
1996-1997	No Conference Affiliation		
1997-1998	No Conference Affiliation		
1998-1999	No Conference Affiliation		
1999-2000	Skyline	10-4	Second-Place Finish, Loss vs. Mount St. Vincent
2000-2001	Skyline	9-7	Fifth-Place Finish, Loss vs. Maritime
2001-2002	Skyline	10-6	Third-Place Finish, Win vs. Stevens Tech Loss vs. Manhattanville
2002-2003	Skyline	4-12	Eighth-Place Finish, Win vs. Maritime Loss vs. Kings Point
2003-2004	Skyline	6-9	Eighth-Place Finish, Win vs. Stevens Tech; Loss vs. Old Westbury
2004-2005	Skyline	8-7	Seventh-Place Finish, Win vs. Maritime Loss vs. Mount St. Mary
2005-2006	Skyline	9-6	Sixth-Place Finish, Loss vs. Mount St. Mary
2006-2007	Skyline	8-8	Seventh-Place Finish, Loss vs. Stevens Tech

2007-2008	Skyline	7-11	Sixth-Place Finish, Win vs. Old Westbury Loss vs. St. Joseph's Patchogue
2008-2009	Skyline	5-13	Seventh-Place Finish, Missed playoffs
2009-2010	Skyline	11-9	Sixth-Place Finish, Loss vs. SUNY Purchase
2010-2011	Skyline	7-13	Seventh-Place Finish, Missed playoffs
2011-2012	Skyline	5-13	Eighth-Place Finish, Missed playoffs
2012-2013	Skyline	7-11	Sixth-Place Finish, Loss to Mount St. Mary

Conference Teams

73-74: Knick:[76]	Brooklyn; Hunter; Kings Point; Lehman; Pace; Pratt; Queens; Stony Brook
74-75: Knick:	Brooklyn; Hunter; Kings Point; Lehman; Pace; Pratt; Queens; Stony Brook
74-75: IAC:	Brooklyn Poly Tech; Drew; Maritime; New Jersey Institute Technology; Stevens Tech
75-76: Knick:	Brooklyn; Hunter; Kings Point; Lehman; Pace; Pratt; Queens; Stony Brook
75-76: IAC:	Brooklyn Poly Tech; Drew; Maritime; New Jersey Institute Technology; Stevens Tech
76-77: Knick:	Pace; Pratt; Stony Brook
76-77: IAC	Brooklyn Poly Tech; Drew; New Jersey Institute Technology; Stevens Tech
77-78: IAC	Brooklyn Poly Tech; Drew; New Jersey Institute Technology; Stevens Tech
78-79: IAC	Brooklyn Poly Tech; Drew; New Jersey Institute Technology; Stevens Tech

---

[77] Knickerbocker Athletic Conference

79-80: IAC	Brooklyn Poly Tech; Drew; New Jersey Institute Technology; Stevens Tech
80-81: IAC	Brooklyn Poly Tech; Drew; Maritime; New Jersey Institute Technology; Stevens Tech
81-82: IAC	Brooklyn Poly Tech; Drew; Maritime; New Jersey Institute Technology; Stevens Tech
82-83: IAC	Brooklyn Poly Tech; Drew; Maritime; New Jersey Institute Technology; Stevens Tech
83-84: IAC	Brooklyn Poly Tech; Drew; Maritime; New Jersey Institute Technology; Stevens Tech
84-85: IAC	Brooklyn Poly Tech; Maritime; New Jersey Institute Technology; Stevens Tech; Western Connecticut
85-86: IAC	Brooklyn Poly Tech; Maritime; New Jersey Institute Technology; Stevens Tech;Western Connecticut
86-87: IAC	Brooklyn Poly Tech; Maritime; New Jersey Institute Technology; Stevens Tech; Western Connecticut
87-88: IAC	Brooklyn Poly Tech; Maritime; New Jersey Institute Technology; Stevens Tech; Western Connecticut
88-89: IAC	Brooklyn Poly Tech; Maritime; New Jersey Institute Technology; Stevens Tech; Western Connecticut
89-90: IAC	Brooklyn Poly Tech; Maritime; Mount St. Vincent; New Jersey Institute Technology; Stevens Tech; Western Connecticut
90-91: IAC	Brooklyn Poly Tech; Maritime; Mount St. Vincent; New Jersey Institute Technology; Stevens Tech; Western Connecticut
91-92: IAC	Bard; Brooklyn Poly Tech; Maritime; Mount St. Vincent; New Jersey Institute Technology; Stevens Tech
92-93: IAC	Bard; Brooklyn Poly Tech; Maritime; Mount St. Vincent; New Jersey Institute Technology; Stevens Tech
93-94: IAC	Bard; Brooklyn Poly Tech; Maritime; Mount St. Vincent; New Jersey Institute Technology; Stevens Tech
94-95: IAC	Bard; Brooklyn Poly Tech; Maritime; Mount St. Vincent; New Jersey Institute Technology; Stevens Tech
95-96: IAC	Bard; Brooklyn Poly Tech; Maritime; Mount St. Vincent; New Jersey Institute Technology; Stevens Tech

96-97	No Conference Affiliation
97-98	No Conference Affiliation
98-99	No Conference Affiliation
99-00: Skyline:	Manhattanville; Maritime; Mount St. Mary; Mount St. Vincent; Old Westbury; St. Joseph's; Patchogue; Kings Point
00-01: Skyline:	Manhattanville; Maritime; Mount St. Mary; Mount St. Vincent; Old Westbury; Stevens Tech; St. Joseph's Patchogue, Kings Point
01-02: Skyline:	Manhattanville; Maritime; Mount St. Mary; Mount St. Vincent; Old Westbury; Stevens Tech; St. Joseph's Patchogue, Kings Point
02-03: Skyline:	Manhattanville; Maritime; Mount St. Mary; Mount St. Vincent; Old Westbury; Stevens Tech; St. Joseph's Patchogue, Kings Point
03-04: Skyline:	Centenary; Farmingdale; Manhattanville; Maritime; Mount St. Mary; Mount St. Vincent; Old Westbury; Stevens Tech; St. Joseph's Patchogue; Kings Point
04-05: Skyline:	Centenary; Farmingdale; Manhattanville; Maritime; Mount St. Mary; Mount St. Vincent; Old Westbury; Stevens Tech; St. Joseph's Patchogue; Kings Point
05-06: Skyline:	Centenary; Farmingdale; Manhattanville; Maritime; Mount St. Mary; Mount St. Vincent; Old Westbury; Stevens Tech; St. Joseph's Patchogue; Kings Point
06-07: Skyline:	Centenary; Farmingdale; Manhattanville; Maritime; Mount St. Mary; Mount St. Vincent; Old Westbury; Stevens Tech; St. Joseph's Patchogue; Kings Point
07-08: Skyline:	Bard; Brooklyn Poly Tech; Farmingdale; Maritime; Mount St. Mary; Mount St. Vincent; Old Westbury; Stevens Tech; St. Joseph's Patchogue; Kings Point
08-09: Skyline:	Bard; Brooklyn Poly Tech; Farmingdale; Maritime; Mount St. Mary; Mount St. Vincent; Old Westbury; St. Joseph's Patchogue; Kings Point
09-10: Skyline:	Bard; Brooklyn Poly Tech; Farmingdale; Maritime; Mount St. Mary; Mount St. Vincent; Old Westbury; Sage; St. Joseph's Patchogue; SUNY Purchase

10-11: Skyline: Bard; Brooklyn Poly Tech; Farmingdale; Maritime; Mount St. Mary; Mount St. Vincent; Old Westbury; Sage; St. Joseph's Patchogue; SUNY Purchase

11-12: Skyline: Brooklyn Poly Tech; Farmingdale; Maritime; Mount St. Mary; Mount St. Vincent; Old Westbury; Sage; St. Joseph's Patchogue; SUNY Purchase

12-13: Skyline: Brooklyn Poly Tech; Farmingdale; Maritime; Mount St. Mary; Mount St. Vincent; Old Westbury; Sage; St. Joseph's Patchogue; SUNY Purchase

Won-Lost Records (1930-2013)

1930-1931	3-1	Club team
1931-1932	2-2	Club team
1932-1933	7-5	
1933-1934	8-5	
1934-1935	No Records	
1935-1936	5-4	
1936-1937	7-4	
1937-1938	11-5	
1938-1939	10-5	
1939-1940	11-8	
1940-1941	9-10	
1941-1942	8-13	
1942-1943	10-5	
1943-1944	9-6	
1944-1945	12-8	
1945-1946	5-14	
1946-1947	6-13	
1947-1948	3-8	
1948-1949	4-11	
1949-1950	8-9	

1950-1951	6-10
1951-1952	4-14
1952-1953	10-10
1953-1954	10-10
1954-1955	13-8
1955-1956	16-2
1956-1957	12-7
1957-1958	9-12
1958-1959	14-4
1959-1960	11-9
1960-1961	3-14
1961-1962	10-10
1962-1963	6-14
1963-1964	7-12
1964-1965	7-13
1965-1966	7-13
1966-1967	5-15
1967-1968	7-14
1968-1969	8-13
1969-1970	3-17
1970-1971	2-17
1971-1972	2-16
1972-1973	4-15
1973-1974	1-19
1974-1975	5-14
1975-1976	3-18
1976-1977	4-17
1977-1978	5-15
1978-1979	3-17
1979-1980	6-14
1980-1981	3-20

1981-1982	9-13		
1982-1983	6-14		
1983-1984	5-15		
1984-1985	11-8		
1985-1986	14-9		
1986-1987	10-13		
1987-1988	16-9	ECAC	Jersey City, 77-89
1988-1989	12-11		
1989-1990	12-10		
1990-1991	15-10	ECAC	Lebanon Valley, 63-76
1991-1992	13-9		
1992-1993	12-12	ECAC	Jersey City, 62-76
1993-1994	12-10		
1994-1995	12-10		
1995-1996	13-12		
1996-1997	15-6	ECAC	Staten Island, 50-80
1997-1998	15-8		
1998-1999	16-7		
1999-2000	16-8		
2000-2001	13-10		
2001-2002	14-12		
2002-2003	8-17		
2003-2004	11-14		
2004-2005	14-11		
2005-2006	13-12		
2006-2007	15-11		
2007-2008	11-16		
2008-2009	7-17		
2009-2010	12-14		
2010-2011	7-18		
2011-2012	5-20		
2012-2013	11-16		

Appendix A

MTA Junior Varsity Players (1966-1972)[78]

Name	Season		Record	
Chanales, Alan	1966-1967		5-5	
Dachs, Harvey	1966-1967			
Davis, Kenny	1966-1967			
Dolinsky, Arthur	1966-1967			
Faber, Albie	1966-1967			
Goldman, Marty	1966-1967			
Jacobson, Shaye	1966-1967			
Koslowe, Mark	1966-1967			
Cohen. Judah	1967-1968			
Faber, Albie	1967-1968	Captain	14-3	
Fisher, Tzvi	1967-1968			
Freimann, Howard	1967-1968			
Hoenig, Robert	1967-1968	Captain		
Josefowitz, Arnold	1967-1968			
Kaufthal, Uri	1967-1968			
Lander, Guy	1967-1968			
Levmore, Saul	1967-1968			
Lunzer, Robert	1967-1968	Manager		
Morgenstern, Jonathan	1967-1968			
Newmark, Avery	1967-1968	Manager		
Pollack, Joey	1967-1968			
Pollack, Michael	1967-1968			

---

[78] I would like to express my appreciation to Mr. Leo Klein for his assistance in gathering the names of the 1966 through 1972 junior varsity players.

Tannenbaum, Elliot	1967-1968			
Wilzig, David	1967-1968			
Zuberman, Izzy	1967-1968			
Aber, David.	1968-1969		5-4	
Apfel, Dov	1968-1969			
Bacon, Ari	1968-1969			
Cohen, Judah	1968-1969	Captain		
Freireich, Austin.	1968-1969			
Goldberg, Alan	1968-1969			
Goldgrab, Shelby	1968-1969	Manager		
Jetter, Robert	1968-1969			
Lebovics, Irving	1968-1969			
Lebowitz, David	1968-1969	Manager		
Miller, Howard	1968-1969			
Safier, Judah	1968-1969	Manager		
Schlussel, Nathan	1968-1969			
Shapiro, Benjamin	1968-1969			
Sonicker, Hilton	1968-1969			
Spira, Elliot	1968-1969	Manager		
Stadler, Michael	1968-1969			
Wenig, Bruce	1968-1969	Captain		
Amsel, Alan	1969-1970		8-6	Lost in finals 50-60
Apfel. Dov	1969-1970			
Bacon, Ari	1969-1970			
Berman, Donnie	1969-1970			
Chanales, Sheldon	1969-1970	Manager		
Eckstein, Kenneth	1969-1970			
Friedman, David	1969-1970			

Goldberg, Alan	1969-1970			
Greenspan, Louis	1969-1970			
Kolb, Melvin	1969-1970			
Miller, Howard	1969-1970			
Rozmaryn, Leo	1969-1970	Manager		
Singer, Gary	1969-1970			
Weiss, Robert	1969-1970	Manager		
Wenig, Bruce	1969-1970			
Werber, Jeffrey	1969-1970			
Amsel, Alan	1970-1971		11-5	Championship 42-40
Berman, Donnie	1970-1971	Captain		
Eizik, Barry	1970-1971			
Dorman, Paul	1970-1971			
Edelstein, Howard	1970-1971			
Friedman, David	1970-1971			
Goldstein, Steven	1970-1971			
Gross, Mike	1970-1971			
Hoenig, Mark	1970-1971			
Kuflick, Paul	1970-1971			
Landa, Harold	1970-1971			
Lipner, Stuart	1970-1971			
Merkin, Sol	1970-1971			
Rifkin, Terry	1970-1971			
Stadtmauer, Gary	1970-1971			
Stern, Leon	1970-1971			
Waldman, Alex	1970-1971			
Weitzen, Andy	1970-1971			
Cooper, Stanley	1971-1972		11-3	Championship 63-59 (OT)

Eisenman, Alan	1971-1972			
Farkas, Barry	1971-1972	Manager		
Goldstein, Steven	1971-1972	Captain		
Heller, Jonathan	1971-1972			
Katz, Avram	1971-1972	Manager		
Klapper, Phillip	1971-1972			
Klein, Leo	1971-1972			
Kolatch, Jonathan	1971-1972			
Landa, Harold	1971-1972			
Merkin, Sol	1971-1972	Captain		
Plawner, Jacob	1971-1972			
Rose, Billy	1971-1972			
Rosenbloom, Robert	1971-1972			
Singer, Barry	1971-1972			
Spett, David	1971-1972			
Stadler, Harry	1971-1972			
Wind, Ira	1971-1972			

Appendix B

<u>1977,1978 and 1979 Yeshiva University High School
Jewish All Stars Basketball Teams</u>

1977

NORTH

Name		School
Morris Beyda	Brooklyn, New York	Yeshiva Flatbush
David Diamond	Atlanta, Georgia	The Lovett School
Mark Hirschberg	Atlanta, Georgia	Briarcliff High School
Michael Kosterlitz	Pittsburgh, Pennsylvania	Alderdice High School
Peter Kinicstein	Bayonne, New Jersey	Bayonne JCC
Jeffrey B. Mazin	Port Chester, New York	Blind Brook High School
Stuart Shapiro	Brooklyn, New York	Sheepshead Bay High School
Allan Silverman	Bronx, New York	Columbus High School
Harrison Sterling	W. Orange, New York	YM-YWHA Metropolitan N. J.
Bruce Valinsky	Pittsburgh, Pennsylvania	Alderdice High School
Wayne Weinzoff	Brooklyn, New York	Hebrew Educational Society

1977

SOUTH

Name		School
Ed Berlin	Plainview, New York	Plainview High School
David Eagle	New Hyde Park, New York	Herricks High School
Michael Eisenman	Brooklyn, New York	Lafayette High School
Michael Feigenbaum	N Woodmere, New York	Lawrence High School
Ricky Gorden	E. Meadow, New York	E. Meadow High School
Ian Harris	Port Chester, New York	Blind Brook High School
Robert Scheinfeld	E. Rockaway, New York	Lynbrook High School
Harvey Sheff	Lawrence, New York	HILI
Danny Schayes	Dewitt, New York	James Dewitt High School
John Sices	Huntington, New York	Cold Spring Harbor High School
Russel Weisenberg	Long Beach, New York	E. Meadow High School

1978

NORTH

Name		School
Morris Beyda	Brooklyn, New York	Yeshiva Flatbush
Larry Gerschwer	Brooklyn, New York	S. Shore High School
Scott Kleber	Atlanta, Georgia	Riverwood High School
Joe Lafonde	Brooklyn, New York	Manhattan Beach JCC
Neil Levinson	Houston, Texas	Houston JCC
Ethan Lipman	New York, New York	Seward Park High School
Sanford Savitz	Syracuse, New York	Dewitt High School
Kenny Silber	Brooklyn, New York	Midwood High School
Bruce e Valinsky	Pittsburgh, Pennsylvania	Alderdice High School
Howie Yormack	Brooklyn, New York	Canarsie High School
Sam Young	Harrison, New York	Harrison High School

1978

SOUTH

Name		School
Ian Behar	Valley Stream, New York	Valley Stream S. Falcons
Peter Blodnick	Plainview, New York	Friend's Academy
Michael Feigenbaum	N. Woodmere, New York	Lawrence High School
Ricky Gordon	E. Meadow	E. Meadow High School
Doug Katz	Glen Cove, New York	Glen Cove High School
Jeff Konigsberg	Port Chester, New York	Blind Brook High School
Johnny Landsberg	Long Beach, New York	Long Beach High School
Steve Rosen	Roslyn Hts, New York	Wheatley High School
Allen Sapadin	N. Woodmere, New York	HILI
Gregg Weisenberg	Long Beach, New York	E. Meadow High School
Russ Weisenberg	Long Beach, New York	E. Meadow High School

1979

NORTH

Name		School
Joel Bell	Philadelphia, Pennsylvania	George Washington High School
Martin Bernstein	Queens, New York	John Adams High School
Danny Epstein	Mamaroneck, New York	Mamaroneck High School
Samson Gris	Atlanta, Georgia	Yeshiva of Atlanta
Bill Haskell	Scarsdale, New York	Scarsdale High School
Al Jaffe	W. Orange, New Jersey	Mountain High School
Steven Kadish	Queens, New York	Yeshiva University High School
Barry Klein	Atlanta, Georgia	Yeshiva of Atlanta
Randy Kuptsow	Philadelphia, Pennsylvania	Lincoln High School
Daniel Liebman	Bayonne, New Jersey	Bayonne High School
Allen Sapadin	N. Woodmere, New York	HAFTR

1979

SOUTH

Name		School
Ian Behar	Valley Stream, New York	Valley Stream S.
Jason Dratell	Brooklyn, New York	Abraham Lincoln High School
Stuart Epstein	LawrenÎ, New York	Lawrence High School
Michael Feigenbaum	N. Woodmere, New York	Lawrence High School
Harland Greenberg	E. Meadow, New York	Sheepshead Bay High School
Robert Kirsner	Port Chester, New York	Lafayette High School
Erick Krittcher	E. Rockaway, New York	Seaford High School
Steven Pollack	Lawrence, New York	Valley Stream C.
Eddie Tawil	Dewitt, New York	Yeshiva of Flatbush
Jeffrey Wein	Huntington, New York	Abraham Lincoln High School
Alan Weinberg	Long Beach, New York	Unknown

Appendix C

Schools that participated in the Original Yeshiva University
Yeshiva High School Invitational Basketball Tournament

1978:
Bialik High School, Quebec, Canada
Hebrew Academy of Montreal, Canada
Herzliah St. Laurent, Canada
Hebrew Institute of Long Island, New York
Hillel High School, Deal, New Jersey
Rogosin High School, Jersey City, New Jersey
Yeshiva High School of Flatbush, New York
Yeshiva High School of Washington, Silver Spring, Maryland.
Champion Tier I: Yeshiva High School, Flatbush

1979:
Frisch School, Paramus, New Jersey
Hebrew Academy Five Towns Rockaway, Woodmere, New York
Hebrew Academy of Montreal, Canada
Herzliah Snowdon, Canada
Herzliah St. Laurent, Canada
New England Academy of Torah, Providence, Rhode Island
Yeshiva Atlanta, Georgia
Yeshiva High School of Flatbush, New York
Yeshiva High School of Washington, Silver Spring, Maryland
Yeshiva University High School Brooklyn, New York
Champion Tier I: Hebrew Academy Five Towns Rockaway
Champion Tier II: Yeshiva Atlanta

1980:
Akiba Hebrew Academy, Bala Cynwyd, Pennsylvania;
Frisch School, Paramus, New Jersey
Hebrew Academy, Montreal, Canada
Herzliah Snowdon, Canada
Herzliah St. Laurent, Canada
Maimonides High School, Boston, Massachusetts

New England Academy of Torah, Providence, Rhode Island
Yeshiva High School of Washington, Silver Spring, Maryland.
Yeshiva University High School New York
Champion Tier I: Akiba Academy, Bala Cynwyd
Champion Tier II: Maimonides, Boston

1981:
Akiba Hebrew Academy, Bala Cynwyd, Pennsylvania
Charles E. Smith Jewish Day School, Rockville, Maryland
Jewish Educational Center, Elizabeth, New Jersey
Maimonides High School, Boston, Massachusetts
New England Academy of Torah, Providence, Rhode Island
Ramaz High School, New York
Rogosin High School, Jersey City, New Jersey
Yeshiva University High School New York
Champion Tier I: Ramaz,
Champion Tier II: Charles E. Smith Jewish Day School

1982:
Akiba Hebrew Academy, Bala Cynwyd, Pennsylvania
B'nai Akiva, Toronto, Canada
Charles E. Smith Jewish Day School, Rockville, Maryland
Hebrew Academy Five Towns Rockaway, Woodmere, New York
Jewish Educational Center, Elizabeth, New Jersey
Maimonides High School, Boston, Massachusetts
New England Academy of Torah, Providence, Rhode Island
Ramaz High School, New York
Yeshiva University High School New York
Champion Tier I: Charles E. Smith Jewish Day School
Champion Tier II: No Record

1983:
Akiba Hebrew Academy, Bala Cynwyd, Pennsylvania
B'nai Akiva, Toronto, Canada
Charles E. Smith Jewish Day School, Rockville, Maryland
Frisch High School, Paramus, New Jersey
Hebrew Academy Five Towns Rockaway, Woodmere, New York
Hebrew Academy of Greater Washington, Silver Spring, Maryland

Hillel High School, Dayton, Ohio
Maimonides High School, Boston, Massachusetts
Sephardic High School, Brooklyn, New York
Yeshiva of Baltimore, Maryland
Yeshiva University High School New York
Young Israel, New York
Champion Tier I: Yeshiva University High School New York
Champion Tier II: Maimonides, Boston

About the Author

Jonathan Halpert played college basketball for Yeshiva University's legendary coach Red Sarachek from 1962 to 1966 and began his college coaching career in 1972. He was winner of the College Basketball Official's Sportsmanship Award in 1980 and 1997, recipient of the Metropolitan Basketball Writer's Good Guy Award in 1998, and was Skyline Conference Coach of the Year in 2000 and 2010.

He is currently the longest-tenured college coach in New York City history, fourth among all currently active NCAA coaches. In 2012, he became the seventh coach in New York City history to earn 400 victories. He received a BA and BHL degree from Yeshiva College in 1966, an MA degree from New York University in 1967, and a PhD in Special Education from Yeshiva University's Ferkauf Graduate School of Humanities and Social Sciences in 1978. For twenty-five years he was the CEO of Camelot, a not-for-profit agency that provided residential, transportation and day-program services for developmentally disabled and traumatic brain injured adults.

He is married to the former Aviva Margolis and has five children and nineteen grandchildren.